Political Science Statistics

KUL B. RAI
Southern Connecticut
State College

JOHN C. BLYDENBURGH
Eagleton Institute of Politics
Rutgers University

Archon Books

Hamden, Connecticut

1979

© 1973 Kul B. Rai and John C. Blydenburgh

First published 1973 by Holbrook Press, Inc. (Allyn and Bacon),

470 Atlantic Avenue, Boston.

Reprinted 1979 with permission

in an unabridged and unaltered edition as an Archon Book,

an imprint of The Shoe String Press, Inc.,

Hamden, Connecticut 06514

Library of Congress Cataloging in Publication Data

Rai, Kul B
Political science statistics.

Reprint of the ed. published by Holbrook Press, Boston.
Includes bibliographies and index.
1. Political statistics.
I. Blydenburgh, John C., joint author.   II. Title.
[JA74.R26   1979]   519.5   79-11923
ISBN 0-208-01820-4

CONTENTS

PREFACE

Almost two decades ago, V. O. Key, Jr., wrote in the first chapter of his book *A Primer of Statistics for Political Scientists* (Crowell, New York, 1954): "Most political scientists, accustomed as we are to other modes of analysis, bristle at the sight of even the most common statistical symbol." Key was probably right about political science as it existed before the behavioral revolution. Since then the methodology of political science has become sufficiently sophisticated that no apology for the writing of a book on statistics for political scientists is necessary. The question now is not whether to use statistical methods for the study of politics but how to use them. Unfortunately, the use of statistics for studying politics has become so fashionable in the past decade—the increasing availability of quantitative data and the use of computers facilitate this—that some overzealous analysts not infrequently misuse statistics. The most common problem in the misuse of statistical methods is the lack of attention to the underlying assumptions of the statistical models. The main object of this text is to remedy this problem.

The approach of this book to the study of statistical methods is unusual in three ways. First, it emphasizes statistics as used and usable in political science. The models explained and the examples given were selected because of their value to a political science curriculum.

Second, in this book an attempt is made to present statistics from an intellectual, or deductive, approach. Statistical models are explained first and then they are followed from their assumptions through their implications and modifications.

The third way that this book is unique is in the emphasis placed on the limitations of each statistical model. The point is repeatedly made that a particular statistical model can be used fruitfully only if its assumptions are met. A particular model may be excellent for studying certain aspects of politics, but it may be inappropriate for other research.

Thus, in this book, more emphasis is placed on intuitive understanding of statistics; that is, understanding models is more important than understanding operations. We believe that undue emphasis on operations misleads students: They cannot see the forests (models) because the trees (operations) are in the way. If students of politics are able to specify the assumptions of a statistical model, they are less likely to misuse it.

We are conscious that the traditional emphasis on operations suffers from our emphasis on concepts. But, in fact, it does not suffer much because very few modern social scientists calculate statistics by hand. But it may still be argued that something is lost by our approach because we place less emphasis on notations, symbols, operations, etc. To compensate in part for this loss, we have separated out all prerequisite symbols and operations and have included them in an optional chapter (Chapter 2). The chapter may be used as a separate lesson or a glossary.

Furthermore, the deemphasis of operations should not be interpreted as a deemphasis of mathematics. Statistical models are, after all, mathematical models. Our very point is that the traditional emphasis on operations has handicapped understanding of mathematical models.

By writing this book on statistics we are not espousing the view that the phenomena of politics can be understood and explained only by quantitative methods In fact, we find fault with a political scientist who relies so heavily on esoteric quantitative techniques that his research is meaningless even for political scientists who, by contemporary standards, have a strong background in methodology. Nor do we agree with some "traditionalists" who scoff at any mention of quantification in the study of politics. We believe that the qualitative interpretations of politics can be appreciably improved by the use of the quantitative methods, although we realize that not everything in politics can be quantified.

We do not plan to challenge the commonly accepted definition of statistics, that is, that it provides methods for making decisions in situations of risk and uncertainty. What we do hope to do in this book is to reduce the element of error when such decisions are made with the help of statistics. Finally, we agree with Abraham Kaplan (*The Conduct of Inquiry*, Chandler, San Francisco, 1964) that statistical techniques are tools for exercising thought and not substitutes for thought.

ACKNOWLEDGMENTS

We wish to express our heartfelt thanks to Christine D. Shaw of Eagleton Institute of Politics, Rutgers University, who typed several drafts of the manuscript with the spirit and humor that the task required. We are indebted to the Literary Executor of the late Sir Ronald A. Fisher, F.R.S., and to Oliver & Boyd, Edinburgh, for permission to reprint Tables III, IV, and VII in their book *Statistical Tables for Biological, Agricultural and Medical Research*. We also wish to acknowledge with thanks the permission of the Chemical Rubber Company to reproduce the Table of Random Numbers and the permission of the Iowa State University Press to reproduce the Table of the Distribution of F from *Statistical Methods* by George Snedecor.

Chapter 1

MODELS IN RESEARCH

We believe that one of the main barriers to the achievement of an understanding of statistics is the student's failure to recognize that statistical tests are based on abstract models of reality and not on real characteristics of the world. A common misconception is that statistical tests are means of measuring reality, while in fact they are merely alternative models of reality no one of which, per se, is necessarily better than any other. It is usually late in an introductory statistics course that the student gets that flash of insight and everything "comes together." That is, the student recognizes the internal logic of statistical models. But even then, the student may be seeing only the relationship among the concepts and constructs he has learned, and he may not recognize the arbitrary nature of the basic assumptions of the models. This leads, in many cases, to a failure to appreciate these rather strict assumptions at a conscious level and a failure to comprehend fully that these assumptions are critical to the successful employment of statistical models.

It is our primary objective, therefore, to prepare the student so that he will begin his exposure to statistics with the conscious knowledge that he is being asked to understand abstract models. Thus, perhaps, he may begin his study with a flash of insight and build toward acquiring a thorough understanding of the critical features of the models. In this way the emphasis in learning statistics may be shifted from learning mathematical operations to understanding the necessary conditions for successful application.

To help the student reach an understanding of statistical models qua models, we provide an epistemological argument in this chapter. We recognize that there are other epistemologies that complement successful research methods, but the argument presented here places emphasis on points that complement the goals of this book. The basic assumption of the forthcoming argument is that a formal system for acquiring knowledge should be analogous to the system human beings actually use. We first present, at a general level, a view of the process of learning, and then attempt to present the process more formally. The formalized process, we believe, fairly characterizes a scientific method. The chapter concludes by showing the formal role that statistical models can play in this process.

MODELS IN HUMAN COGNITION

Whether out of natural curiosity or a quest for power, man has sought to understand his environment. This understanding has aimed, directly or indirectly, at achieving a measure of control over his environment: A convincing argument can be made that the pursuit of knowledge is aimed at eliminating human insecurity. In the course of building an understanding of his environment, the only source of information on which man can rely is sense experience. Events or processes that demand explanation are perceived in terms of attributes which can be seen, heard, touched, smelled, or tasted. In the pursuit of knowledge the senses have been both an aid and a hindrance. As an aid, sense experience has provided man with the ability to experience his environment directly. On the other hand, experience sometimes hinders understanding because the senses are indiscriminate. They feed enormous quantities of information to the brain without any priority or organization. Thus, for man to understand his environment, it is necessary that he acquire means to reduce the scope of the problem of understanding by constructing techniques for organizing his perceptions and focusing his attention.

One of the most useful tools for understanding is the analogy. When confronted with a new set of circumstances, one naturally seeks, consciously or unconsciously, to find similarities to familiar circumstances. When confronted with a new process, or sequence of events, a natural reaction is to attempt to relate the process to elements of a familiar process. Knowledge of the familiar process leads to hypotheses about the critical aspects of the unfamiliar process. The familiar process is used as a *model* of the new process and serves to organize perceptions and focus attention; thus the observer does not have to digest all information about the new process. As more information about the unfamiliar event is digested, the model is accepted, modified, or rejected. In the latter case, either another model is tried or a new model created.

When we use the term *model*, we are not referring to a paper diagram or a physical structure. When one finds elements of a familiar process that help him understand an unfamiliar process, the familiar process itself is not the model. The model is the way in which critical aspects of the familiar process are logically related. The word "model," as we use it here, refers to a purely abstract form, with no empirical reference. We call these models *cognitive* models because they are the tools we use to come to know or to understand. They are null intellectual structures, stored in the brain for use in understanding new phenomena. Let us illustrate.

Chomsky's argument about the linguistic ability of children is useful in this connection. (See Chomsky, 1959.) He argued that rules of grammar can be understood by a two-year-old because of the human ability to intuit patterns of sense experience with only fragmentary evidence. Chomsky dismissed the stimulus-response theory as appropriate for explaining a child's linguistic ability because a two-year-old does not have enough experience to learn language in that fashion. Furthermore, children can construct words and word structures that are out of their experience, but which are consistent with the rules of grammar. Chomsky argued that on hearing language, the child attempts to make sense out of his perception of sound patterns. He organizes the sound patterns by intuiting rules of grammar. The rules enable him to discriminate among sounds and therefore understand a language. A child intuits grammatical rules and then generalizes them to unfamiliar cases, enabling him to speak and understand a language after relatively little exposure to it. Evidence in support of Chomsky's argument is found in the fact that children overgeneralize grammatical rules. Many of the corrections we make in a child's grammar after three years of age concern exceptions to the rules. For example, the rule of agreement leads to "he do," "they does," and rules for plurals produce "gooses," "mouses," "sheeps," etc. Chomsky's argument illustrated the acquisition and use of models drawn from no obvious source. The cognitive model that enables generalization, in its most abstract form, is one of consistency: The child learns to expect things to be consistent, so when he discovers a pattern he intuits a rule that seems to "explain" the pattern.

As another example consider a classic political case of the application of a familiar model to an unfamiliar process. A problem facing United States foreign policy makers in the mid-1950s was whether or not to make some military commitment in Southeast Asia. The area was one of great political instability, as nationalist and "communist" groups sought a role in government. United States policy makers operated from an internationalist point of view, so they had to decide whether international interests of the United States were at stake in the disruptions of the Indo-Chinese status quo. It was decided that vital interests were at stake and therefore U.S. intercession was necessary. This conclusion followed from an analysis of international affairs drawn from the model used to characterize the problem. All the pro-western underdeveloped nations of the world were conceived as a row of dominoes. If one fell, it was argued, then all would fall. The model implied that the vital interests of the United States were tied to the stability of each of these nations. This argument led to the commitment of a large number of ground troops in an Asian land war, something western military strategists have opposed for centuries. At its peak, the war cost the United States $30 billion annually—more than the total annual economic production of all Southeast Asia. The cognitive model here, in its most abstract form, is of a chain reaction. Both consistency and chain reaction are cognitive models as we wish the term to be understood. Neither has a specific empirical reference and both are purely abstract concepts.

Legitimately, you might ask how a model is chosen or a new one created. A great deal of ink has been spilled on attempts to characterize formally the process of cognition. It has not been done successfully and probably it will not be done because the process is not formal. We can list rules ad infinitum for the use of deductive or inductive logic, but the rules will not lead to the process whereby we come to understand some phenomena. Rules of induction may lead to valid generalizations, and the rules of deduction may lead to valid inferences from a hypothetical understanding of the phenomena. But no prescriptive rules can be established leading to the "imaginative leap, a flight of fancy, taken to account for observed phenomena" (Goldberg, 1962, pp. 26–35). Stated another way, we are saying that there are no formal rules that lead to choosing a model, or analogy, or familiar process, or which account for a newly observed phenomenon. The flash of insight by which a model is selected is a purely creative process. Goldberg, in citing Hanson (1958), identified the process of retroduction as distinct from deduction or induction:

Deduction proves that something *must* [logically] be; induction shows that something *actually* is operative [to the extent of observations]; ... [retroduction] merely suggests that something *may be*. (Goldberg, 1961, p. 31.)

However we label it—intuition, insight, creative imagination, or retroduction—the process is one that cannot be formalized by definition. The only formalized aid to the selection of cognitive models is education. The more models one fully comprehends, the more choices for that "imaginative leap."

The fact that the process of the selection of a model cannot be formalized does not imply that no formal system of acquiring knowledge is possible. Presumably, the scientific method is a formalization (to the extent that it can be formalized) of the process of cognition as described and illustrated, but executed consciously by the scientist. Science is the formal acquisition of knowledge in the sense that, ideally, scientists are conscious of the models they employ, the rules they use to accept or reject a model, and the system they use for acquiring information about the process or event under study. The scientist must engage in two clearly different activities. One, he must hypothesize an explanation for some phenomenon based on the evidence he has about it. This entails applying a cognitive model to the process and thereby constructing a theory. The second distinct activity is the testing of the theory. Some theories are tested "automatically"; that is, they are rejected on the basis of some obvious evidence. Other tests require formal structures that measure nonobvious relationships deduced from the theory. It is for these tests that we require statistical models.

The remainder of this chapter is divided into two parts paralleling the divisions of the scientist's labor. First, we present and discuss some cognitive models in politics. Second, we discuss the role of statistical models in testing theories.

COGNITIVE MODELS IN POLITICS

Cognitive models pervade political science research and are the motivation of a great deal of political and social behavior. Perhaps the most common model used in political analysis, albeit crude, is the reification of some aspect of the political process. Plato's classic dictum—the state is but the "individual writ large"—is an example that continues to infest our intellect. Terminology currently used to describe the state is illustrative of reification: There is a *head* of state, the *arms* of government, a *body* of law, the *heart* of the government, and beneath the feet are the grass roots of support for the regime. Explanations of voter behavior employ the model extensively. We refer to the *body* politic, the *mood* of the voter, and use phrases like "uppermost in the voter's *mind.*" We talk about subgroupings of voters as if they were single individuals: the labor vote, the Black vote, the white-collar vote, etc. Such terms are not so commonly used among political scientists as they once were, but they are an integral part of many persons' understanding of politics.

A somewhat less widely employed model is that of conservation, the presumption that a variable phenomenon exists in finite quantities. Of course in some cases the model is accurate, but in many others its value is suspected. A misapplication would be a poor person's rationalization for his condition: The rich man cannot be happy (you can't have everything). Theories of equilibrium always employ the conservation model. Pre-Keynesian economics mistakenly held that the demand for capital always expanded to consume savings. As an economy contracted, and savings increased, investment would increase correspondingly, thus expanding the economy again. This application of the conservation model, implying a constant relationship between savings and investment, was debunked by Keynes as well as by the Great Depression. The result was a revolutionary change in the role of government in the economy. Keynes argued that the relationship between savings and investment was not as the classical economic theorists held, but that savings and investment had to be manipulated, presumably by government, into equilibrium. Successful applications of the conservation model can be found in political science and economics in theories relying on the concepts of marginal costs and opportunity costs. They assume that a consumer has utility for a finite amount of a product; thus, as this limit is reached, each additional unit of the product is valued less. Applied in these theories, the conservation model enables the theorist to make some reasonable statements about cost and utility functions and then to draw nonobvious inferences from them.

A model that has permeated western scholarship since the Renaissance is the mechanistic model; that is, looking at processes as precision machines, with each action determined by a single previous action. The industrial revolution, by making machines commonplace, brought the model into popular usage. The model has led the conception of events in terms of linear cause and effect. In the social sciences that product has been social or historical determinism. Marx's historical determinism, resting on the borrowed model of a dialectical process, clearly has had great impact on human behavior. A more contemporary use of the mechanistic model, however, is found in the "funnel of causation," in *The American Voter* (Campbell, 1966). Campbell and his associates specified multiple causes for events, but the funnel is deterministic. Stimulus-response explanations of human behavior are based on mechanistic models and are present in political science under the label "behavioralism." Behavioral theories account for human behavior by seeking in the human environment those stimuli that produce reactions in the organism, which in turn affect some behavior. It is a generally accepted proposition among behavioralists that attitudes (predispositions to action) are the parts of the organism that undergo change as a result of stimulation. Therefore, we find behavioralists spending a great deal of their time trying to study "political attitudes." If machines outlive their usefulness, perhaps we shall lose the mechanistic model, but it does not seem very likely to occur.

Political scientists have borrowed much knowledge of research techniques from the biological sciences and along with the techniques have borrowed one of their models as well. The model is that of a living organism. Each of the components of the organism's structure performs some function that enables it to continue living. Structural-functionalism is the basis for some of the most ambitious efforts in the social sciences. Examples are given by Parsons and Shils (1951), Lowi (1963), and Almond and Verba (1964). The essence of the model is to identify formal institutions, informal institutions, values, and norms by the functions they perform in the maintenance of the object of study. Mitchell (1962) showed the functions of various structures in U.S. society in maintaining the stability of the system. The structural-functional model is fairly common, perhaps because it has been borrowed from a life science and is clearly a model and therefore acceptable as a research tool.

Another model currently found in political science research, one that is conceptually related to structural-functionalism, is Darwin's natural-selection-evolution model. This model has served numerous purposes since its articulation. In the early part of the twentieth century, Social Darwinism had a great following in the United States. The model was used on the one hand to justify the status quo by arguing that this is the best of all possible worlds; on the other hand, the model was used to point out social injustice by arguing that the strong dominate the weak. Also, the model was used to substantiate arguments about differences between the races, and thus to justify segregation as a social policy. Elements of the Darwinian model are evident in the basic writings of the Nazi philosophers. Nazi ideology argued that the Aryan race, because it was the pinnacle of evolution, had the right and responsibility to dominate the inferior races of the world.

In political science research the Darwinian model is found in theories built on the development of complementary interests among groups with separate and distinct goals. Downs' (1956) theory of the party system postulated the existence of political parties and voters with distinctly different goals, but with an incentive to exploit each other. The relationship between the two develops toward satisfying both because each stumbles upon better ways of exploiting the other, thus evolving toward a new status quo in which each improves its position. Downs' parties adapt in the same way that "improved" mutants eventually drive out the dominant species: Those who adapt are more successful and those who do not die off (or lose elections).

Another model that is conceptually related to structural-functionalism and the natural-selection-evolution model is the cybernetics model. Deutsch's (1963) explication of this model's utility in political theory has produced a number of insights into previously unexplained phenomena, and has offered new accounts for some already "understood" phenomena. Easton's (1965) systems analysis is admittedly based on a cybernetics model. His "black box," the set of decision rules in a cybernetics system, has become as familiar to contemporary students of politics as Aristotle's *Politics* was to another generation. Furthermore, "feedback loops" are commonly found as an essential feature of many contemporary explanations of complex political phenomena.

Perhaps it is the versatility of these six cognitive models that enables them to survive. All six are enjoying continued usage because they have been found useful in solving problems confronting us. They have aided man in producing knowledge, and therefore have increased his power over his environment. These six models are certainly not the only models man finds useful, but they are fairly common and they serve to illustrate what we mean by cognitive models.

Now we are about to move into a discussion of the role of statistical models in testing hypotheses. Before we do, it is necessary to digress slightly and explain the philosophical problems of testing a hypothesis. Logical positivists have demonstrated that, empirically, it is not possible to prove any general proposition to be true (in the sense of validity, not Truth). One can only find out if a general proposition is *not false*. This follows from the fact that it is impossible to investigate all components of a generalization. Thus, researchers must be content to observe a number of tests of a proposition and, on finding no evidence to reject it as false, tentatively accept the proposition as true. If one of many observed cases demonstrates that the proposition is false, then the proposition is rejected. The falsifiability criterion is one of the basic tenets of research.

STATISTICAL MODELS AS TESTS FOR THEORIES

Statistical models are characteristically different from cognitive models, and they play a somewhat different role in the production of knowledge. The role of statistical models is to establish the correspondence between a theory and the "reality" the theory is intended to represent. After the researcher has chosen a cognitive model, translated it into a theory, and tentatively accepted the theory as representing the essence of the phenomenon under observation, he must devise formal tests of propositions drawn from the theory. Statistical models facilitate such tests. One of the fundamental points we would like to make here is that statistics should be approached as a study of mathematical models.

A mathematical model is a set of concepts and operating rules that allow us to explore the logical relationship among mathematical statements. They are tools that can be used to state problems in their most abstract form and to seek solutions at that level. They enable us to define a problem in its most essential elements and to explore the possible meanings of those elements. Mathematical models are useful because they enable us to solve generic classes of problems. It is of little value per se to know that if $a \cdot b = c$, then $a = c/b$. But if we wish to know how long it would take to go c miles at b miles per hour, then knowing $a \cdot b = c$ tells us that it would take c/b hours. We can easily solve this problem because we can look to its generic class; that is, the mathematical model that captures the essence of the problem. We are able to conclude that $a = c/b$ follows from $a \cdot b = c$ directly as a result of assumptions we made about a, b, and c, as well as the meaning of the symbols $(\cdot)$ and $(=)$. Because of these assumptions and definitions, $a = c/b$ necessarily follows from $a \cdot b = c$. Thus, we can say that $a \cdot b = c$ is a mathematical model, albeit a simple one. The implications we can draw from this model enable us to solve the class of problems for which the assumptions and definitions of the model are met, such as distance–rate–time problems.

Statistical models are mathematical models in the same sense as $a \cdot b = c$ is a mathematical model. The chief difference is that statistical models make a greater number of more complex assumptions. The model $a \cdot b = c$ contains three values of the same type. They are called *parameters* and they are constants. All we need to know in order to use the model is the value of each parameter a, b, and c (or perhaps values of any two and a definition of the third). In mathematics a parameter is defined as a quantity, the value of which is determined arbitrarily. In the generic model, a, b, and c have no values and the model per se places no restrictions on them. But we can plug in any combination of values for the parameters (which is consistent with the assumptions and definitions of the model) and the model tells us the specific numerical relationship among them. Once specific values are assigned to a, b, and c, they may have only these values. Statistical models contain parameters, but they also contain variables. Whereas a parameter (a constant) legitimately can take on only one value, a variable legitimately can take on a range of possible values. Perhaps the most interesting aspect of statistical models is that we find the values of the parameters by making assumptions about the relationship among variables and then use the observed values of the variables. The essential idea of using a statistical model is to answer the question: Assuming a specific type of mathematical function defines the relationship between variables, and given the data available (the variable or variables being observed), what are the most likely values of the parameters of the model? This point probably does not impress you now, before being exposed to statistical models, but is quite valuable and worth referring to after further study.

Procedurally, we test a theory with a statistical model by selecting a model that organizes and places restrictions on data so that the model reflects the assumptions of the theory. An appropriate statistical model is set up so that model parameters represent the important characteristics of the theory. The theory predicts the characteristics of the parameters (their sign and relative magnitude) in the statistical model. Then assumptions are made about the character of the data, and values for the parameters are calculated as prescribed by the statistical model; that is, propositions that were drawn from the theory are drawn from the statistical model. Next, the truth-value of the theoretical propositions are tested through observing the corresponding inferences drawn from the statistical model. This means that if the parameters meet the requirements or predictions of the theory, then the theory is accepted; if they do not, then a new or modified theory must be sought.

To illustrate, let us consider the cognitive model of adaptation applied to voting behavior. The model underlies rationality theories of voting. Voters are assumed to be rational; that is, they maximize political utility by efficiently pursuing their goals. In a two-party system where one party favors a particular policy and the other party opposes it, we would expect rational voters whose goals were promoted by that policy to favor the first party. Suppose we observe that the Republican party supports business interests. Then the applied cognitive model, our theory of voting behavior, predicts that voters whose goals are closely tied to business interests will support the Republican party. Up to this point we have applied the cognitive model of adaptation to voting behavior and have drawn a specific, testable statement from it. For data, suppose we have in-depth interviews with a random sample of voters. Now a statistical model must be set up. We decide on a way to measure the Republican voting, R, and the business interests, I, of a set of voters. For simplicity we assume that the relationship between R and I is linear. We can now state our hypothesis formally. The generic model of linear relationships is $Y = a + bX$. The terms a and b are the parameters in the model, and Y and X are variables. Suppose we define a as the net Republican vote due to exogenous factors and b as the effect of business interests on the Republican vote.

$$R = a + bI$$

The theory predicts that b will be positive. That is, higher values of I produce higher values of R. Needless to say, there is a statistical model available, designed precisely for such a problem. The model enables the estimation of the sign and relative magnitude of the parameters a and b. After having made assumptions about the important features of the measures of R and I, the model specifies how a and b are to be calculated. The estimates of these parameters enable the researcher to make a decision to keep or to reject the theory. There are, of course, numerous other parametric statistical models available for numerous other generic types of problems. Many models will be introduced in this text, but none assumes a mathematical function more complex than a linear function.

Parametric statistical models are used to estimate the true value of a parameter in a population while using data about only a sample from the population. One of the most valuable aspects of parametric statistical models is that each produces a measure of the reliability of the conclusions drawn from it. That is, each model gives an indication of how much confidence can be placed in the estimates of the parameters calculated from it. Since the models help the researcher to make decisions about hypotheses, it is quite valuable to the researcher to have a clear indication of how accurate the estimate is. This means that before the tests are performed, the researcher can decide what type of relationship would best test the propositions he has drawn from the applied cognitive model, *and* he can decide the critical level of reliability of the relationship at which he would accept or reject the proposition. Although such pretest decision rules do not eliminate bias, they discourage it.

We hasten to point out that parametric statistical models are not the only statistical models available for testing hypotheses. The researcher has the option of creating his own model or of using some of the wealth of nonparametric models available. The most common distinction between parametric statistics and nonparametric statistics is that the former is inferential and the latter is descriptive. Parametric statistical models are used to make inferences about a population from a sample of the population. Nonparametric statistical models are used to describe the characteristics of a data set, be it sample or population. Parametric statistical models are more powerful because they produce a measure of the reliability of their estimates, whereas nonparametric tests afford no such measure. On the other hand, nonparametric statistics can be used to analyze data to which parametric tests are inapplicable. Parametric tests can be used only if data are measured by at least an interval scale. Nonparametric tests are available for use on nominal and ordinal scales. We argue that a choice of tools of analysis should suit the sophistication of the data being analyzed. Where the data fit, one should use the more powerful tool—parametric statistical models.

OTHER USES OF STATISTICAL MODELS

It would be unfair, if not invalid, to argue that statistical models may be used only to test theoretical propositions. Other uses of statistical models are consistent with the preceding epistemological argument.

It was stated that models facilitate understanding by reducing the scope of a problem, focusing attention, and implying tentative explanations. Goldberg (1964) suggested the name "retroduction" for the dialogue between data and model which converges on an explanation. But what about the case where no model suggests itself to the researcher? Surely, we cannot advocate that if you draw a blank, then you ought not to study a phenomenon. For the sake of argument let us assume that there is a phenomenon for which no model offers obvious promise of satisfaction. The problem, then, becomes one of reducing the phenomenon to manageable proportions and refining perceptions of its features. This could mean inspecting it from various points of view or carefully examining small parts of it. In either case, arbitrary decisions must be made as to where to begin and how to conduct observation. One way to conduct such an investigation is to search for relationships between or among features of the phenomenon.

Statistical models may be used as an aid to perception in such an endeavor because a statistical model can simplify the task of the research by reducing the scope of the problem. Sophisticated statistical models can be employed only on quantitative data, and the process of quantification always simplifies; therefore, use of a statistical model may force the researcher to reduce the amount of data with which he must deal. Presumably, by reducing the amount of information the researcher must digest, the likelihood of discovering a model may be correspondingly increased. (Note the use of the conservation model here, based on the assumption that there is a finite amount of information with which a human being can deal effectively.)

A second way in which statistical models can be valuable in this connection would be as a tool for searching systematically for patterns in the phenomena under study. This would entail the application of varieties of alternative statistical models. Goldberg's retroduction, or Deutsch's (1963) "ah ha" experience, comes into play when the scientist suddenly puts together empirical relationships that entail some simplifying principles. Applying alternative statistical models to the same data might produce the relationships leading to explanation.

Statistical models *can* be used legitimately for functions other than testing hypotheses. We recognize this practice, but we do not recommend it, especially to the novice. In the first place, situations in which no model of a phenomenon applies are unlikely. There is almost always some possible explanation for a phenomenon. In the second place, the discovery of patterns in data may lead a researcher to "believe" in them. An excellent example of this possibility is the body of political science research predicated on the psychologist's stimulus-response model. Many students of politics "believe" in the existence of attitudes and predispositions and do not recognize that they are merely occasionally useful concepts. This miscomprehension has grown out of attempts to construct theories of voting behavior consistent with patterns found in political survey data. Such surveys, having been designed by psychologists of the stimulus-response school, probed attitudes and predispositions of voters. Since there were no theories of voting behavior, political scientists looked for patterns in the data to help them out. The patterns in the survey data led to explanations based on what the psychologists attempted to measure, a stimulus-response model of voting behavior. Only recently is political science research recovering from this approach to voting behavior. Hopefully, we have learned our lesson. One way to avoid the recurrence of this kind of problem is to employ statistical models for testing propositions consciously drawn from consciously applied cognitive models and, only under the most extreme conditions, to use statistical models to organize data.

The best epistemological argument against this practice is presented by Churchman (1963). In criticizing the popular view of scientific method, Churchman took to task the position that "observations are thought to be an anchor—or system of anchors—which supply rigidity to the structure of science" so that its resultant theories do not "float away." This view of scientific method holds that scientific endeavor is a process of going from the simple to the complex. The process runs from observation of facts to measurement, through hypothesis construction to theory: Simple observations build into complex theories. Churchman first pointed out that no phenomena occur with perfect certainty, but some phenomena occur with greater certainty than others. As phenomena occur with greater certainty, we are more likely to accept the phenomena as facts. But, he argued, the belief in fact entails theorizing. Churchman offered two examples of propositions that could be classified as facts:

1. An observed object X weighs k pounds.
2. An observed object X is blue.

These facts, he argued, are methodologically incomplete. The complete statement should read, "If X is observed under any of the conditions C_i belonging to the class of conditions C, by any observer O_j belonging to the class of observers O, the recorded observations will all belong to a class of propositions P." Statements 1 and 2 become facts because we believe that the test of the extended version of the proposition will validate them. But it is clear that there is a model of stability, or of consistency, underlying the acceptance of the proposition as fact. The expectation that the test will support the proposition is a belief in the model's successful operation. The model, of course, is the theoretical base of statements 1 and 2.

We are not arguing that one should not make assumptions; rather, we are arguing that it is not possible to avoid making assumptions, even when dealing with "facts." Hypothesis testing limits the researcher's problem by focusing his attention on relatively clearly defined method-ological problems. When he is conscious of the assumptions underlying the data, all pertinent relationships can be considered carefully. Pattern searching, on the other hand, is an open-ended process in which few limitations are placed on the scope of the data to be observed. Therefore, there are no limits placed on compounding assumptions about the data. In the case of the latter, the researcher is less likely to be conscious, prior to data analysis, of assumptions he is making. Therefore, results of a search for patterns in data are less likely to be reliable.

We believe a reasonable alternative to using statistical models for pattern searching is to search consciously for cognitive models of the process under study. This approach is more likely to produce meaningful results, for two reasons. First, it provides a systematic method for dealing with a complex problem. In the search for models, many models can be eliminated prior to data analysis, on grounds of inconsistency or their untestable structure. Second, the scope of the researcher's problem is reduced because he can deal with each model separately. Therefore, he can be more conscious of the assumptions he is making. A recurrent theme of this chapter has been that science is a pragmatic approach to producing knowledge: A search for models is probably better than a search for patterns in the data because the former is more likely to produce useful results.

SUMMARY

We have been prompted to compile this volume because of what we per-ceive to be a serious problem in political science research. Namely, statistics frequently has been misunderstood if not misapplied as a research tool. The problems in understanding and application, we believe, stem mostly from a lack of attention to the assumptions of statistical models. Too many students are exposed to a "cookbook" approach to research methods. The approach to research outlined above is, we believe, characteristic of what has come to be called the postbehaviorial revolution in political science. We place a great deal of emphasis on viewing the study of statistics as the study of models, for we believe this approach will lead to the deepest understanding of the subject matter.

Our epistemological position is presented in part to give the student a point of view from which to see statistical models. It also argues for a specific interpretation of the role of statistics in research. The approach implies that statistical models are appropriately used to test hypotheses. Put another way, statistical models are best used to make research decisions. A likely objection to this position is that it excludes many of the uses of statistics to describe data. Our rejoinder is lucidly argued by Churchman (1963, chap. 4). There are no facts quo facts; each definition and each category with which we identify a fact is theoretically based. Thus, to use a statistical model to describe data is to apply some theory or theories unconsciously to the data. Very little of importance is likely to be discovered by such a haphazard procedure. Furthermore, the latter approach to data analysis (strictly defined) does not enjoy popularity. Occasionally one finds some research for which this was the apparent procedure, but in each case there are restrictions on admissible variables, restrictions on measurement, etc., suggesting that the researcher had oriented his research toward a theoretical base, even though he may not have been conscious of it. We argue that such a researcher should state his theory clearly in advance of his research. Only then will he be able to establish clear decision rules for the acceptance or rejection of a theory. The chances of producing knowledge are few if one is not able to state the theory clearly prior to undertaking data analysis. For these reasons, we believe that the approach to research outlined here is more likely to be productive.

Also implied by this view of research is the position that scientific method is a pragmatic endeavor. The value of a cognitive model lies in the results that can be derived from it. The model should be judged by the utility of its results. We conclude, with Churchman (1963, p. 89), "that science is identified by its aims; that science does not have any clearly identifiable actions which are 'best' with respect to its aims; that all scientific aims must be examined in the light of their effectiveness as strategies or tactics."

However, it is not necessary to accept our view of research in order to understand statistical models as we present them. Even the brute empiricist would benefit from knowing the assumptions underlying the statistical models he employs. We are confident that this volume can be of value to the student of politics who intends to pursue data analysis at a sophisticated level, regardless of his epistemology. Hopefully, this discussion, as a thesis or antithesis, will improve the comprehension of the study of statistics as a study of models.

REFERENCES   Chapter 1

Almond, Gabriel, and Sidney Verba. *The Civic Culture*. Princeton: Princeton University Press, 1964.

Campbell, Angus, et al. *The American Voter*. New York: Wiley, 1966.

Chomsky, Naom. "Review of Skinner," *Language*, Vol. 35, No. 1 (1959) pp. 26–57.

Churchman, C. West. *Prediction and Optimal Decision*. Englewood Cliffs, N.J.: Prentice-Hall, 1963, pp. 87–89.

Deutsch, Karl W. *The Nerves of Government*. New York: The Free Press, 1963.

Downs, Anthony. *An Economic Theory of Democracy*. New York: Harper & Row, 1956.

Easton, David. *A Systems Analysis of Political Life*. New York: Wiley, 1965.

Goldberg, Arthur. "Political Science as Science." In *Politics and Social Life: An Introduction to Political Behavior*, Nelson Polsby, Robert A. Dentler, and Paul A. Smith (eds.). Boston: Houghton Mifflin, 1964.

Hanson, Norwood R. *Patterns of Discovery*. Cambridge: Cambridge University Press, 1958, p. 85.

Lowi, Theodore J. "Toward Functionalism in Political Science," *American Political Science Review*, Vol. LVII (1963), pp. 570–583.

Marx, Melvin H. (ed.). *Learning: Theories*. London: Macmillan, 1970.

Meehan, Eugene. *Explanation in Social Science: A System Paradigm*. New York: Dorsey Press, 1968.

Mitchell, W. C. *The American Polity*. New York: The Free Press of Glencoe, 1962.

Northrop, Filmer S. *Logic of the Sciences and the Humanities*. New York: Macmillan, 1947.

Parsons, Talcott, and Edward Shils. *Toward a General Theory of Action*. Cambridge: Harvard University Press, 1951.

Chapter 2

BACKGROUND FOR THE STUDY
OF STATISTICS

In this chapter we introduce the student to some elementary definitions, notational symbols, and concepts, the understanding of which is assumed throughout this book. In the usual approach to the study of statistics these conventions are dealt with as they arise, but we feel that this approach may divert the reader's attention from studying statistical models per se. Thus, we have separated out a good deal of the mechanics of employing statistical models and methodological problems in order to avoid confusing them with the study of statistical models. We assume the reader to be acquainted with the basic concepts of elementary algebra.

VARIABLES

A variable is a quantity that can take on any value. The range of many variables is unlimited theoretically, but in practice the feasible values of most variables occur within a specified range. Common variables in physical science are height, strength, and speed. Common political examples are power, participation, and political party strength. The range of a variable defines its limits, its maximum and minimum possible values. We denote the variable with a capital letter, usually X or Y. Subscripted X's are used to denote specific values of the variable. For example, let the variable X represent percent electoral support for a Democratic candidate for governor in five counties in some state. This can be represented by the following hypothetical data:

X: $X_1 = 48.4$, $X_2 = 51.3$, $X_3 = 60.1$, $X_4 = 39.8$, $X_5 = 49.8$

The subscripts to the X's—1, 2, 3, 4, and 5—identify each X_i as a county. If we desire to refer to the X's in general, in this case for example, to define how Democratic support was calculated, we use the subscript i.

$$X_i = \frac{\text{county Democratic vote in year } k}{\text{total county turnout in year } k}(100)$$

Read: For county *i* (any given county in the set X) a value of the variable X is determined by the ratio of Democratic vote for governor in county *i*, in year *k*, to total vote in county *i*, year *k*. The range of the variable is 0 to 100. The actual observed values are the five values of X_1 through X_5 for respective counties.

· A particular type of variable, a *random variable*, is very important to the logic of statistical models. A random variable is one whose values have probabilities associated with them. Each value in the range of the variable has a number associated with it, describing the likelihood that the value will turn up purely by chance. The face-up side of a fair die has six possible values for each roll. The probability of any one of the values is 1/6. When two dice are rolled, the number of possible values (the sum of the faces) is increased to 11, and the respective probabilities of the values are not equal. There are 36 possible different combinations of faces of the dice and only 11 possible outcomes; thus, some values must be more likely than others. The value 2 can be achieved only one way $(1,1)$, but the value 5 can be achieved four ways $(4,1)$, $(3,2)$, $(2,3)$, $(1,4)$.

Table 2-1

Random Variables

Value	2	3	4	5	6	7	8	9	10	11	12
Frequency	1	2	3	4	5	6	5	4	3	2	1
Probability	1/36	2/36	3/36	4/36	5/36	6/36	5/36	4/36	3/36	2/36	1/36

The probabilities of the values of most real-world random variables increase as they get closer to the midpoint of the range of the variables, just as they do in the dice example. Variables that have a single peak in roughly the center of their range are variables comprising compounds of independent random processes. See Table 2-1. The values of random variables, as in the example of two dice, are independent of each other, and each value of each is determined randomly.

A Political Example

Suppose we had reason to believe that elections officials, in counting minority candidate ballots (in a place where there are no voting machines), systematically counted inaccurately. Suppose that, where one party clearly was the winner, elections officials rounded off the number of votes for the minority rather than go through the trouble of counting accurately. The variable to investigate would be *vote count*. Assuming that most rounding would show up in the digit column, the range of the variable would be 0 to 9. It is a random variable because each of its values has a probability associated with it; by chance, each digit would show up as 1/10 of the observations. But the lazy-counter hypothesis would lead us to expect the values 0 or 5 to occur more often than once in ten observations because they are "natural" rounding points. To explore this question, we would count the absolute frequency of the occurrence of each digit in the returns from election districts (precincts). The absolute frequency is the number of observations of each value of the variable. These frequencies are shown in column 2 of Table 2-2. But to have a standard measure to compare among categories, we compute a relative frequency. This is found in column 3. The *relative frequency* is the ratio of the number of observations in each category to the total number of observations, and it is a good way to summarize the figures in column 2. We see that categories 0 and 5 have .234 of the observations, while the average of the remaining four pairs of eight categories is .194. There may be some truth in the lazy-counter hypothesis.

Table   2-2

Vote Count Frequencies

| *1* | *2* | *3* |
X	Absolute frequency	Relative frequency
0	51	.117
1	43	.099
2	45	.103
3	38	.087
4	39	.089
5	51	.117
6	43	.099
7	48	.110
8	34	.078
9	44	.101
Total	436	1.000

Before leaving the topic of variables we should consider an important distinction in the way variables can be measured. In our first example, Democratic support is measured by a ratio that presumably could take on any value between 0 and 100. There are no natural dividing points between values of the variable. If we conceive of a straight line between 0 and 100, the values of the variable could fall anywhere on that line. That is to say that there is a continuity of possible values of the variable. Appropriately, such a variable is called a *continuous variable*. In our third example, however, the possible values of the variable are restricted to ten. There are dividing points between categories, and only certain values are possible. This kind of variable is called a *discrete variable* because there are discrete differences between the possible values it could take on. Occasionally, it becomes necessary to convert a continuous variable to a discrete variable.[1] This is accomplished by collapsing the continuous variable (that is, arbitrarily defining discrete intervals for the continuous scale), and then treating all observations within the interval as having the same value. For example, one might convert the almost continuous variable income to a discrete variable by grouping the data in intervals of $3000. The first category would be 0–$2999, the second $3000–$5999, and so forth. Some possible values of the discrete variable would be the midpoint of the interval, $1500, $4500, etc., consecutive integers, the average of the group, or some other value that reasonably represents it. Converting a continuous variable to a discrete one results in the loss of some information, but sometimes it is necessary to simplify data in order to comprehend them. One should take care that the simplification does not result in too much distortion. This is largely a question of the researcher's judgment.

In summary, we have offered intuitive definitions of the concepts of variable and random variable, illustrated some of their features with absolute frequency distributions and relative frequency distributions, and concluded by defining continuous and discrete variables. We turn now to other techniques for describing variables, building on the concepts presented here.

NOTATION, SYMBOLS, AND OPERATIONS

In our discussion of variables we mentioned that the subscript was used to identify individual observations of a variable. Usually, the subscript i is used to identify individual observations as a general case, but frequently a double subscript is encountered; for example, Y_{ij}. The double subscript identifies a cell in a matrix. The i refers to row and the j to column; therefore Y_{ij} identifies individual cells in a matrix as a general case. In denoting a simple variable, the subscript i may be considered matrix notation identifying a row of a matrix. As such, a variable is a one-column multiple-row matrix with the reference to a column dropped. If the column reference were included, each value of the variable would be subscripted Y_{i1} with the i referring to row and the 1 to the single column.

Since we shall encounter matrices in the study of statistics, it is useful to review matrix notation. Essentially, a matrix is a cross-classificatory scheme. A given set of units of observation are simultaneously classified by two attributes or variables. Suppose we have a population of Congress-

		Vote	
		Yea	Nay
Region	South	n_{11}	n_{12}
	non-South	n_{21}	n_{22}

FIGURE 2-1

men who can be classified as either from the South or not, and as having voted for or against some bill before Congress. See Figure 2-1. The n_{ij} refer to the number in each cell of the matrix. The term n_{12} means row 1, column 2. If one wanted to stipulate that no cell in the matrix has less than 50 Congressmen in it, we would write $n_{ij} \geqslant 50$: It is a general characteristic of the matrix that no cell has less than 50 observations.

A summation sign, $\sum$ (sigma), should not bother the student who has an acquaintance with college-level mathematics. The sign is usually written thus

$$\sum_{i=1}^{N}$$

with some terms following it. The $i = 1$ below the sigma and the N above it should be read as follows: "Add up the values, beginning with the first value and ending with the Nth." The N can be any number. If the whole expression is

$$\sum_{i=1}^{5} X_i$$

it means: "Add up the first five values of X." The i under the summation sign refers you to the i after the variable following the summation sign:

$$\sum_{i=1}^{5} X_i = X_1 + X_2 + X_3 + X_4 + X_5$$

If the expression is

$$\sum_{i=2}^{3,5} X_i$$

it means: "Add up values 2, 3, and 5 of the X's." That is,

$$\sum_{i=2}^{3,5} X_i = X_2 + X_3 + X_5$$

Consider a 5 by 2 matrix of X's. Suppose we wish to sum the first column only. This would be indicated by

$$\sum_{i=1}^{5} X_{i1}$$

The sum of the second column only would be indicated

$$\sum_{i=1}^{5} X_{i2}$$

The sum of the whole matrix is

$$\sum_{i=1}^{5} X_{i1} + \sum_{i=1}^{5} i2 = \sum_{i=1}^{5} \sum_{j=1}^{2} X_{ij}$$

A double summation instructs you to sum the sums. That is, add all the columns and then total the sums of the columns:

$$
\begin{array}{ll}
X_{11} & X_{12} \\
X_{21} & X_{22} \\
X_{31} & X_{32} \\
X_{41} & X_{42} \\
X_{51} & X_{52}
\end{array}
$$

$$\sum X_{i1} + \sum X_{i2} = \sum_{i=1}^{5} \sum_{j=1}^{2} X_{ij}$$

The summation sign conforms to a few logical rules. Recall from elementary algebra that in expanding an expression, you always work from the inside out. This rule follows for the summation sign. Whatever the operation to be performed on the quantity being summed, always perform the operation first.

$$\sum_{i=1}^{N} X_i Y_i \quad \text{(multiply the X's times the Y's before summing)}$$

$$\sum_{i=1}^{N} \frac{X_i}{Y_i} \quad \text{(divide the X's by the Y's before summing)}$$

$$\sum_{i=1}^{N} X_i^2 \quad \text{(square the X's before summing)}$$

You should verify that

$$\sum_{i=1}^{N} X_i^2 \neq \left(\sum_{i=1}^{N} X_i \right)^2$$

The rules for addition and subtraction are straightforward:

$$\sum_{i=1}^{N} (X_i + Y_i) = \sum_{i=1}^{N} X_i + \sum_{i=1}^{N} Y_i$$

$$\sum_{i=1}^{N} (X_i - Y_i) = \sum_{i=1}^{N} X_i - \sum_{i=1}^{N} Y_i$$

Finally, there are rules for dealing with constants. Let A represent a constant:

$$\sum_{i=1}^{N} A X_i = A \sum_{i=1}^{N} X_i$$

$$\sum_{i=1}^{N} \frac{X_i}{A} = \frac{1}{A} \sum_{i=1}^{N} X_i$$

$$\sum_{i=1}^{N} A = NA$$

The reader should verify each of these rules.

MEASUREMENT

Perhaps the reason statistical models had not been applied in political research before the age of the computer is that political scientists had been unable previously to develop very sophisticated measures of political variables. The problem is still with us, though it is being dealt with, and it is one to which we should all be sensitive because only certain types of scales are amenable to sophisticated statistical analysis.

To measure a thing is to characterize formally some of its properties. As we shall see below, the formal characterization may range from simple labeling to complex mathematical functions. Our ability to understand a phenomenon is directly related to the sophistication with which we can describe its important properties. The more subtle and discrete the tools of measurement, the more comprehensive is the characterization of the phenomenon. It follows that the levels of measurement (that is, types of scales) available as tools for the researcher are critical. Students of measurement theory generally identify four types of scales: nominal, ordinal, interval, and ratio. The four differ in their mathematical properties, and therefore vary in the degree of analytic sophistication for which each can be used.

Torgerson (1965, chap. 2), in his discussion of the types of scales, approached classification in a useful way. Suppose we look at measurement as the assignment of numbers to represent properties of phenomena.

The problem of measurement is to assign numbers so that there is a one-to-one correspondence between the characteristics of the numbers and the characteristics of the properties they are intended to represent. Without any rules to tell us how to do this, we are left with an infinity of sets of numbers to represent properties of phenomena. Each level of measurement provides a set of rules that reduces the possible sets of numbers corresponding to the properties they represent. "Each of the [four] types of scales accomplishes this basic feature of reducing the completely arbitrary element in the assignment of numbers to represent the property to a different degree" (Torgerson, 1965, p. 16).

Nominal Scales

A nominal scale is the simplest means of measuring the amount or degree of a property. It entails a simple taxonomy and labeling, the assignment of names to categories. The degree of mathematical sophistication of a nominal scale is described with equal ease: A nominal scale permits no mathematical operations on the scale values. Some examples of nominal scales are names of persons, names of nations, names of political parties, identification of blocs of nations or of voters, etc. Of course any of these sets of alphabetic labels could be replaced by unique numbers. The function of the label is to set the category apart from other categories, and since any name (or number) that accomplishes this is an appropriate label, the labels themselves have no meaning. It follows that any meaning attached to the labels by mathematical operations is equally meaningless. The mathematical weakness of a nominal scale leads us to refer to it as the "lowest" level of measurement. Any set of unique numbers can constitute a nominal scale.

Ordinal Scales

Proceeding up the ladder of mathematical sophistication and reducing the set of possible numbers representing the characteristics of a property, we encounter ordinal scales. An ordinal scale is one that, by the magnitude of numbers, ranks a property by degree. Any set of numbers is suitable as long as it reflects the rank ordering of the property being measured. An ordinal scale is constructed by ranking the observations of the property and then assigning numerical values consistent with the ranking. A common source of ordinal scales in social research is sample-survey data. A survey respondent may be asked to rank a number of candidates for office or rank political issues on a conservative-to-liberal scale. The respondent indicates a "more than" ($>$) or "less than" ($<$) relationship. Suppose he ranks four candidates, A, B, C, and D, as conservative to liberal. Any of the sets of numbers in Table 2-3 would accurately reflect

Table 2-3

Ordinal Scaling

	1	2	3	4	5
Conservative	A	1	1	4	1,000,000
	B	2	1.1	3	.3
	C	3	1.2	2	.2
Liberal	D	4	4	1	.1

this ordering. There is no clear direction in which the ranking should go in Table 2-3; thus, the values in columns 2 through 5 are equally valid. In many cases an ordinal scale will describe an order of magnitudes of a phenomenon, or a sequence of events such as the order in which nations join a coalition. In these cases it would be natural to assign lower values to "higher" ranks so that scale magnitude would reflect sequential order.

Although ordinal scales do not permit mathematical operations on their values, the numerical value has some meaning per se. For example, scale values can be used to compare *among* observations. If $A > B$, then A is ranked higher on the scale than B, even if we do not know how much higher. Furthermore, since the scale progresses in one direction, transitivity holds: If $A > B$ and $B > C$, then $A > C$. By stating this meager mathematical potential for ordinal scales, we have exhausted the possibilities for their manipulation. There are, however, a number of useful statistical tests based on ordinal scales, so the reader should not dismiss ordinal data because of their mathematical limitations. Siegel (1956, chap. 9) listed and explained these tests.

Interval Scales

An interval scale is the minimum required level of measurement for the use of most of the statistical models presented in this book. Like ordinal scales, interval scales have no natural zero point. Unlike ordinal scales, the relative distances between observations, as expressed by the scale values of the observations, are meaningful. A familiar example of an interval scale is *time*. There is no natural zero point of time, and therefore any set of numbers that preserves the intervals in lengths of time between events is an adequate scale.

An example of an interval scale in social research is the Von Neuman utility experiment cited by Luce and Raffia (1957, chap. 2). In the case of three alternatives (x, y, z), the object is to measure a respondent's value for the alternatives in "utiles." First the respondent is asked to rank-order the alternatives. Assume that he ranks the alternatives x, y, z in descending order of preference. Then he is offered a series of lotteries. He is offered a choice between the second alternative for certain and a lottery between the first and third. For example, he is offered y for certain or x with a probability of .9 and z with a probability of .1. New lotteries are offered until a set of probabilities are found (for x and z) such that the respondent is unable to make up his mind. Suppose the respondent cannot decide whether to choose between y for certain and a lottery consisting of x with a probability of .6 and z with a probability of .4. Then it is concluded that $.6y = x$, and if $y = 1$, then $x = .6$ and $z = 0$. This set of numbers, $y = 1$, $x = .6$, and $z = 0$, is an interval scale that is a linear function of the respondent's "true" values for x, y, and z. Any set of numbers that preserves these relative intervals, say

$$\frac{y-x}{x-z} = \frac{.4}{.6} = .667$$

adequately represents the respondent's "utiles."

Interval scales allow many more complicated mathematical operations than do ordinal scales. With an ordinal scale, one is stuck with expressing relationships among observations as "more than" or "less than." With a variable measured by an interval scale, it is meaningful to add, subtract, multiply, or divide the *intervals* between variables. It is not, however, legitimate to perform any of these operations on the scale values themselves. Suppose, for example, we have a scale with four points, as shown in Figure 2-2. The distances between the points are shown on the bottom of

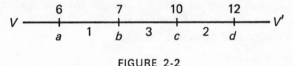

FIGURE 2-2

the line VV' and the scale values for the points are shown above the points (a, b, c, d). It is meaningful to say that the interval between c and d is twice the interval between a and b. It is not meaningful to say that d is twice a. The relationship between the points on the scale is a function of the set of numbers used to represent the scale and is not a "true" scale.

Ratio Scales

Ratio scales, or cardinal scales as they are sometimes called, have a natural zero point, and only one set of numbers adequately represents the scale. This means that any mathematical operation of any kind can be performed on the scale, among values, intervals combinations, etc. Ratio scales are fairly common, once one begins to look for them. Virtually any economic variable can be measured by a ratio scale: education (in years), popular votes, roll-call votes, and a host of demographic indices. In addition, proportions are ratio scales, thus enabling the conversion of many nominal or ordinal scales to ratio scales. If the property being measured is dichotomous (or, in some cases, trichotomous), then the dummy scale might suffice. A dummy variable is constructed by having the scale equal 1 if the property of interest is present, and zero otherwise. A more detailed discussion of the use of dummy variables is taken up in Chapter 9.

This classification of types of scales is cumulative; that is, each level of scale can be legitimately treated as a "lower" level of measurement. All ratio scales may be treated as interval, ordinal, or nominal scales. Interval scales may be treated as ordinal and nominal scales, and an ordinal scale may be treated as a nominal scale. Stepping down from one level of scale to another is easy, and sometimes it makes good sense. But the interesting question is: Are there conditions when it is justifiable to move up one level of sophistication? The most serious jump one could make would be to treat an ordinal scale as an interval scale. Indeed, it is the most tempting leap for a social scientist because so many variables, especially those measured by survey responses, are measured by ordinal scales. We do not believe that it is always unjustifiable to treat an ordinal scale as an interval scale, but we cannot recommend the practice. In order to understand the implications of this assumption, one must have more than a passing understanding of research methods. Furthermore, there are implications and procedures available from scaling theory to guide such a decision. The researcher contemplating the change of a scale should be thoroughly familiar with the techniques of scaling theory. (Refer to Torgerson, 1965.) Finally, there must be sound theoretical reasons for the change in scales. The researcher must have strong reasons to believe that his ordinal scale is actually an interval scale. We would argue that a researcher pursuing a project with methods at the level presented in this book would probably not understand all the implications of changing scales. We conclude that it would be an extremely unwise decision to treat an ordinal scale as an interval scale.

Graphs of Functions

Occasionally it is useful to picture graphically a relationship between two variables. This can be done in a variety of ways, but we are interested here in a particular technique that will aid in the understanding of some basic statistical concepts. In particular, we wish to graph functions on a two-dimensional plane called a *rectangular coordinate* system. The rectangular coordinate system is defined as in Figure 2-3, where a horizontal line XX' intersects a perpendicular line YY' at point 0, called the origin. Line XX' is called the X-axis, and line YY' is called the Y-axis. Values of X to the right of the origin are positive; to the left, X values are negative. Values of Y above the origin are positive, and below the origin Y values are negative. Every point in the XY plane can be defined by a value of X and a value of Y. These values are called the *coordinates* of a point: the X coordinate is called the abscissa and the Y coordinate is called the ordinate.

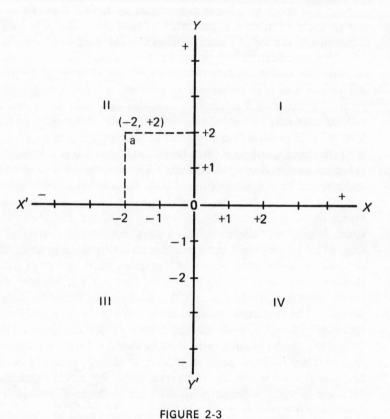

FIGURE 2-3

In identifying a point by its coordinates, the abscissa is written first. The point a in Figure 2-3 is identifiable by the coordinates $(-2, +2)$, that is, $X = -2$ and $Y = +2$.

A brief definition of functions is necessary before a graphical representation of a function is presented. The variable Y is defined as a function of the variable X if, on assigning a value to X, the value of Y is determined. The relationship is denoted $Y = F(X)$. For example, if we define $Y = F(X)$ as $Y = 2X$, then for $X = 2$, $Y = 4$, for $X = 1$, $Y = 2$, etc. Further, we can see that the value of the variable Y depends on the value of X, but X does not depend on anything for its value. Thus, we say that Y is a dependent variable in the function and X is an independent variable.

Let us turn now to some illustrations of the graphical presentation of functions. The simple function presented above, $Y = F(X) = 2X$, is easily shown. By arbitrarily setting X (the abscissa) at a series of values, we can solve for Y (the ordinate) and get a series of coordinates of points in the rectangular coordinate system (Figure 2-4). The graph of the function

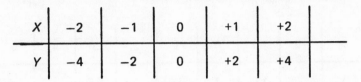

X	-2	-1	0	$+1$	$+2$	
Y	-4	-2	0	$+2$	$+4$	

FIGURE 2-4

(Figure 2-5) turns out to be a straight line passing through all the points defined by the coordinates. Any function that, when graphed, produces a straight line is called a *linear function*. Formally, a linear function is defined as a polynomial of degree 1, that is, a polynomial in which all

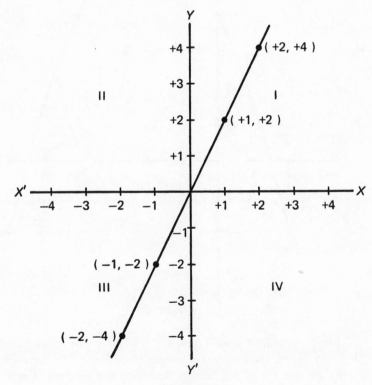

FIGURE 2-5

variables are raised to the first power. Functions that contain variables squared, cubed, etc., produce curved lines when graphed. For example, consider the function

$$Y = -(\tfrac{1}{2}X^2 - 2X - 4)$$

which is displayed in Figures 2-6 and 2-7.

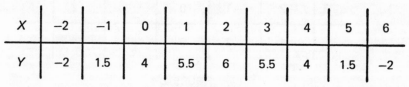

X	-2	-1	0	1	2	3	4	5	6
Y	-2	1.5	4	5.5	6	5.5	4	1.5	-2

FIGURE 2-6

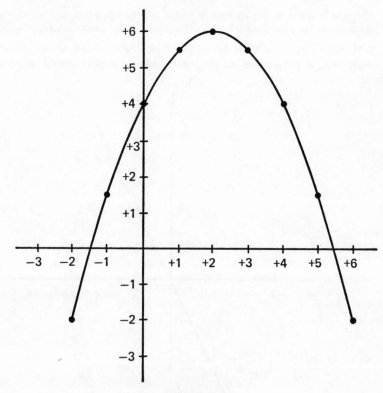

FIGURE 2-7

Linear equations always have one and only one set of coordinates. They are called *single-valued functions*. Nonlinear functions may have more than one set of coordinates satisfying the function. For example, $Y = F(X) = X^2$. If $Y = 25$, $X = \pm 5$.

Any function with two variables can be graphed in a two-dimensional space, regardless of how complicated the function. When a third variable is added, however, a three-dimensional space is required to represent the function pictorially. A function in such a space would be represented by a plane rather than a line. This complicates matters somewhat, but we can conceive a three-dimensional space nevertheless. The problem, conceptually, arises when the number of variables in the function exceeds three. However difficult it is for us to conceive of a four-, five-, or six-dimensional space, such spaces exist in the abstract world of mathematical reasoning. Pictorial representation is another matter entirely.

HISTOGRAMS

Suppose you are advising a Republican candidate in his campaign for assemblyman in the state legislature. His particular assembly seat has a constituency of 50 election districts (precincts). The candidate would like to know, in terms of partisan vote, what he is up against. You compute the percentage of Republican votes in the last assembly race, group the data as in Table 2-4, and count election districts in each group. To assign

Table 2-4

Histogram Data

Republican, %	Midpoint	Absolute frequency	Relative frequency, f_i
33–37.9	35.5	4	.08
38–42.9	40.5	6	.12
43–47.9	45.5	8	.16
48–52.9	50.5	12	.24
53–57.9	55.5	9	.18
58–62.9	60.5	7	.14
63–67.9	65.5	4	.08
Total		50	1.00

dividing points in this discrete data, a value falling between the intervals 37.9 and 38.0 is put in the higher interval if it exceeds 37.95 and in the lower category if it is equal to or less than 37.95. When you show Table 2-4 to your candidate, he says: "That's fine, but I have to use this information to attract campaign contributions. Is there any way to present it so that its importance can be seen more quickly?" Being a resourceful political scientist, you decide to summarize the data in a histogram. That is, you

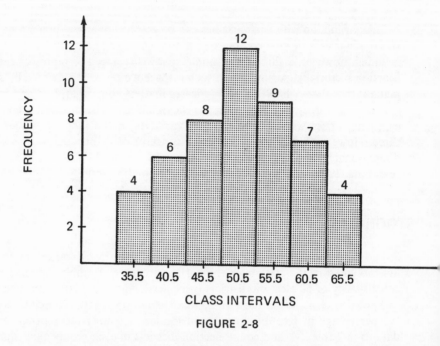

CLASS INTERVALS

FIGURE 2-8

decide to draw a picture of the data for the candidate (Figure 2-8). The base line of the histogram indicates class intervals and the vertical line indicates frequency count. Each interval is identified by its midpoint. The histogram visually displays the absolute frequency count in Table 2-4. The higher the bar, the greater is the density of observations in that interval. It shows the candidate's potential contributors that the greatest concentration of election districts occurs around the 50 percent point and that the distribution of the variable is relatively symmetrical. This should indicate to contributors that, if history is any indicator of things to come, the Republican candidate has a pretty good chance of victory.

The geometry of the histogram is interesting. The frequency of observations in each interval is represented by the height of the bar. By multiplying the height by the class interval, which is taken to be 5, you get the area of the bar for that interval. In Figure 2-8, the interval 38 to 43 contains 6 observations. The area of the bar for that interval is $5 \times 6 = 30$. We take the area of each bar in the histogram and sum the areas:

$$5 \sum_{i=1}^{7} f_i(X_i) = 250$$

where

f_i = frequency count in interval i

$i = (1, 2, ..., 7)$ intervals, identified by their midpoints

It should be obvious that $250 = (\text{interval size})(N)$, or $5(50)$. By dividing the area of each bar by the total area, the relative frequency of each interval is obtained. For the interval 38 to 43, the area of the bar divided by the total area is $30/250 = .12$, the relative frequency of values in that interval. The area of each bar can be used to determine the relative frequency of observations in its interval. By converting each bar of the histogram from an absolute frequency to a relative frequency, a new histogram can be drawn (Figure 2-9). The new vertical axis is the relative

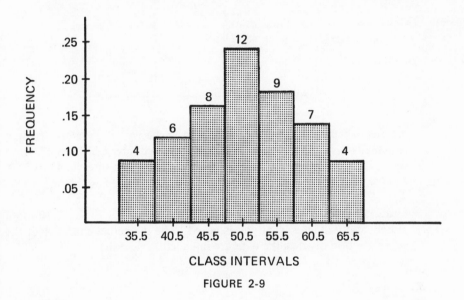

CLASS INTERVALS

FIGURE 2-9

frequency of each interval. The height of the bar, as measured in units on the vertical axis, is the proportion of the total area of all bars. That is, the height of each bar is the relative frequency of that interval. Note that if we set the total area of the histogram equal to 1.0, the area of each bar would be directly interpretable as the relative frequency of observations in its interval.

In this example the histogram was drawn with equal class intervals. This is not a necessary requirement, but caution should be exercised if unequal intervals are used. The height of each bar should be measured in a standard unit, frequencies per interval. In the example, the interval is 5, and all bars are drawn in terms of the frequency of observations per interval of 5.

Suppose the data you gathered for your Republican assembly candidate was somewhat different. You are quite sure that the distribution of support for the Republican assembly candidate was fairly evenly distributed around the 50 percent point, but the results from the preceding election distort this relationship somewhat. Instead of the distribution in Table 2-4, you find the data given in Table 2-5. In order to get the election

Table 2-5

Effect of Observed Data on Distribution

33–37.9	4
38–42.9	6
43–47.9	3
48–52.9	17
53–57.9	9
58–62.9	7
63–67.9	4

returns to represent Republican strength in the way Republican strength is actually distributed, you can collapse the two intervals 43 to 47.9 and 48 to 52.9. Note that there are 20 observations in the interval 43 to 52.9. But the height of the bar representing this interval would not be 20, because 43 to 53 is a double interval. The height of the bar would be measured in frequencies per interval, $20/2 = 10$. The histogram in Figure 2-10 more closely approximates what you believed to be the actual character of the set of election districts the data are intended to describe.

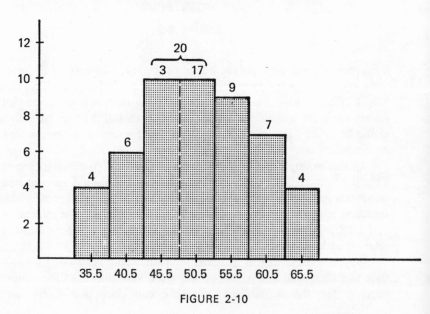

FIGURE 2-10

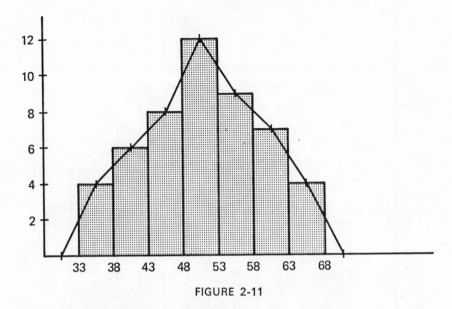

FIGURE 2-11

Visual presentation of the distribution of a variable may be presented alternatively as a frequency polygon. A frequency polygon is a line that connects the midpoints of the bars of a histogram. Figure 2-11 presents the frequency polygon for Figure 2-8. The polygon gives the viewer an idea of the densities of the distribution at various points. The frequency polygon has the advantage of apparently dispersing grouped data. In the example of 50 election districts, the data have been grouped rather arbitrarily. The smoother polygon de-emphasizes the grouping while presenting a reasonable picture of the real distribution of the variable.

Consider a hypothetical case in which a continuous variable has been made discrete by grouping. Using the example in Figure 2-8, notice what happens in Figure 2-12 when the size of the class intervals is reduced by one-half. The new histogram begins to "smooth out" the steps in the histogram in Figure 2-8. Consider a continuing reduction of the intervals of the grouping until steps become smaller and smaller and the distribution appears to be described by a continuous line. This line is called a *frequency curve* (Figure 2-13). The frequency curve describes the absolute frequency distribution of a continuous variable, and describes the frequency density in the same way that the bars of a histogram show the frequency density of a discrete variable.

If we want to know the relative frequency of some values of the continuous variable between two points on its scale, we convert the absolute frequency distribution to a relative frequency distribution and find the area under the frequency curve between the two points. How can this be done? Clearly, the problem is quite complicated. But this mathematical problem,

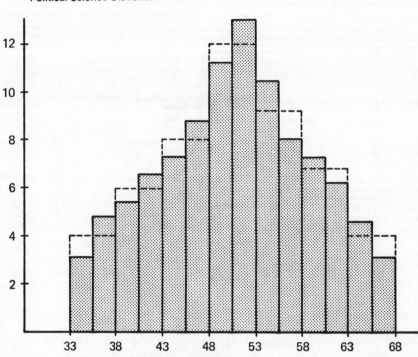

FIGURE 2-12

Frequency Curve

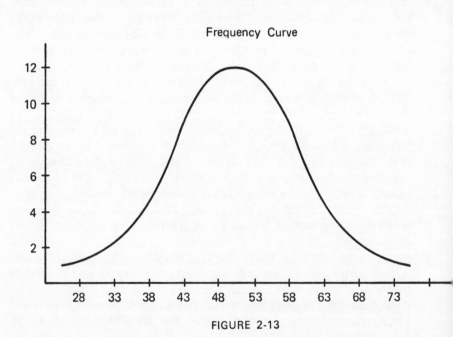

FIGURE 2-13

like most human problems, is not one that we solve, but one for which we find ways to circumvent. In this case, we assume that the actual frequency distribution curve can be reasonably approximated by a hypothetical frequency distribution curve, the properties of which are known. This assumption provides the basis for statistical models and it is thoroughly discussed in Chapter 3.

NOTE   Chapter 2

1. As we shall see in later chapters, it is sometimes useful to treat a discrete variable as a continuous variable.

REFERENCES   Chapter 2

Luce, R. Duncan, and Howard Raiffa. *Games and Decisions.* New York: Wiley, 1957, chap. 2.

Mendenhall, William. *Introduction to Probability and Statistics.* Belmont, Calif.: Wadsworth, 1969 (especially chap. 2).

Moore, Gerald E. *Algebra.* New York: Barnes and Noble, 1964. (College Outline Series.)

Siegel, Sidney. *Nonparametric Statistics.* New York: McGraw-Hill, 1956, chap. 9.

Torgerson, Warren S. *Theory and Methods of Scaling.* New York: Wiley, 1965.

Chapter 3

STATISTICAL MODELS, FUNDAMENTAL ASSUMPTIONS

In the opening chapter we argued that the best way to understand the subject of parametric statistical techniques is to approach it as a study of models. Statistical models are systems of logically related propositions drawn from specific assumptions. If the assumptions are met by the data to which the model is applied, hypotheses about the data can be tested. The hypotheses are interpretations of cognitive models; thus, the appropriate use of statistical models is to test cognitive models. In later chapters we shall explore variations of models and their suitability to test a variety of types of relationships. In this chapter we explore the basic assumptions of statistical models and present some methods for determining if these assumptions are met by the data being analyzed. Some other uses of these methods are discussed also.[1] The chapter concludes with some elementary concepts necessary to understand statistical tests of hypotheses.

Statistical models are useful because of a special characteristic of real-world phenomena. On repeated observation of a quantitative variable, it becomes evident that most observations fall close to the mathematical average observation. That is, for the whole range of values that some variable may take on, substantially more values will be closer to the mean than farther away.

To illustrate the point, consider the variable "height" distributed through a population of male students. Note in Table 3-1 that although height is a continuous variable, we have made it discrete by grouping in 1-inch intervals. The mean of the sample, 68.4, lies in the interval with the most observations. While the range of the variable is 12 inches, approximately 80 percent of the sample falls within 3 inches of the mean. The frequency polygon for this distribution, shown in Figure 3-1, illustrates the distribution of the variable. If we took a very large number of male students and measured their height continuously, presumably the points on the frequency polygon would smooth out. Associated with the resulting line would be a mathematical formula that perfectly described the line on a rectangular coordinate system.

Table 3-1

Distribution of Height in a Sample of Male Students

Height, in.	Absolute frequency	Relative frequency
63	1	.012
64	3	.036
65	6	.074
66	9	.11
67	11	.13
68	14	.171
69	12	.146
70	10	.122
71	7	.085
72	5	.061
73	3	.036
74	1	.012
Total	82	1.000

Repeated observation, trial and error, and some very sophisticated mathematical reasoning has shown that the distribution of most variables, as the number of observations increases, can be approximated by a special mathematical formula known as the *normal distribution function*. It is a particular mathematical expression that produces a bell-shaped curve on a

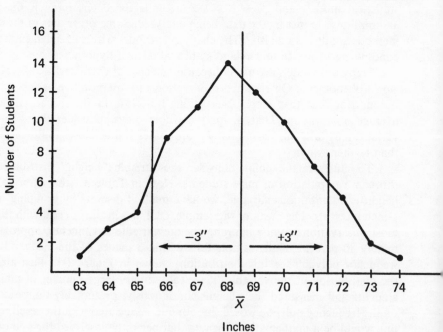

Inches

FIGURE 3-1

rectangular coordinate system. The abscissa X comprises the observations of the variable, and the ordinate Y spans the frequency of occurrences of X. The normal curve has some properties that make it particularly attractive. These will be discussed momentarily. First, it should be made clear that all statistical models discussed in this book, except one, are in some way based on the normal curve. The tests we explain here are based on the assumption that the real distribution of one or more variables is reasonably approximated by a hypothetical normal curve.[2] The appropriateness of the application of the models depends very heavily on whether the normal curve reasonably represents the distribution of the variable(s) being observed. It is critical, therefore, that the characteristics of the frequency distribution of a variable be understood.

MEASURING THE CHARACTERISTICS OF A DISTRIBUTION

Four constants are used to describe the characteristics of a frequency distribution. These use the first four moments of a distribution and measure, respectively, the central tendency of the distribution, its dispersion, asymmetry, and relative height. Each moment can be used to help decide if the frequency distribution from which these measurements were derived is reasonably approximated by the normal curve. The general formula for calculating the moments of a distribution is very simple. The kth moment of the distribution of the variable X is as follows:

$$(3\text{-}1) \qquad \mu_k = \frac{\sum X^k}{N}$$

Translated, the expression dictates that each of the observations of the variable X should be raised to the kth power; then all should be added together[3] and divided by the total number of observations. That is, the kth moment of a distribution is the mean of the distribution after all observations have been raised to the kth power.

Moments are always calculated about a point in a distribution. As described above, the kth moment is calculated about the point zero:

$$(3\text{-}2) \qquad \mu_k = \frac{\sum (X-0)^k}{N}$$

The first moment measure of the character of a distribution is calculated about the point zero, as we shall see below. The second, third, and fourth moment measures, however, are calculated about the mean of the distribution. The kth moment about the mean of a population is defined as

$$(3\text{-}3) \qquad \mu_k = \frac{\sum (X-\overline{X})^k}{N}$$

where $\overline{X}$ is the arithmetic mean of the variable X.

CENTRAL TENDENCY, OR CHARACTERISTIC VALUE OF A DISTRIBUTION

Measures of the central tendency of a distribution are means of locating the central tendency of a distribution rather than measuring its degree of central tendency. The distributions of most variables in the real world tend to cluster around a particular value near the center of the distribution, which we identify as the value that is most characteristic of a distribution. The characteristic value is the one that would be the best guess of the value of any randomly selected individual observation. We commonly summarize a distribution with its most characteristic value when we create average consumers, average businessmen, average drivers, average housewives, etc. This nomenclature enables us to avoid cumbersome phrases like "the mean breakdown of the use of disposable income to purchase goods and services"; it is easier to say "the average consumer."

We identify the characteristic value of a population by μ, the Greek letter mu. The most common method of identifying μ is the arithmetic mean, or average, and throughout this book we shall refer to μ as the population mean. As we point out momentarily, there are cases where alternative methods of finding μ are superior to the arithmetic mean.

The Mean

Calculating means for populations or samples not only has value as a way to locate the characteristic value of a distribution, but also has value per se as a simple index of a variable. For example, the average length of residency might explain differential voter turnout rates in two constituencies; the trend of the average congressional vote in support of foreign aid over the past ten years might tell us something about U.S. foreign policy changes. The mean of a distribution, treated as a characteristic value of the distribution, might tell us something that the whole distribution might conceal.

The first moment of a distribution is a measure of its central tendency. It is clear in expression (3-1) that when $k = 1$, the expression produces the arithmetic mean of the distribution. The mean, for roughly normal distributions, is treated as the most characteristic value of a distribution:

$$(3\text{-}4) \qquad \mu_1 = \frac{\sum X^1}{N} = \frac{\sum X}{N}$$

The mean, the first moment, is conventionally noted without the subscript and is so symbolized throughout this text.

Example 3-1

The formula (3-4) for the mean weights each observation equally, adds all observations, and divides by the number of observations. This procedure is necessary when data are ungrouped, that is, when there are almost as many different values of X as there are observations. In political research we deal frequently with grouped data, namely, continuously measured variables that have been collapsed into discrete measures of equal interval. Table 3-2 presents Democratic voting by election district for the 1968 congressional race in Middlesex County, New Jersey. The election districts are assumed to be of equal size, a condition for which Boards of Election strive. The data have been grouped in intervals of .05. The column f is the frequency of observations for the respective interval.

Table 3-2

1968 Democratic Vote for Congress, Middlesex County, New Jersey*

Interval	X	f	fX
.301–.35	.325	1	.325
.351–.40	.375	11	4.125
.401–.45	.425	28	11.900
.451–.50	.475	59	28.025
.501–.55	.525	81	42.525
.551–.60	.575	70	40.250
.601–.65	.625	48	30.000
.651–.70	.675	28	18.900
.701–.75	.725	18	13.050
.751–.80	.775	9	6.975
.801–.85	.825	4	3.300
.851–.90	.875	2	1.750
Total		359	201.125

*Data in proportion of two-party vote.

Grouping simplifies the calculation of the mean because each observation in an interval is identified by the value of the midpoint of the interval. Taking the interval .501 to .55, for example, multiply 81 times the midpoint .525 instead of adding 81 numbers. The result of the method presented in (3-5) will not exactly equal the mean of the ungrouped data

$$(3-5) \qquad \mu_1 = \frac{\sum fX}{N} = \frac{201.125}{359} = .560236$$

but if the intervals are of reasonable size, the result will always be a very close approximation, or at least sufficiently close to be identified as the mean.

The Median

Occasionally, the mean conceals more information than it produces. The mean is most useful when the distribution of a variable is approximately normal, but it is only one way to arrive at a value characteristic of a distribution, and it is not necessarily the best. The median is sometimes more useful than the mean. The median is defined as the middle value of the distribution; half of the values of the variable lie to its left and half lie to its right. The median is obtained by rank-ordering the values of the observations by magnitude and then choosing the value that is in the middle of the rank order. Suppose, for example, we had a distribution of 13 digits as follows: 2157483964187. Placed in order, the distribution is 1123445677889. The middle value, the seventh in the order, is 5. There are six numbers above 5 and six numbers below 5. When the number of observations is even, the median is halfway between the two middle values. Suppose in our example we eliminate the first value. Now there are 12 values: 123445677889. The middle values are 5 and 6. The median, therefore, is $5\frac{1}{2}$.

Finding the median of a frequency distribution with a large number of observations could be tedious. Fortunately, there exists a method for finding a reasonable approximation of the median. Using the data in Table 3-2, we can employ the following method:

$$(3\text{-}6) \qquad \text{Median} = \begin{pmatrix} \text{lower limit} \\ \text{of median} \\ \text{class interval} \end{pmatrix}$$

$$+ \frac{\left(\dfrac{N}{2}\right) - \begin{pmatrix} \text{total frequencies} \\ \text{in preceding intervals} \end{pmatrix}}{\begin{pmatrix} \text{number of frequencies} \\ \text{in median class interval} \end{pmatrix}}$$

$$\times \begin{pmatrix} \text{size of median} \\ \text{class interval} \end{pmatrix}$$

Example 3–2

Find the median of the data in Table 3-2. First, find the median class interval. This is the interval containing the 180th observation, .501

to .55. Using the formula (3-6),

$$\text{Median} = .501 + \frac{179.5 - (99)}{81} \times (.05)$$

$$= .501 + .0497 = .5507$$

The median is different from the mean (.5602 − .5507) by .0095, a negligible amount. For the data in this example, either the median or the mean would adequately represent the typical value of a distribution. But this is not always the case.

The median is preferable to the mean in cases where the distribution of the variable contains extremely large or extremely small values near its tails. Extreme values would cause the mean to be a poor measure of the characteristic value of the population because the mean weights each observation by its value. The median, on the other hand, counts each value equally; thus, it may be able to single out from a widely dispersed distribution a value more representative than the mean. Like the mean, however, the median is most useful in cases where the distribution of a variable is approximately normal.

Note that when a distribution is symmetrical, the median equals the mean. One might then ask why the mean is ever used in preference to the median. The answer lies in expedience. There is no elegant mathematical technique for calculating a median; thus, it is not so versatile, mathematically, as the mean. The point we emphasize here is that one ought to be careful not to let the expedient operation lead to a bad measure of the characteristic value of a distribution. The distribution of a variable should be carefully investigated before the mean is interpreted as a characteristic value.

The Mode

As stated above, the mean and the median are of value in describing approximately normal distributions. Neither would be appropriate for distributions that were relatively asymmetrical. The value that may be more appropriate is the mode of the distribution. The mode is defined as the value that occurs most frequently in a distribution. For the distribution 2 4 7 6 4 4 3 2, the mode is 4, the most frequently occurring value. If this distribution were graphed, the line would be highest over the value 4; thus, the mode of a distribution is the point at which the distribution is highest over the abscissa, or the point below the line where the ordinate is highest. The mode can be located within the modal interval of a distribution by a simple technique:

$$(3\text{-}7) \qquad \text{Mode} = \begin{bmatrix} \text{lower limit of} \\ \text{modal interval} \end{bmatrix} + \frac{f_m - f_1}{2f_m - f_2 - f_1} k$$

where

f_m = number of observations in modal interval

f_1 = number of observations in preceding interval

f_2 = number of observations in following interval

k = size of modal class

Example 3-3

The application of this technique can be illustrated with the data in Table 3-2. The modal interval is, of course, the one with the most observations, that is, the highest f_1. Again the interval is .501 to .55. Using the formula (3-7),

$$(3\text{-}8) \qquad \text{Mode} = .501 + \frac{81-59}{2(81)-70-59}(.05)$$

$$= .501 + \frac{22}{33}(.05) = .5343$$

The mode for the same data set differs from both median and mean.

The mode has advantages over both mean and median. Its appeal in selecting a value characteristic of a distribution is its choice of the value that appears most often. Of course, if a distribution is symmetrical and unimodal, the mode, mean, and median are equal. Unfortunately, symmetrical and unimodal distributions do not always occur in politics. When a distribution is relatively asymmetrical, the mode might better characterize the central tendency of a distribution than would either mean or median. The mode, like the median, does not possess mathematical elegance; thus, it is used far less frequently than the mean. But again the reader should keep in mind the advantages of using the mode instead of the mean in some special cases, and should be sensitive to cases where the mean misrepresents the data.

The Geometric Mean

Another measure of the central tendency of a distribution is the geometric mean. It is far less commonly used as a measure of central tendency than is any of the three statistics previously described. The geometric mean is found by finding the Nth root of the product of N values:

$$(3\text{-}9) \qquad \text{Geometric mean} = \sqrt[N]{X_1 \cdot X_2 \cdots X_N}$$

A simple illustration would be six observations: 1 1 2 2 4 4. Their product is $1 \cdot 1 \cdot 2 \cdot 2 \cdot 4 \cdot 4 = 64$. The sixth root of 64, the geometric mean, is 2.

Typically, one would not have occasion to calculate a geometric mean as a measure of the central tendency of a distribution. A shortcut method for calculating the geometric mean is to use logarithms. The main advantage of the geometric mean over the arithmetic mean is found in the special case of an asymmetrical distribution with an overload of higher extreme values. The geometric mean weighs extremely large values less heavily than the arithmetic mean; thus, it is less affected by them. However, note that if any value of the distribution is zero, the product of values is zero.

We pointed out that the mean and median were most useful for locating the characteristic value of distributions that were approximately normal. Knowing the location of the characteristic values of a distribution is important, but it is also important to know how the remaining values are dispersed around the characteristic value. Figure 3-2 shows three

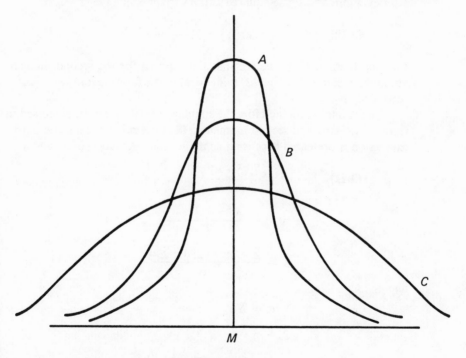

FIGURE 3-2

distributions: M identifies the location of the mean, median, and mode of all three distributions. Although M is an excellent measure of the characteristic value of A, it is an extremely poor measure for C because A, B, and C vary with respect to the way their values are dispersed about M. We turn now to a discussion of techniques for measuring the dispersion of a distribution. Measures of the dispersion of a distribution, like measures of the characteristic value of a distribution, are of value for their own sake. But, in addition, the most common measure is one of the foundation statistics for all models we discuss in later chapters.

DISPERSION

The *standard deviation* of a distribution is defined as the square root of the variance. The variance is the mean of the sum of the squared deviations about the mean. The standard deviation is the measure of dispersion that is indispensable in the construction of statistical models. The variance of a population of N observations of the variable X is given by (3-10). Conventionally, the small Greek letter sigma (σ) is used to represent the standard deviation, and sigma squared is the variance.

$$(3\text{-}10) \qquad \sigma^2 = \text{Var}(X) = \frac{\sum (X - \mu)^2}{N}$$

Looking back to (3-3), we see that the formula for the second moment about the mean (that is, $k = 2$) is identical to the formula for the variance; thus, $\sigma^2 = \mu_2$.

The variance and therefore the standard deviation can be expressed in terms of the first and second moments about the point 0. This alternative expression is presented because it simplifies the calculation of σ^2 and σ.

$$(3\text{-}11) \qquad \sigma^2 = \frac{\sum (X - \mu)^2}{N}$$

$$= \frac{\sum (X^2 - 2\mu X + \mu^2)}{N}$$

$$= \frac{\sum X^2 - 2\mu \sum X + \sum \mu^2}{N}$$

where

$$\sum \mu^2 = N\mu^2$$

$$\sum X = N\mu$$

$$= \frac{\sum X^2}{N} - \frac{2\mu N\mu}{N} + \frac{N\mu^2}{N}$$

thus,

$$= \frac{\sum X^2}{N} - 2\mu^2 + \mu^2 = \frac{\sum X^2}{N} - \mu^2$$

$$(3\text{-}12) \qquad \sigma^2 = \frac{\sum X^2}{N} - \left(\frac{\sum X}{N}\right)^2$$

Therefore, the variance of a distribution may be expressed as the second moment about the point 0 minus the square of the first moment about the point 0. This form of σ^2 eliminates the cumbersome step of subtracting each observation from the mean before squaring.

Example 3-4

By using the data from Table 3-2 and referring to Table 3-3, both methods of calculating population variance can be illustrated. From (3-5), $\mu = .560236$. The difference, $.009963 - .009401 = .000562$ is due to rounding. The short method, (b) in Table 3-3, condenses the three

Table   3-3

Calculating the Population Variance

1 X	2 f	3 $(X-\mu)$	4 $(X-\mu)^2$	5 $f(X-\mu)^2$	6 X^2	7 $f(X^2)$
.325	1	−.235	.055	.055	.106	.106
.375	11	−.185	.034	.374	.141	1.551
.425	28	−.135	.018	.504	.181	5.068
.475	59	−.085	.007	.413	.226	13.334
.525	81	−.035	.001	.081	.276	22.356
.575	70	.015	.0002	.014	.331	23.170
.625	48	.065	.004	.192	.391	18.768
.675	28	.115	.013	.364	.456	12.768
.725	18	.165	.027	.486	.526	9.468
.775	9	.215	.046	.414	.601	5.409
.825	4	.265	.070	.280	.681	2.724
.875	2	.315	.099	.198	.766	1.532
	359			$\sum f(X-\mu)^2 = 3.375$		$\sum f(X)^2 = 116.254$

(a) $\sigma^2 = \dfrac{\sum f(X-\mu)^2}{N} = \dfrac{3.375}{359} = .009401$

(b) $\sigma^2 = \dfrac{\sum f(X)^2}{N} - \left(\dfrac{\sum f(X)}{N}\right)^2 = \dfrac{116.254}{359} - (.560236)^2 = .009963$

steps of columns 3, 4, and 5 to two steps, columns 6 and 7. We will use $\sigma = (.009401)^{1/2} \doteq .097$. The histogram is shown in Figure 3-3.

The standard deviation is useful in deciding if it is reasonable to assume that a variable is normally distributed. An approximately normal distribution must conform to a particular pattern of dispersion with regard to the standard deviation. Specifically, in a normal distribution, approximately

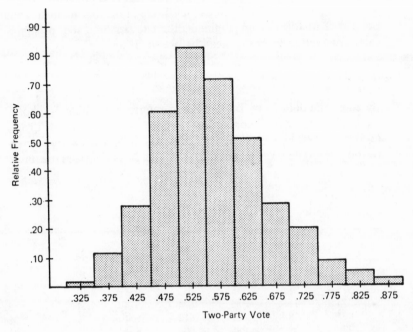

FIGURE 3-3

two-thirds of the observations of the variable will lie in an interval of one standard deviation from the mean. About 95 percent of the observations will lie within two standard deviations of the mean, and virtually all observations (99.7 percent) will fall within three standard deviations of the mean. Thus, conventionally, a variable is described by its mean followed by its standard deviation.

With this information we can decide whether it is reasonable to assume that a variable is normally distributed. The guidelines for this decision are arbitrary and those we offer here are on the conservative side. If between 60 and 75 percent of the observations fall in the interval defined by plus and minus one standard deviation around the mean, normalcy can be assumed. An interval defined by two standard deviations around the mean should contain between 85 and 99 percent of the observations. For the distribution described in Example 3-4, we find that the interval defined by one standard deviation about the mean, $.56 \pm .097 = .463$ to .657, contains approximately 69 percent of the observations. Two standard deviations about the mean, $.56 \pm 2(.097) = .366$ to .754, contain approximately 94 percent of the observations. By our criteria it is reasonable to assume that this distribution is normal.

Example 3–5

The standard deviation is also used to test hypotheses. Sometimes very important features of a variable are discovered by observing its dispersion. For example, both Union and Atlantic Counties in New Jersey are commonly considered Republican strongholds. But in recent years Union County's population has undergone change while Atlantic's has been fairly stable. Nevertheless, Union County contains only one municipality that regularly votes Democratic and Atlantic County contains only two. We would like to know whether Union County's Republican party strength differs from Atlantic County's Republican strength. One way to find out is to devise a measure of party strength for each municipality, and compare the two counties' distributions of the measure.[4] An index of voter independence is used to measure party strength:

$$\left| \left(\begin{array}{c} \% \text{ Republican for} \\ \text{party office} \end{array} \right) - \left(\begin{array}{c} \% \text{ Republican for} \\ \text{salient office} \end{array} \right) \right|$$

A salient office is one in which there is a great deal of voter interest. We assume that the stronger the support for the Republican party in a municipality, the lower is voter independence. This index was calculated for all municipalities in the two counties. The variance of the distribution for Atlantic County is $\sigma^2 = .000543$, $\sigma = .0233$. For Union County, $\sigma^2 = .002088$, $\sigma = .0457$. The data indicate that the distribution of the index of party support is more widely dispersed in Union County than in Atlantic County. From these data we conclude that support for the Republican party in Union County is "weaker" than support for the Republican party in Atlantic County.

SKEWNESS

In our discussions of measures of central tendency—the mean, the median, and the mode—we made reference to the symmetry of distributions. A unimodal distribution that is asymmetrical is called a *skewed distribution* (Figure 3-4). We identify a left-skewed distribution as one for which the longer tail of the distribution is to the left of the mode. Since graphs are conventionally drawn with higher values to the right and lower values to the left, a left-skewed distribution is identified as a distribution skewed toward negative values, or negatively skewed. Right-skewed distributions have a longer tail to the right of the mode, and these are identified as skewed toward positive values, or positively skewed. In applying a statistical model, we are likely to encounter skewed variables that we would like

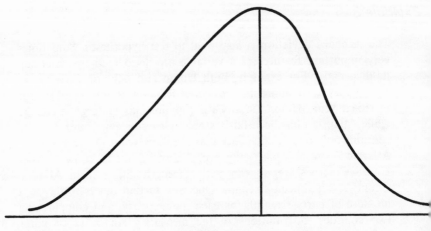

FIGURE 3-4

to assume were normally distributed. It is therefore important that we have some means of measuring the degrees of skewness in order to make an intelligent decision about whether or not a variable is normally distributed.

The third moment about the mean of a distribution will tell whether a distribution is positively or negatively skewed. The third moment will be positive if a distribution is positively skewed:

$$(3\text{-}13) \qquad \mu_3 = \frac{\sum (X-\mu)^3}{N}$$

It will be negative if negatively skewed, and zero if the distribution is symmetrical. A negatively skewed distribution will have more values farther from the mean to the left than to the right. When cubed, these negative values will outweigh the closer positive values to the right; thus, the sum of all cubed deviations about the mean will be negative. The opposite will be true of a positively skewed distribution. The cube of the greater number of extreme values to the right will outweigh the cubed values closer to the left. For a symmetrical distribution, the cube of the values on the left will equal the negative of the cubed values on the right, and the third moment will equal zero.

As pointed out above, many distributions are skewed so that we are very likely to get a nonzero value for the third moment about the mean. But the sign of the third moment tells only the direction of the skewness; it does not measure the magnitude of skewness. Thus, the third moment per se is not very helpful in deciding whether it is appropriate to assume that a distribution is normal. A generally accepted, standardized measure of skewness is available, however:

$$\alpha_3 = \frac{(X-\mu)^3/N}{\sigma^3}$$

This measure can be expressed in terms of the second and third moments about the mean:

$$(3\text{-}14) \qquad \alpha_3 = \frac{\mu_3}{\sigma^3} = \frac{\mu_3}{(\sigma^2)^{3/2}}$$

$$\alpha_3 = \frac{\mu_3}{(\mu_2)^{3/2}}$$

Sigma (σ) is, of course, the standard deviation. This measure α_3, will be positive for right-skewed distributions and negative for left-skewed distributions. Some conventionally accepted guidelines may be employed in using α_3 to decide if a distribution is unreasonably skewed. If the absolute value of α_3 is 2 or greater, the assumption of a normal distribution cannot be made. It is reasonable to assume that a distribution is normal if the following inequality is true: $-2 \leqslant \alpha_3 \leqslant +2$.

This same measure is sometimes referred to as β_1.

Example 3–6

The histogram for Table 3-2, presented in Figure 3-3, indicates that the distribution is skewed. Values for $\sigma = .097$ (Example 3-4) already have been computed. Now, referring to Table 3-4,

$$\sigma^3 = .097^3 = .000913$$

$$\alpha_3 = \frac{.172029/359}{.000913} = \frac{.000479}{.000913} \doteq .52$$

The value of $\alpha_3 = .5$ is well within the limit of 2 and, as Figure 3-3 indicates, the distribution is positively skewed.

Another measure of skewness, developed by Karl Pearson, relies on the fact that in a symmetrical distribution the mean equals the median equals the mode. Skewness does not affect the location of the mode, but it does affect both the mean and the median by pulling each in the direction of the skewed tail. Thus,

$$(3\text{-}15) \qquad \text{Skewness} = \frac{\text{mean} - \text{mode}}{\sigma}$$

The division of the distance between the mode and the mean by the

Table 3-4

Example 3–6

X	f	$f(X-\mu)^3$
.325	1	−.012978
.375	11	−.069652
.425	28	−.068880
.475	59	−.036226
.525	81	−.003483
.575	70	.000210
.625	48	.013200
.675	28	.042588
.725	18	.080856
.775	9	.089442
.825	4	.074440
.875	2	.062512
Totals	359	+.172029

standard deviation standardizes the measure. An alternative formulation, based on the relative distances of the mean and median, is

$$(3\text{-}16) \qquad \text{Skewness} = \frac{3(\text{mean} - \text{median})}{\sigma}$$

This formulation relies on the fact that the distance between the mean and the median is about one-third the distance between the mean and the mode for most skewed distributions. By inspecting these formulas, it can be seen that this measure, as with the third-moment measure, is positive for right skewness and negative for left skewness. Conventionally, a distribution is assumed to be approximately normal if the value of this measure is less than 1.0. This means that if the mean is within one standard deviation of the mode, it is reasonable to make the assumption of normalcy.

One of the immediately obvious advantages of Pearson's measure over the third-moment measure is its mathematical simplicity. In deciding which measure to use, one must decide whether it would be easier to locate the mode or the median for the Pearson measure rather than execute the cumbersome calculations of the third-moment measure.

Example 3–7

The mean, median, and mode for the data presented in Example 3-1 have been computed:

Mean $\doteq$ .56

Median $\doteq$ .551

Mode $\doteq$ .535

Pearson's measure of skewness is expressed as follows:

$$\frac{.56-.535}{.098} \doteq .255 \quad \text{or} \quad \frac{3(.56-.551)}{.098} = .276$$

The interpretation of this statistic is that the mean is approximately $.25\sigma$ away from the mode, well within the limit of 1σ. Note that the distance between the mean and the mode is approximately 2.8 times the distance between the mean and the median.

KURTOSIS

Thus far we have developed measures of central tendency dispersion and the symmetry or asymmetry of a distribution. We have yet to develop a measure of the "peakedness" of a distribution or the relative height of the mode. The term used for this characteristic of a distribution is *kurtosis*. The normal distribution has a specific height with respect to its dispersion; thus we must be able to measure the height of a distribution to help us decide whether the normal distribution reasonably approximates its distribution. The measure we present, as you probably guessed, is based on the fourth moment about the mean of the distribution.

A distribution is called *mesokurtic* if its peak is the height of the normal distribution. If the distribution is abnormally flat, it is called *platykurtic*. A distribution with an unusually high peak is called *leptokurtic*.

The measure of kurtosis, α_4, is analogous to the skewness measure, α_3. This measure is sometimes referred to as β_2, and it is a standard measure of kurtosis. It is difficult to give an intuitive explanation of this measure that is as appealing as the explanations of the dispersion and skewness measures. Perhaps the most important feature is the numerator, the fourth moment about the mean, in that it places very heavy emphasis on extreme values in the distribution.

$$\alpha_4 = \frac{\sum(X-\mu)^4/N}{\sigma^4} = \frac{\sum(X-\mu)^4/N}{(\sigma^2)^2}$$

In terms of moments we have

$$(3\text{-}17) \quad \alpha_4 = \frac{\mu_4}{(\sigma^2)^2} = \frac{\mu_4}{(\mu_2)^2}$$

As more values of a variable go farther from its mean, the sum of the values raised to the fourth power increases at a rapidly increasing rate. Thus, we would expect the fourth moment of a relatively flat distribution to have a higher value for its fourth moment than that of a relatively more peaked distribution. That is, for two distributions with the same mean and measured in the same scales, the fourth moment for a more leptokurtic distribution will be smaller than a relatively more platykurtic distribution. However, the divisor σ^4 weighs extreme values less heavily than the fourth moment does, so that α_4 for a leptokurtic distribution will be larger than for a platykurtic distribution. A normal distribution will produce a value $\alpha_4 = 3$ by this measure. Platykurtic distributions produce values below 3 and leptokurtic distributions produce values greater than 3.

Example 3–8

Referring again to Table 2-2, α_4 can be calculated for the distribution. See Table 3-5.

Table   3-5

Example 3–8

X_i	f_i	$f(X_i-\mu)^4$
.325	1	.00305
.375	11	.012881
.425	28	.009296
.475	59	.003068
.525	81	.000162
.575	70	.000000
.625	48	.000864
.675	28	.004900
.725	18	.013338
.775	9	.019233
.825	4	.019728
.875	2	.019692

$$\sum(X-\mu)^4 = .106212$$

$$\alpha_4 = \frac{\sum(X-\mu)^4/N}{\sigma^4} = \frac{.106212/359}{(.097)^4} = \frac{.00295}{.000089} = 3.315$$

We conclude that our distribution is slightly leptokurtic.

THE NORMAL CURVE

We have stated that all statistical models we present here are based on or related to the normal distribution. That is, one or more of the variables in each test is *assumed* to be normally distributed. In the foregoing section we presented techniques to measure four properties of any distribution, and gave rules for deciding whether to assume that a distribution is reasonably normal. We found that in a normal distribution the mean, median, and mode are equal as measures of the characteristic value of the distribution. The standard deviation of a normal distribution places specific limits on its dispersion. The measure of skewness of a normal distribution, α_3, equals zero, and the measure of kurtosis, α_4, equals 3.

The normal curve is a specific mathematical function with specific characteristics. For the hypothetical variable X,

$$(3\text{-}18) \qquad F(X) = \frac{1}{\sigma(2\pi)^{\frac{1}{2}}} \, e^{-(X-\mu)^2/2\sigma^2}$$

The ordinate of the graph, $F(X)$, is the relative frequency of X. The abscissa is, of course, the variable X. Suppose that the variable X is a continuous variable with a very large number of observations and that its distribution is perfectly normal. In expression (3-18) the numbers 2, π, and e are known. If we had values for μ and σ, we could find $F(X)$ for each value of X and graph the results, and the outcome would be a perfect normal curve.

The problem of finding the relative frequency of intervals of the values of a variable, say, between X_1 and X_2, is not an uncommon one in practical research problems. One way we could find this relative frequency is to find the relative frequencies of small intervals of X between X_1 and X_2 and then sum these relative frequencies. If we knew μ and σ, then we could simply enter a value of X in (3-18) for each interval between X_1 and X_2, and then sum the results. But this method would be tedious at best.

STANDARDIZATION OF VARIABLES

Fortunately, it is not necessary to go through these cumbersome calculations in order to solve the problem. It should be evident that if we could measure all variables in the same units, that if all variables had the same mean and all variables were normally distributed, then we could set up a table that specified the relative frequencies for all intervals of values in a distribution. This can be done much more simply than it may at first seem. We standardize the measurement of a variable by a two-step process. First, the mean of the variable is shifted to zero. This is accomplished by subtracting the mean from each individual observation. We stated earlier that statistical tests require only interval-scale levels of measurement and that any ratio scale can be treated as an interval scale. Shifting the mean of the variable to zero is consistent with these principles. Graphically, this shift can be seen in Figure 3-5.

The second step in the process of standardization is to divide each value of the variable by σ, its standard deviation. With a mean of zero,

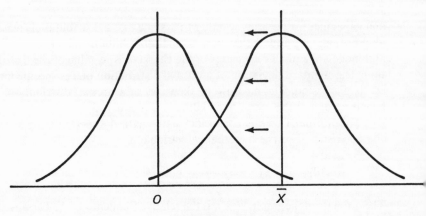

O　　　X

FIGURE 3-5

each value of the variable is then measured by its relative distance from the mean in units of σ. What we have done is to apply a simple linear transformation of the type $a+bX$ to the variable X. The constant $a = -\mu$ and $b = 1/\sigma$. This two-step process transforms the scale in which the variable is measured from some idiosyncratic units to units in which all variables can be compared.

A standardized variable is noted as $X^* = (X-\mu)/\sigma$. The transformed X, X^*, has some interesting properties. First, it can be shown that the variance of X variable is unchanged by shifting its mean to zero. In order to prove this, we must first establish that the variance of a constant is 0:

$$(3\text{-}19) \qquad \frac{\sum (a-a)^2}{N} = \frac{\sum (0)^2}{N} = 0$$

Second, the variance of a variable plus a constant is equal to the variance of the variable:

$$(3\text{-}20) \qquad \mathrm{Var}(X+a) = \frac{\sum [(X+a)-(\mu+a)]^2}{N}$$

$$= \frac{\sum (X-\mu+a-a)^2}{N} = \frac{\sum (X-\mu)^2}{N}$$

$$= \mathrm{Var}(X)$$

Since μ is a constant, the variance of X minus μ is equal to the variance of X:

$$(3\text{-}21) \qquad \mathrm{Var}(X-\mu) = \frac{\sum [(X-\mu)-(\mu-\mu)]^2}{N} = \frac{\sum (X-\mu)^2}{N}$$

Third, when $\mu = 0$, the variance of X is

(3-22) $$\frac{\sum(X-\mu)^2}{N} = \frac{\sum X^2}{N}$$

Having taken these steps, we can find the variance of a standardized variable, X^*:

(3-23) $$\text{Var}(X^*) = \frac{\sum((X-\mu)/\sigma)^2}{N} = \frac{1}{\sigma^2} \frac{\sum(X-\mu)^2}{N}$$

$$= \frac{\sigma^2}{\sigma^2} = 1$$

Therefore, the variance of a standardized variable is 1, and of course the standard deviation, $(\text{Var}(X^*))^{\frac{1}{2}}$ equals 1 also. These features of a standardized variable, $\overline{X}^* = 0$, $\sigma^2 = 1$, will prove valuable later in more detailed discussion of statistical models.

We conclude this discussion of standardization with a word on the notation of normally distributed variables and standardized normal variables. When a variable is assumed to be normally distributed with a mean of μ and a standard deviation of σ, we note it thus: X is $N(\mu, \sigma)$. When a normal variable has been standardized, it is noted X is $N(0, 1)$. The understanding of a standardization is very important for the understanding of much of what is to follow.

STATISTICAL TESTS ON STANDARDIZED VARIABLES

Having found a means of converting all variables to standard units of measurement, the task remains to find a table of values for all intervals of a variable. Calculating values for such a table requires the use of a great deal of higher mathematics. Fortunately, some enterprising statisticians have set up tables that are more easily read than calculated.

We refer the reader to Table A-1, "Normal Distribution" in the Appendix. This table presents areas under a hypothetical normal curve to the right of points on the abscissa. The left-hand column, Z, is the measure of the distance on the abscissa from the mean, μ, in units of standard deviation.

Now, if we were interested in knowing the area under the normal curve between μ and one standard deviation ($Z = 1$), the first step would be to look in the column marked Z in Table A-1, follow down to 1.0, and find the value .1587. (See Figure 3-6.) This value tells us the area under the

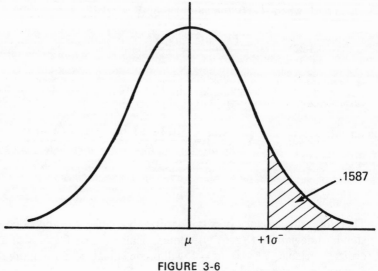

FIGURE 3-6

curve between $Z = 1$ and the right tail of the distribution. To get the rest of the area, we subtract $1 - .1587 = .8413$. (See Figure 3-7.)

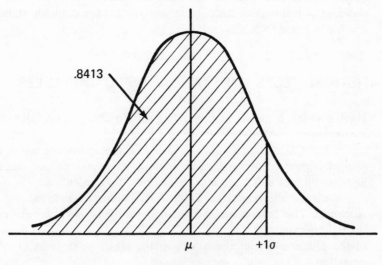

FIGURE 3-7

The problem, however, was to find the area under the curve bounded by the mean and one standard deviation away from the mean. The Z score for the mean is obviously zero. Looking up $Z = 0$ in Table A-1, we find

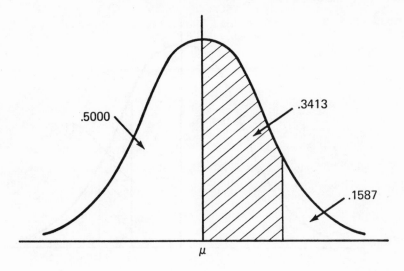

FIGURE 3-8

.5, which is the area under the curve between the mean and one tail. (See Figure 3-8.) Subtracting $.8413 - .5 = .3413$, which is shown in Figure 3-8. Knowing that the normal distribution is symmetrical, one can follow a simple process of subtraction and find the area under the normal curve between any two points, as long as they are measured in units of σ.

To illustrate further, let us find the area under the normal curve between the two values of a normally distributed variable for which $\mu = 10$, $\sigma = 5$. For $X = 15$,

$$Z(X) = \frac{15-10}{5} = 1.0$$

For $X = 13$,

$$Z(X) = \frac{13-10}{5} = .6$$

From Table A-1, the area between $Z = .6$ and the right tail of the distribution is found to be .2743. We have already established that the area to the right of $Z = 1.0$ is .1587. The area between the two points is $.2743 - .1587 = .1156$. (See Figure 3-9.)

The technique of dealing with negative values of Z, or left-tail points, is equally easy. When Z is negative, the values in Table A-1 should be read as the distance between the Z score and the left tail of the distribution. Suppose, for the same distribution as given above, $X = 7$ and $\mu = 10$. Then $(7-10)/5 = -.6$. We wish to find the area under the normal curve between $Z = -.6$ and $Z = 1$. The area to the left of $-.6$ is .2743.

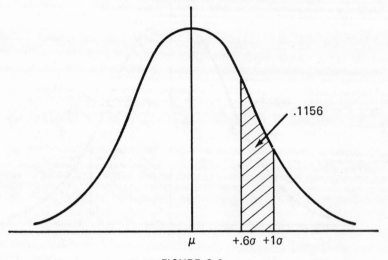

FIGURE 3-9

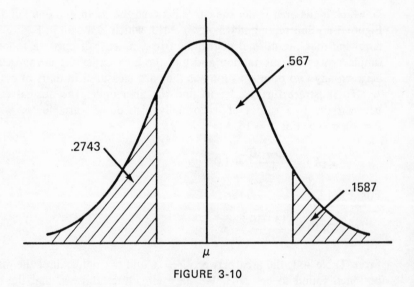

FIGURE 3-10

To the right of $Z = 1$ is .1587. (See Figure 3-10.) The area we seek is everything between $Z = -.6$ and $Z = 1.0$. It is easily found:

$$1 - (.2743 + .1587) = 1 - .433 = .567$$

Table A-1, "Normal Distribution," is simple, and with a little practice the technique of using it is easily mastered.[5]

FREQUENCIES AND PROBABILITIES

By this time the astute reader will have seen the implied relationship between relative frequencies and probabilities. Relative frequencies are the observed rates of occurrences of phenomena. Probabilities are predictions of the likely rates of occurrences of phenomena. One of the most important uses of statistics is to formalize the process of basing probability statements on observed frequency counts. It is in this connection that we assume that the normal *frequency* distribution is a normal *probability* distribution. The point may seem trivial to some, but nevertheless it is important. The assumption that frequency distributions can be approximated by probability distributions is purely arbitrary. We do not mean, however, that this assumption is unreasonable. Indeed, it is necessary if we are to make any inferences about future phenomena from past experience. The assumption is so fundamental that it is usually ignored; yet, because it is fundamental and philosophically controversial, especially among persons who disparage statistical methods, the student should be consciously aware of it.

When we make the leap from frequencies to probabilities, we acquire the power that statistical models promise. We return to the examples of how to read Table A-1 and reinterpret the areas under the curve in terms of probabilities. In the preceding example, $\mu = 10$ and $\sigma = 5$, we sought the area under the curve between $X = 15$ and μ, and found it to be .3413. This is interpreted as follows: Given the whole population of a normally distributed X, the probability of randomly choosing a value between 10 and 15 equals .3413. That is, assuming that the variable X is normally distributed with the stated mean and standard deviation, then there is slightly better than one in three chances of randomly choosing a value between 10 and 15. The assumption of a normal probability distribution for a variable enables us to make fairly precise statements about its distribution. It enables us to state the likelihood of any range of values of the variable, knowing only the mean and standard deviation of the variable. The accuracy of the statement depends on how well the variable distribution is approximated by the normal distribution.

ESTIMATION

We have emphasized that the assumption of normalcy for a variable permits making statements about its distribution when only μ and σ are known. The problem to which we now turn is the way in which to arrive at values for μ and σ. We stated earlier that the mean and standard deviation represented these parameters of the normal frequency distribution. But now we must modify our earlier position after making an important distinction about the phenomena we study. The mean and the standard deviation as previously defined are exactly equal to μ and σ when we deal with a *whole* population, but if we are dealing with a *sample* of that population, as we almost always do in political science, then some account for this fact must be recognized in our calculations. When we deal with a sample of a variable, we do not actually calculate μ and σ. In fact, we use the data from the sample to *estimate* μ and σ. Notationally, population parameters are represented by Greek letters. Estimates of parameters are usually represented by arabic letters, as in the case of $\overline{X}$ as an estimator of μ, or Greek letters with a circumflex accent, or "hat" (such as $\hat{\sigma}$ as an estimator of σ), although we frequently drop the circumflex. A population size is denoted N and a sample is denoted n.

There are, of course, ways of measuring the appropriateness of estimators of population parameters. There are four criteria that acceptable estimators must meet, but we shall discuss only three. The fourth, sufficiency, is not considered here. The first criterion of an estimate is that it be *unbiased*. Formally, an unbiased estimator is one for which the expected value of the statistic is equal to the parameter it estimates. Let us briefly explain expected value, or mathematical expectation.

The mathematical expectation of a random variable is the value of the variable, assuming that the a priori probabilities of the observations are operative. Expectation can be best explained by tentatively defining it as a long-run average. If a fair die is rolled a very large number of times, the relative frequency of each face will approach 1/6, so the a priori probability of each value is 1/6. Then the long-run average value of the variable will be

$$1/6(1) + 1/6(2) + 1/6(3) + 1/6(4) + 1/6(5) + 1/6(6)$$

$$1/6 + 2/6 + 3/6 + 4/6 + 5/6 + 6/6 = 21/6 = 3 \ 1/2$$

Consider another example. When flipping a fair coin, a man wins $1.00 for every head that turns up and loses $.50 for every tail. What is the expected value of the wager? The a priori probability of each face of the coin is one-half: $(1/2)(\$1.00) - (1/2)(\$.50) = \$.50 - \$.25 = \$.25$. In the long run, the man should win about $.25 per toss. But as Keynes was fond of saying, in the long run we are all dead. Mathematical expectation is a means of evaluating a variable or event before it is observed; it is not a means of describing what happens in the long run.

We can define the expected value of the variable X as $E(X) = \sum p_i X_i$, where p_i is the probability of the occurrence of event X_i. Given that each value of X is equally likely,

$$E(X) = \sum \left(\frac{1}{N}\right)(X) = \frac{\sum X}{N}$$

This expression is identical to the mean of variable X, where p_i is the relative frequency of X_i. Later, the concept of expected value will be used to draw inferences from statistical models. In particular, each parameter of a statistical model has an expected value. When the expected value of each population parameter is defined in terms of frequencies in the long run, then the parameters can be estimated from the frequency distributions of samples of the population.

It is easily shown that $\overline{X}$ is an unbiased estimator of μ, once we have introduced a result from the Central Limit theorem. The Central Limit theorem is not simple and the inference we present from it is not obvious. We beg the reader's indulgence, and ask that he accept this result without proof, referring him to Yamane (1962, pp. 20–23) for further discussion. If we had a large population of any shape distribution (not necessarily normal) and then we took a number of samples from the population and calculated the mean of each sample, we would have a distribution of sample means. The relevant results from the Central Limit theorem are as follows: Each sample would have the same variance, σ^2, the unbiased estimate of the population variance. This distribution of sample means would be normal, with a mean $\overline{X}$, the expected value of which is μ, the population mean. The variance of this distribution of sample means is σ^2/n. This result holds regardless of the distribution of the population. Proving that $E(\overline{X}) = \mu$ is now an easy task. Since $\overline{X}$ is a member of a distribution of sample means, its expected value is the mean of the distribution. The expected value of that mean, $\overline{X}$, in turn is μ:

$$(3\text{-}24) \qquad E(\overline{X}) = E\left[\frac{\sum \overline{X}}{N}\right] = E\left[\frac{N\overline{X}}{N}\right] = E(\overline{X}) = \mu$$

Thus, $\overline{X}$ is an unbiased estimator of μ.

The second criterion for measuring the appropriateness of an estimator is *consistency*. An estimator is consistent if it approaches the population parameter as the sample size increases toward total enumeration of the population. Clearly, if a population is normally distributed (if only it is unimodal and symmetrical), $\overline{X}$ for the population will equal μ. Other estimates, like the median or the mode, are susceptible to variations in the particular sample chosen, and are drawn away from μ by skewed sample distributions. For a skewed sample, the mean of the sample is always closer to the population mean of a normal distribution than to either the median or the mode.

The third measure of an estimator is *efficiency*. An efficient estimator is a minimum variance estimator. The importance of the variance of an estimator should be clear. The variance measures the dispersion of the estimator so that the narrower the dispersion, the closer the estimator is likely to be to the population parameter. Again, the advantage of the mean over the median or the mode lies in estimating from skewed distributions. It should be clear from our discussion of second-moment measures of dispersion that the variance of a skewed distribution, using either the median or the mode, will be greater than the variance computed by using the mean. The latter requires the squaring of fewer extreme values than either of the former two. By a rather complicated mathematical proof it can be shown that the mean of a sample is *the* minimum variance estimator; that is, no estimator of μ may have a smaller variance than the mean. (See Yamane, 1962.)

There are two ways we can go about estimating population parameters, but thus far we have presented only one. We have calculated a point estimate, a single value for a parameter, rather than an interval estimate, a range of possible values for the parameter. That is, the method of estimation we have introduced produces a single value (point) to represent the parameter. For most uses of statistics in political science, point estimates are all that is necessary. In some cases, however, it will be useful to calculate an interval estimate for population parameters. These cases and other problems are taken up in greater detail in Chapter 6, "Hypothesis Testing."

Thus far we have not discussed an estimation for σ (or σ^2). Two important points must be made about estimating σ^2 by means of formula 3-10. First, the expression $\sum (X - \bar{X})^2 / n$ is a biased estimate of σ^2. Second, even after compensating for the bias, the new formula for σ (or σ^2) may seriously distort the variance of small samples of small populations. For the first point, let us prove as an exercise that $\sum (X - \bar{X})/n$ is a biased estimator of σ^2. The strategy of this proof is to find the expected value of the expression in terms of σ^2. If it is unbiased, its expected value will equal σ^2. Suppose we have a sample of size n. We begin by inserting $\mu - \mu$ in the expression:

$$(3\text{-}25) \qquad \frac{1}{n} E \sum [(X - \mu) - (\bar{X} - \mu)]^2$$

Multiplying out the square,

$$\frac{1}{n} E \sum [(X - \mu)^2 + (\bar{X} - \mu)^2 - 2(X - \mu)(\bar{X} - \mu)]$$

Distributing the summation signs,

$$\frac{1}{n} E [\sum (X - \mu)^2 + \sum (\bar{X} - \mu)^2 - 2 \sum (X - \mu)(\bar{X} - \mu)]$$

$$\text{where} \quad \sum (X - \mu) = \sum X - \sum \mu = n\bar{X} - n\mu;$$
$$\sum (\bar{X} - \mu) = n(\bar{X} - \mu)$$

$$\frac{1}{n} E [\sum (X - \mu)^2 + n(\bar{X} - \mu)^2 - 2n(\bar{X} - \mu)^2]$$

$$\frac{1}{n} E [\sum (X - \mu)^2 - n(\bar{X} - \mu)^2]$$

$$\frac{1}{n}[\sum E[(X-\mu)^2] - nE[(\overline{X}-\mu)^2]]$$

$$\text{where} \quad E(X-\mu)^2 = \sigma^2;$$

$$E(\overline{X}-\mu)^2 = \sigma^2/n$$

We state, without proof, a result from the Central Limit theorem:

$$E(\overline{X}-\mu)^2 = \frac{\sigma^2}{n}$$

$$\frac{1}{n}\left[n\sigma^2 - \frac{n\sigma^2}{n}\right] = \frac{1}{n}[n\sigma^2 - \sigma^2]$$

$$\sigma^2 - \frac{\sigma^2}{n} = \left(1 - \frac{1}{n}\right)\sigma^2$$

or

$$(3\text{-}26) \qquad \left(\frac{n-1}{n}\right)\sigma^2$$

This proves that $\sum(X-\overline{X})^2/n$ calculated from a sample is a biased estimator of σ^2, the population variance. But, practically speaking, $(n-1)/n\sigma^2$ is not a severe bias. The way to overcome the bias is to multiply the mean sum of squares $\sum(X-\overline{X})^2/n$ by the reciprocal of the bias, $n/(n-1)$, producing $\sum(X-\overline{X})/(n-1)$. But for larger samples this procedure does not seem worthwhile. The bias for $n = 100$ is only $-.01$, which probably would not be very important in most cases. Unless the researcher has some reason to be extremely precise, the correction $n/(n-1)$ may be ignored for large samples.

The second problem in estimating σ^2 is encountered when the modified formula is used for a sample from a relatively small population. The classic illustration of the problem is a box containing a small number of colored balls, some white, some black. The problem is to estimate the proportionate breakdown of black and white balls. If we take one ball out at a time, inspect it, and then set it aside, the probability of getting a black ball or a white ball changes after every ball is removed. As the balls are removed, the proportion of each color remaining changes. In statistical terminology, the trials (the observations of the variables; in this case, the selection of a ball) are not independent of each other. Practically speaking, $\sum(X-\overline{X})^2/(n-1)$ can lead to useless results.

Example 3–9

Suppose you have a population of six equal-sized election districts from a relatively homogeneous constituency, and you have calculated their turnout rates, as in Table 3-6, taking a sample of five. You wish to characterize the distribution of turnout for the population. The estimate for σ, .16, is disconcerting. It means that the 95 percent of the observations of X fall between .38 and 1.02 ($\pm 1.96\sigma$ about μ). This is clearly unacceptable.

Table 3-6

Example 3-9

District	Turnout	$(X - \bar{X})^\dagger$	$(X - \bar{X})^2$
X_1	.9	.2	.04
X_2	.8	.1	.01
X_3	.7	0	0
X_4	.6	$-.1$	.01
X_5	.5	$-.2$	.04
		$\sum(X - \bar{X})^2 =$	.10

$$\frac{\sum(X - \bar{X})^2}{n-1} = \frac{.10}{4} = .025$$

$$\sqrt{.025} \doteq .16$$

$\dagger$ Where $\bar{X} = .7$.

To overcome problems created by samples from small populations, a ratio called the *finite population correction* (fpc) must be used. It corrects the variance to account for the dependence among observations of the variable. Note that the population size is represented by N and the sample size by n. For Example 3-9, the following calculations are more realistic.

$$(3\text{-}27) \qquad \frac{\sum(X_i - \bar{X})^2}{n} \cdot \frac{N-n}{N-1}$$

where

$$\frac{N-n}{N-1} = \text{fpc}$$

Then

$$.025\left(\frac{6-5}{6-1}\right) = .025\left(\frac{1}{5}\right) = .00500$$

Thus, the corrected standard deviation is a little over .07, and the .95 percent interval about the mean is a more realistic .56 to .84.

It should be obvious that as N gets larger, and consequently n is a smaller proportion of N, the finite population correction is less important. When N is very large, $N - n$ will not be very different from $N - 1$; thus the fpc ratio approaches 1. To illustrate, suppose we drew a sample of 5000 persons from the total population of the United States. The ratio would be .99975. If we took a sample of one million, the ratio would be .995! Statisticians vary on a rule of thumb for determining when the fpc can be dropped from estimates. A more liberal rule would be to use the fpc if $n/N \geqslant .10$; a more conservative rule is to use fpc when $n/N \geqslant .05$. We opt for the more conservative rule, and note that if one uses a computer, the calculation is practically costless and certainly harmless.

ESTIMATION FOR DISTRIBUTIONS OF PROPORTIONS

The mean and variance for a distribution of proportions has some special features of interest to us. In Example 3-1 we assumed that the election districts were of equal size. We treated each election district as a case, thus defining the possible range of the variable X as $0 \leqslant X \leqslant 1$, and the number of cases was 359 election districts. But suppose we treated each voter as a separate case. We would then have 143,600 cases (assuming 400 voters per election district). Furthermore, the new variable Y would be limited to only two values: $Y = 1$ if the voter voted Democratic, and $Y = 0$ if not. Variables of this form are called *binomial* variables, after *bi* meaning 2 and *nomial* meaning number. They can take on only two values.

We wish to find the mean of this binomial variable. From earlier discussions we defined in (3-5) the mean of the variable X as

$$\mu = \frac{\sum f_i X_i}{N}$$

where f_i is the frequency count in group i, $N = 359$ election districts, and X_i is the proportion Democratic in district i; that is,

$$(3\text{-}28) \qquad X_i = \frac{\sum Y_j}{W}$$

where Y_j is the binomial variable representing individual voters and $W = 400$ is the size of an election district ($NW = 143,600$).

Then the mean of X for the population can be restated as

$$(3\text{-}29) \qquad \frac{\sum f_i X_i}{N} = \frac{\sum f_i (\sum Y_j / W)_i}{N}$$

$$= \frac{\sum f_i (\sum Y_j)_i}{NW} = \pi$$

which can be simply stated as

$$\frac{\text{Number of voters voting Democratic}}{\text{Number of voters}} = \frac{\text{proportion voting}}{\text{Democratic}}$$

The population mean π is the proportion of Y's for which $Y = 1$. The *sample* proportion is written p and $E(p) = \pi$. It should be evident that the sample proportion is an unbiased, consistent, and efficient estimator of π, since it is strictly analogous to $\overline{X}$ as an estimate of μ.

The variance of a binomial variable is appealing because of its simplicity. We derive a simple formula for the *population* variance of Y as follows:

$$(3\text{-}30) \qquad \text{Var}(Y) = \frac{\sum (Y - \mu)^2}{N} = \frac{\sum (Y - \pi)^2}{N}$$

Since Y equals either 1 or 0,

$$\frac{\sum (1 - \pi)^2 + \sum (0 - \pi)^2}{N}$$

There will be $N\pi$ ones and $N(1 - \pi)$ zeroes; thus,

$$\frac{N\pi(1 - \pi)^2 + N(1 - \pi)(0 - \pi)^2}{N}$$

since $(0 - \pi)^2 = \pi^2$, and factoring $N\pi(1 - \pi)$ gives

$$\frac{N\pi(1 - \pi)[(1 - \pi) + \pi]}{N} = \frac{N\pi(1 - \pi)}{N} = \pi(1 - \pi)$$

So, the variance of a binomial variable Y is

$$(3\text{-}31) \qquad \sigma_Y^2 = \pi(1 - \pi)$$

The mean of Y is π and the variance of Y is $\pi(1 - \pi)$. From the Central Limit theorem we know that if we take a number of samples from a population, the expected value of the mean of the distribution of sample means is the population mean (π) and the variance is σ^2/n; that is, $(\pi(1 - \pi))/n$.[6] In the examples we have presented thus far (especially Example 3-1), our interest has been in the distribution of π. Thus the statistic of value to us is the variance of π:

$$\sigma_\pi^2 = \frac{\pi(1 - \pi)}{n}$$

Estimations of σ_π^2 are straightforward. Using the *sample* proportion p as an estimate of the population proportion π, we employ the same correction to $\hat{\sigma}^2$, as in previously stated estimates of σ^2. Then

$$(3\text{-}32) \qquad \hat{\sigma}^2 = \left(\frac{p(1 - p)}{n}\right)\left(\frac{N - n}{N - 1}\right)$$

where N is the population size and n is the sample size. However, most populations for which the binomial distribution is applicable are quite large; therefore,

$$(3\text{-}33) \qquad \hat{\sigma}^2 = \frac{p(1-p)}{n}$$

will be adequate.

Example 3–10

Suppose you wanted to estimate how a committee of 20 members voted on a particular measure, but you only have time to interview 10 of its members. Of your 10 interviewees, 7 voted for the measure and 3 voted against it. You set up the problem as follows:

$$N = 20$$

$$n = 10$$

$$p = \frac{\sum Y}{n} = \frac{7}{10} = .7$$

The sample mean is .7, but we want to get an idea of how much confidence can be placed in this estimate of π. Of course we want to estimate the standard deviation of the distribution of sample means:

$$\hat{\sigma}^2 = \frac{p(1-p)}{n} \cdot \frac{N-n}{N-1}$$

$$= \frac{.7(.3)}{10} \cdot \frac{20-10}{19}$$

$$= \frac{.21(10)}{10(19)} = \frac{2.10}{190} \doteq .011$$

Therefore

$$\hat{\sigma} = (.011)^{\frac{1}{2}} \doteq .105$$

A standard deviation of .105 means that $p \leqslant .5$ lies almost two standard deviations away, suggesting that it is quite likely that the measure passed.

SUMMARY

In this chapter we have sought to point out the important assumptions common to all statistical models based on the normal distribution. We presented measures that help decide whether or not it is reasonable to assume that a distribution is normal. We discussed the normal distribution function and its implications. The method of standardization of variables was presented and the use of the Table A-1, "Normal Distribution," was illustrated. Finally, we concluded the discussion of the normal distribution with methods of estimating its parameters, μ and σ.

There are three important points in this chapter that are critical to the successful employment of statistical models. The first is that in order to use a statistical model, some highly restrictive assumptions have to be accepted about the data to which the model is applied. One assumption is that all scales of measurement are at least interval scales. If they were not interval scales, we would not be able to perform the mathematical operations we have described. Another assumption is that the distribution of the variable is approximately normal. The limits of deviation from normalcy are measurable by the moment measures that were discussed. The normal distribution can be employed in restricted cases where the population is not normally distributed. All these cases are tests of hypotheses dealing with a distribution of sample means. This follows from the Central Limit theorem. The assumption of a specific probability distribution for a random variable is also important. We must know the probabilities of observations of a variable in order to calculate its expected value. Expected values, in turn, enable the estimation of the parameters μ and σ. This leads to the second important point.

Statistical models enable a researcher to make calculated guesses about a population when he has information only about a sample of the population. Thus, you should keep in mind the difference between population parameters and sample estimates of the parameters. When you assume that a population variable is normally distributed, you assume that the distribution of the population variable can be characterized by the normal distribution function (3-18). From a sample we glean data that indicate, through estimates of μ and σ, what the population is most probably like. The use of sample data thus enables the researcher to make probability statements about the population.

Our third important point is the tacit but important assumption in statistical models that frequencies in the present can be treated as probabilities in the future. This assumption, as we stated earlier, is controversial among some epistemologists, but its acceptance is necessary if our science is to do anything more than describe political history. Chapter 4 provides an introductory discussion of probability theory.

The final point we wish to emphasize in this conclusion is an assumption tacitly made throughout this chapter. When we make inferences about a population from a sample, we cannot use just any sample. Valid samples must be selected in accordance with inferences from probability theory, and so we dedicate Chapter 5 to drawing these inferences and thoroughly discussing the theory of sampling.

NOTES   Chapter 3

1. Technically, these methods may be employed as nonparametric statistical tests, but their understanding is so important that these uses are explained.

2. As we shall see in Chapter 7, this assumption may be ignored when the χ^2 distribution is used.

3. Throughout this book the subscripts are ignored in summation expressions when the symbolism is unambiguous. Precisely stated, (3–1) should be

$$\frac{\sum_{i=1}^{N} X^k}{N}$$

4. Such a measure assumes that each municipality is equally important as a measure of strength, regardless of size.

5. For discrete data with broad intervals and a relatively narrow range, it is necessary to make a continuity correction to the Z transformation. In most political research the correction is of negligible importance. This example illustrates the need for the continuity correction. The likelihood of getting a value between 7 and 10 is actually the likelihood of getting a value between 6.5 and 10 because of the way we round off continuous values to include them in discrete categories. Any value between 6.5 and 7.4 is identified as 7.0. The continuity correction allows for this rounding. Where discrete categories merit it, the Z transformation should be $(|X—.5| — \mu)/\sigma$.

6. This result will be explained further and put to use in Chapter 5.

REFERENCES   Chapter 3

Ferber, Robert. *Market Research*. New York: McGraw-Hill, 1949. (See especially chap. ii.)

Mendenhall, William. *Introduction to Probability and Statistics*. Belmont, Calif.: Wadsworth, 1969. (See especially chap. 7.)

Yamane, Taro. *Mathematics for Economists*. Englewood Cliffs, N.J.: Prentice-Hall, 1962. (See especially chaps. 13 and 14.)

Chapter 4

PROBABILITY

In Chapter 3 we said that when we make the leap from frequencies to probabilities, we acquire the power that statistical models promise. In Chapter 5 we shall show that sampling procedures are designed to control the probability of selecting various types of samples and the probability of each member of the population's being included in the sample. Decision rules based on probability statements are crucial to the subject matter of Chapters 6 through 9. Since probability theory plays such an important role in statistical models, it is important that you understand it thoroughly.

MAIN APPROACHES TO PROBABILITY

There are two main approaches to probability: subjective (or subjectivist) and objective (or objectivist). It is the objective approach (in fact, a certain type of objective approach, which we shall soon discuss) that has been investigated extensively by statisticians and which is essential for the understanding of the statistical models presented in this book. However, the subjective approach, which statisticians dismiss as unscientific and consequently irrelevant, is often used in the statements made about political events. For example, when a person speculates that a particular candidate (say, candidate A) will probably win, he uses subjective approach to probability. Even when "Jimmy the Greek" lays 3:2 odds that so and so will be elected president, his rather precise odds are merely the reflection of his judgment. He uses subjective approach to probability. The main point here is that since the probability is subjective, another person making prediction about the same candidate may come up with an entirely different assessment of the chances of that candidate winning.

An interesting aspect of the subjective approach to probability is that the mathematical model of the objective approach to probability is applicable to it also. The statement that the chances of candidate A winning in a two-way race are 3 to 2 can be interpreted as follows: The probability of candidate A winning equals 3/5, or .6, and the probability of the second candidate winning equals 2/5, or .4; if more than two candidates are running, then the probability of candidate A winning equals 3/5, or .6, and the combined probabilities of all other candidates winning equal 2/5, or .4. In both cases, .6 + .4 = 1. We shall show presently that this model is similar to the model of the objective approach to probability. The greatest problem, however, with the subjective approach (besides its being different for different persons) is that, as an event becomes complicated, it becomes very difficult to calculate subjective probabilities.

The objective approach to probability is of two types: a priori and relative frequency in the long run. Some social scientists writing in the field of statistics confuse one for the other and mistakenly regard the former more important than the latter. The fact of the matter is that it is probability in the sense of the relative frequency in the long run that has received extensive treatment from statisticians, and it is this type of probability that we also emphasize. However, let us first explain what we mean by a priori probability. The main idea of a priori probability is that we make a probability statement on the basis of abstract reasoning or prior assumptions about an event. We also assume symmetry (that is, equivalent conditions) in a priori probability. (Symmetry is assumed for the second type of the objective probability also.) Thus, when we say that the probability of getting the head in a toss of a fair coin is 1/2, we may make this statement on the basis of prior assumptions about coin tossing and by assuming that the coin is fair (fairness of the coin is called *symmetry*).

Probability in the sense of the relative frequency in the long run is based on experience, or rather on a large number of experiments, and this makes it more important than a priori probability. As indicated above, it also assumes symmetry or equivalent conditions. A third assumption of this type of probability is randomness; that is, the result of a single observation or experiment is variable and cannot be predetermined. Thus, if we conduct 500 experiments of tossing a fair coin, we can say that the relative frequency of obtaining the head would approach 1/2. We denote the number of experiments (500 in this case) by n and the number of heads by m. So, we are saying that m/n, when $n = 500$, approaches 1/2. We call m/n the relative frequency of obtaining the head. This objective approach to probability is based on such relative frequencies in the long run. In other words, probability in this case refers to the result obtained from observation and expressed in precise terms in our model. In the example of a fair coin, even after a million trials, the relative frequency of obtaining the head may not be exactly 1/2. But in the model we assume that the probability of obtaining the head is exactly 1/2.

VOCABULARY OF PROBABILITY

In the discussion of probability certain terms are often used. These terms are *simple events, compound events, sample points, sample space, set, complementary set, exclusive events, intersection of events,* and *union of events.* Let us define these terms.

Simple Events

By simple events we mean outcomes or results that cannot be further subdivided.

Example 4-1

Consider three candidates (*A, B,* and *C*) running for office. Three outcomes or results are possible: (1) candidate *A* can win; (2) candidate *B* can win; (3) candidate *C* can win. Each of these outcomes is considered a simple event.

Example 4-2

If a coin is tossed, two simple events are possible: (1) head can turn up; (2) tail can turn up.

Compound Events

A compound event may be further subdivided into two or more simple events. In Example 4-1, suppose *C* is the weakest of the candidates, and we can say that either *A* or *B* will win. This is a compound event, since the probability that either *A* or *B* will win can be subdivided into two simple events: (1) *A* will win; (2) *B* will win.

Sample Points

Sample points are the same as simple events. In Example 4-1, there are three sample points, which are shown in one-dimensional space in Figure 4-1.

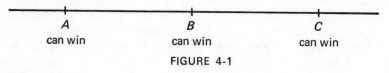

FIGURE 4-1

Example 4–3

Now consider another election, in which four candidates (*D, E, F,* and *G*) are running for office. In this case there are four sample points. However, if we consider the election of Example 4-1 as well as the

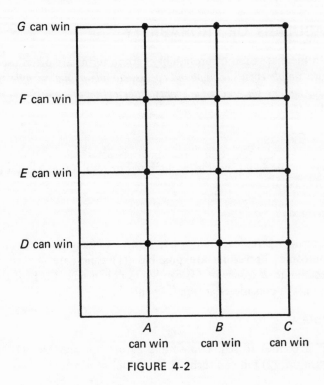

FIGURE 4-2

election of this example, we have 12 sample points, as shown in two-dimensional space in Figure 4-2.

Sample Space

The collection of all sample points is called sample space. Thus, in Figure 4-1, the sample space consists of 3 sample points, and in Figure 4-2 the sample space consists of 12 sample points.

Set

The sample space is also referred to as *set*. When we use the term *set*, we call the sample points *elements* of the set. We use braces to denote a set. Thus, $\{A, B, C\}$ is a set with 3 elements. To say that A is a member of the set $\{A, B, C\}$, we write $A \in \{A, B, C\}$. To say that D is not a member of the set $\{A, B, C\}$, we write $D \notin \{A, B, C\}$. If a set has no element in it, we call it an empty, or null set. Now consider $\{A, B\}$ and $\{A, B, C\}$. We say that $\{A, B\}$ is a subset of $\{A, B, C\}$, since every element of the former is an element of the latter. If we denote $\{A, B\}$ by S_1 and $\{A, B, C\}$ by S, then the notation used is $S_1 \subset S$. Read $\subset$ as "contained in."

Complementary Set

Consider two subsets S_1 and S_2 of the set $S = \{A, B, C\}$, where $S_1 = \{A, B\}$ and $S_2 = \{C\}$. Then, as shown in Figure 4-3 also, no elements in S_1 or S_2 are common to either subset. In such a case we say that S_1 is a *complement* of S_2 or that S_2 is a complement of S_1. We write the complement of a subset by placing a bar over it. Thus, the complement of S_1 is $\bar{S}_1$, which, as we know, is equal to S_2. The complement of the set S is an empty set, since it contains no element. Note that the elements in a set are simple events.

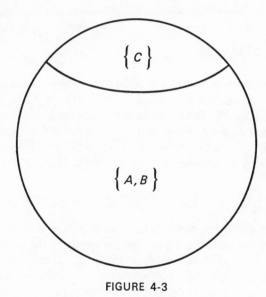

FIGURE 4-3

Exclusive Events

No common simple event belongs to either of the events that we consider exclusive.

Example 4–4

Consider four candidates (A, B, C, and D) running for office. We can consider success of A or B as a compound event and success of C as a simple event (ignore D for the time being). Then, we can say that the compound success event of A or B and the simple success event of C are exclusive. This is shown in Figure 4-4. Note in Figure 4-4, because of the presence of D, we cannot say that the subset $\{C\}$ is the complement of the subset $\{A, B\}$.

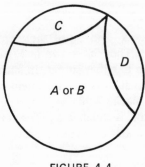

FIGURE 4-4

Intersection of Events

Suppose a compound event E consists of simple events AB, AC, AD, BA, CA, DA and another compound event F consists of simple events AB, BA, BC, BD, CB, DB. Then, we can say that simple events AB and BA are in both E and F. We call this the *intersection* of the two events E and F and write it $E \cap F$; that is, the notation $\cap$ (the "cap" symbol) is used to denote intersection. Alternatively, $E \cap F$ is written E and F.

Example 4–5

Consider a situation in which four candidates A, B, C, and D run for office and the winner must receive a majority of the valid votes cast. If none of the candidates receives a majority of the votes, then there is a second election in which all the four candidates run again, but this time the winner is decided by the plurality. The members of the French National Assembly are elected by this electoral system.[1] Let us consider a candidate receiving plurality of votes in the first election to be a simple event, and a candidate receiving plurality of votes in the second election to be also a simple event. Then, we have four simple events in the first election and four simple events in the second election.

If we consider both elections together, then we get 16 simple events or sample points, which we can show in a sample space as follows:

AA	*AB*	*AC*	*AD*
BB	*BA*	*BC*	*BD*
CC	*CA*	*CB*	*CD*
DD	*DA*	*DB*	*DC*

AA means that A receives plurality of votes in the first election as well as in the second election. AB means that A receives plurality of votes in the first election and B receives plurality of votes in the second election. The rest of the simple events can be interpreted similarly. Now consider two compound events in this sample space: (1) A receives plurality of votes in one of the elections, which is represented by the compound event E consisting of AB, AC, AD, BA, CA, DA; and (2)B receives plurality of votes in one of the elections, which is represented by the compound event F consisting of AB, BA, BC, BD, CB, DB. Note that two simple events, AB and BA, are common to both compound events. We show this in Figure 4-5.

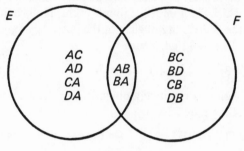

FIGURE 4-5

Union of Events

In the preceding example, if we consider all the simple events in the two compound events, then we have 12 simple events. These 12 simple events are regarded as the union of E and F. The main point here is that all 12 simple events are in E or in F or in $E \cap F$. The union of events is written $E \cup F$; that is, the notation $\cup$ denotes the operation of uniting. Alternately, $E \cup F$ is written E or F.

BASIC POSTULATES OF PROBABILITY

We now discuss the basic postulates of probability, emphasizing, as indicated above, probability in the sense of the relative frequency in the long run. These postulates apply to a priori probability as well as to the subjective approach to probability.

We write the probability of a simple event A_i as $P(A_i)$. $P(A_i)$ is a nonnegative number and varies between 0 and 1. In other words, the first basic postulate of probability is

(4-1) $0 \leqslant P(A_i) \leqslant 1$

The long-run relative frequency of A_i is m/n, m being the number of times A_i occurs and n being the total number of experiments. The expression in (4-1) is, in fact, the equivalent of

$$0 \leqslant \frac{m}{n} \leqslant 1$$

In a large number of experiments, m/n approaches $P(A_i)$.

The first postulate applies to compound events also. If E_i is a compound event, then

(4-2) $0 \leqslant E_i \leqslant 1$

The discussion of probability assumes that we are considering situations in which the number of simple events is more than 1. If in a situation we write the probability of each of the possible simple events $A_1, A_2, \dots A_n$ as $P(A_1), P(A_2) \cdots P(A_n)$, then

(4-3) $P(A_1) + P(A_2) + \cdots + P(A_n) = 1$

This expression is intuitively obvious. For illustration, consider tossing a coin or rolling a die. Then,

$P(T) + P(H) = 1$ (in the case of tossing a coin)

$P(1) + P(2) + P(3)$

$+ P(4) + P(5) + P(6) = 1$ (in the case of rolling a die)

If the coin and the die are fair, then

$P(T) = P(H) = \frac{1}{2}$ and $P(1) = P(2) \cdots = P(6) = \frac{1}{6}$

This is often called a *uniform probability model*, since each of the simple events has the same probability. However, postulate (4-3) also applies to situations in which the probabilities of the simple events are unequal.

Consider again the example of three candidates (A, B, and C) running for office. We know that the probabilities of the simple events A winning, B winning, C winning are unequal (even though they cannot be calculated). We can also say, using postulate (4-3), that

$P(A) + P(B) + P(C) = 1$

The probability of a compound event can be understood in terms of the probabilities of the simple events, of which it is composed. If a compound event E is composed of the simple events A_1, A_3, and A_5, then

(4-4) $P(E) = P(A_1) + P(A_3) + P(A_5)$

In the case of a uniform probability model, the probability of a compound event can be very easily calculated.

Example 4–6

Consider the compound event of a die showing more than 4 points. This compound event is composed of two simple events, showing of 5 points and showing of 6 points. If the die is fair, the probability of the compound event equals $\frac{1}{6} + \frac{1}{6} = \frac{2}{6} = \frac{1}{3}$.

As a general rule, if E is a compound event composed of simple events, each of which has the same probability, then

$$(4\text{-}5) \qquad P(E) = \frac{n(E)}{n}$$

where $n(E)$ is the number of simple events in E and n is the total number of simple events.

The next postulate of probability concerns exclusive events. Exclusive events were explained above and shown in Figure 4-4. If E and F are exclusive events, then

$$(4\text{-}6) \qquad P(E \cup F) = P(E) + P(F)$$

The sixth postulate applies to *any number* of exclusive events, and not only to *two* exclusive events.

Example 4–7

Suppose we have 3 black, 3 white, 3 red, and 3 blue balls in an urn, and we draw one ball at a time with replacement. The probability of drawing a white or a red or a blue ball is

$$P(w \cup r \cup b) = P(w) + P(r) + P(b) \qquad \text{(since they are}$$
$$\text{exclusive events)}$$

$$= \tfrac{3}{12} + \tfrac{3}{12} + \tfrac{3}{12} = \tfrac{3}{4} = .75$$

If two events E and F are not exclusive—that is, one or more simple events are in $E \cap F$, then

$$(4\text{-}7) \qquad P(E \cup F) = P(E) + P(F) - P(E \cap F)$$

The last postulate of probability that we mention concerns complementary events, in which we extend the postulate regarding exclusive events. Note that complementary events are exclusive events. The complement of the event E is $\bar{E}$ and

$$P(E) + P(\bar{E}) = 1$$

Therefore,

$$(4\text{-}8) \qquad P(E) = 1 - P(\bar{E})$$

CONDITIONAL PROBABILITY

When we want to find the probability of an event, given that another event has already occurred, we call it *conditional* probability because the occurrence of the event in which we are interested depends on the condition that another event has preceded it. If we want to find the conditional probability of the event *B*, given that the event *A* has occurred, we write it $P(B|A)$. Let us extend the explanation of conditional probability and give examples of its use.

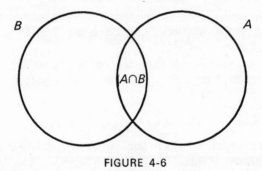

FIGURE 4-6

Consider Figure 4-6, which is similar to Figure 4-5. We use the following notations:

$$n(A) = \text{number of simple events in } A$$

$$n(B) = \text{number of simple events in } B$$

$$n(A \text{ and } B) = \text{number of simple events in } A \cap B$$

$$n = \text{total number of simple events in sample space}$$

If we seek to find $P(B|A)$, then we restrict ourselves to the sample space of the events in *A*, since the certain occurrence of *A* is assumed. Now $n(A \text{ and } B)$ may be considered some of the simple events in this sample space, and $P(B|A)$ may be considered the ordinary probability (as opposed to conditional probability) of a compound event consisting of $n(A \text{ and } B)$ simple events in the same sample space. (If $n(A \text{ and } B)$ contains only one simple event, then $P(B|A)$ is the ordinary probability of a simple event in this sample space.) Assuming a uniform probability model, we can use postulate (4-5) and write

$$\textbf{(4-9)} \qquad P(B|A) = \frac{n(A \text{ and } B)}{n(A)}$$

To derive a formula for $P(B|A)$ in terms of $P(A \text{ and } B)$ and $P(A)$, we perform certain algebraic manipulations. Again assuming a uniform probability model and using postulate (4-5), we have

$$P(A) = \frac{n(A)}{n}$$

$$P(A \text{ and } B) = \frac{n(A \text{ and } B)}{n}$$

Therefore,

$$\frac{P(A \text{ and } B)}{P(A)} = \frac{n(A \text{ and } B)}{n} \cdot \frac{n}{n(A)}$$

$$= \frac{n(A \text{ and } B)}{n(A)}$$

$$= P(B|A)$$

or

(4-10) $$P(B|A) = \frac{P(A \text{ and } B)}{P(A)}$$

In deriving formulas (4-9) and (4-10) for $P(B|A)$, we have assumed a uniform probability model. It can be shown, however, that formula (4-10) holds, even if a uniform probability model is not assumed. $P(B|A)$ may be considered the conditional probability of a compound event, and this compound event is considered as composed of the simple events, each of which is assigned a conditional probability. In the uniform probability model, by restricting ourselves to the sample space of the events in A, we assumed the ordinary probability of each of these simple events to be the same. If we again restrict ourselves to the sample space of the events in A, but do not assume a uniform probability model, then

$$P(B|A) \neq \frac{n(A \text{ and } B)}{n(A)}$$

Instead, we write

$$P(B|A) = \sum P(A_i|A)$$

where A_i is a simple event in $A \cap B$ and i ranges from 1 through k so that $A_1, A_2, \ldots A_k = A \cap B$. Note that $P(A_i|A)$ is the conditional probability of the simple event A_i in $A \cap B$, and may be considered an ordinary probability of the event A_i if we restrict ourselves to the sample space of the events in A. It can be shown that

$$P(A_i|A) = \frac{P(A_i)}{P(A)}$$

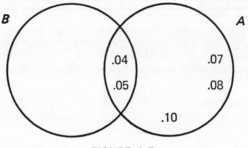

FIGURE 4-7

Consider an example with probabilities of some of the simple events indicated in Figure 4-7, where $A \cap B$ is shown composed of two simple events with probabilities .04 and .05. Event A is a compound event composed of five simple events with probabilities as shown. The remaining events are not shown because they are not relevant to our purpose. Now consider $P(A_1|A)$, where A_1 is a simple event in $A \cap B$ with .04 probability. If we consider $P(A_1|A)$ an ordinary probability of A_1 in the sample space of the events in A, then

$$P(A_1|A) = \frac{4}{34}$$

(assuming the probabilities of the other four simple events in the sample space of the events in A to be 5/34, 7/34, 8/34, and 10/34).

In the original sample space,

$$P(A) = .04 + .05 + .07 + .08 + .10 = .34$$

and

$$P(A_1) = .04$$

Therefore,

$$\frac{P(A_1)}{P(A)} = \frac{.04}{.34} = \frac{4}{34}$$

which means that

$$P(A_1|A) = \frac{P(A_1)}{P(A)}$$

Hence,

$$P(B|A) = \sum P(A_i|A)$$
$$= \frac{P(A_1)}{P(A)} + \cdots + \frac{P(A_k)}{P(A)}$$
$$= \frac{P(A \text{ and } B)}{P(A)}$$

which is formula (4-10). If $A \cap B$ is a simple event, which we denote by A_1, then $P(B|A) = P(A_1)/P(A)$.

Using formula (4-10), we write

(4-11) $P(A \text{ and } B) = P(A)P(B|A)$

This is known as the *multiplication rule*. It is easily shown that

$$P(A|B) = \frac{P(A \text{ and } B)}{P(B)}$$

and

$$P(A \text{ and } B) = P(B)P(A|B)$$

Therefore

(4-12) $P(A)P(B|A) = P(B)P(A|B)$

Example 4–8

Consider again Example 4-5 of four candidates running for office in a two-stage election procedure. In that example the sample space consisted of 16 simple events (or sample points). We also mentioned two compound events: (1) Candidate A receives plurality of votes in one of the elections, and (2) candidate B receives plurality of votes in one of the elections. Now, using that example and assuming a uniform probability model for simplicity, we want to find the conditional probability of B's receiving plurality of votes in one of the elections, given that A receives plurality of votes in one of the elections (that is, in the other election). Earlier we used F to denote B as receiving plurality of votes in one of the elections, and E to denote A as receiving plurality of votes in one of the elections. Using the same notation, we want to find $P(F|E)$. Note that both E and F are compound events. As shown in Figure 4-5, E is composed of AB, AC, AD, BA, CA, DA; F is composed of AB, BA, BC, BD, CB, DB. AB and BA are in $E \cap F$. Then, using formula (4-9),

$$P(F|E) = \frac{n(E \text{ and } F)}{n(E)} = \frac{2}{6} = \frac{1}{3}$$

Example 4–9

Suppose we have a population of 90 voters, 50 of whom are registered Democrats and 40 are registered Republicans. We ask them how they voted in the last presidential election. We receive the following information:

40 registered Democrats voted for the Democrat presidential candidate

10 registered Democrats voted for the third-party candidate

30 registered Republicans voted for the Republican presidential candidate

10 registered Republicans voted for the third-party candidate

Now, from our population of 90 voters, we select one voter at random. Random selection means that each of the 90 voters has the same probability, 1/90, of being selected. The question we ask is: What is the probability that the selected person voted for the third-party candidate, given the information that he is a Democrat? In other words, we want to find $P(T/D)$, where T means voting for the third-party candidate and D means a registered Democrat. Again assuming a uniform probability model and using formula (4-9), we find

$$P(T/D) = \frac{n(T \text{ and } D)}{n(D)} = \frac{10}{50} = \frac{1}{5}$$

If we want to find the probability that the selected person voted for the third-party candidate, given that he is a Republican, then this conditional probability would be (assuming a uniform probability model) $10/40 = 1/4$.

In Examples 4-8 and 4-9, we assumed a uniform probability model. However, in a large number of the interesting political situations this assumption cannot be met. When we consider the difficulties of the calculation of subjective probability, we realize that some interesting conditional probabilities are virtually impossible to calculate. We give an example to illustrate this.

Example 4-10

At the time of this writing the Republican governor of Connecticut was preparing to submit his annual budget to the Democrat-controlled General Assembly of the state. An interesting question is: What is the *conditional* probability that the Republican governor's budget will be approved, given the fact that the Democrats control the General Assembly? Those who understand state politics in Connecticut would say that this conditional probability is very low, but the question is: How low? If we say that this conditional probability is close to 0, then the question is: How close to 0? The question obviously cannot be answered in terms of exact conditional probability.

BAYES' THEOREM

We now discuss a special case of conditional probability. In some cases the calculation of conditional probability is quite tedious. In such cases we use Bayes' theorem (also called Bayes' formula), which expresses in a systematic manner how the calculation is to be done.[2] We first explain this theorem and then show its use with an example.

Suppose we have a two-stage experiment. In the first stage there are k possible outcomes, which we write $H_1, H_2, ..., H_k$. We assume that $P(H_i)$ is known. It is called the *prior* probability of H_i. For the second stage of the experiment, suppose we have l possible outcomes, which we write $A_1, A_2, ..., A_l$. Now we want to find $P(H_1|A_1)$; that is, the conditional probability of H_1, given A_1. This is called the *posterior* probability, since the entire experiment is performed. H_i is often referred to as a hypothesis, since $P(H_i)$ is known. A_i is always referred to as an event.

Using formula (4-10), we get

$$P(H_1|A_1) = \frac{P(A_1 \text{ and } H_1)}{P(A_1)} = \frac{P(H_1 \text{ and } A_1)}{P(A_1)}$$

We know from (4-11), the multiplication rule, that

$$P(H_1 \text{ and } A_1) = P(H_1)P(A_1|H_1)$$

Note that $P(H_1)$ is given and $P(A_1|H_1)$ can be easily calculated. Now we have to express $P(A_1)$ in a form that can be easily calculated. A_1 can occur along with H_1 or H_2 or ... H_k. If A_1 occurs along with H_1, then, using the multiplication rule, we can write

$$P(A_1 \text{ and } H_1) = P(H_1 \text{ and } A_1) = P(H_1)P(A_1|H_1)$$

The probabilities of the occurrences of A_1 along with other H_i's may be written similarly. All events A_1 occurring with any H_i are exclusive. Using formula (4-6) for the exclusive events, we get

$$P(A_1) = P(H_1)P(A_1|H_1) + P(H_2)P(A_1|H_2)$$
$$+ \cdots + P(H_k)P(A_1|H_k)$$
$$= \sum_{i=1}^{k} P(H_i)P(A_1|H_i)$$

Therefore,

$$(4\text{-}13) \qquad P(H_1|A_1) = \frac{P(H_1)P(A_1|H_1)}{\sum\limits_{i=1}^{k} P(H_i)P(A_1|H_i)}$$

This is called Bayes' theorem, or Bayes' formula.

Example 4–11

Suppose we have two populations, each of ten persons. Further, suppose the first population consists of six Democrats and four Republicans; the second population consists of six Republicans and four Democrats. We first select at random one of these populations and then select again at random one person from the selected population. We notice that the selected person is a Democrat. We do not know whether the selected population was the first or the second. We want to find the probability of the selected person's belonging to the second population. In this case, the first population is H_1 and the second population is H_2. $P(H_1)$ and $P(H_2)$ are known (half in each case) and are the *prior* probabilities. We want to find $P(H_2|D)$, which is a *posterior* probability. Using Bayes' formula, we get

$$P(H_2|D) = \frac{P(H_2)\,P(D|H_2)}{P(H_1)\,P(D|H_1)+P(H_2)\,P(D|H_2)}$$

$$= \frac{\frac{1}{2}\times\frac{4}{10}}{\frac{1}{2}\times\frac{6}{10}+\frac{1}{2}\times\frac{4}{10}} = \frac{2}{5} = .4$$

INDEPENDENCE IN PROBABILITY

Two events, A and B, are considered statistically independent if

(4-14) $P(A \text{ and } B) = P(A)P(B)$

First, we derive this formula and then discuss its relevance to the study of politics.

Suppose we want to select a random sample[3] of two persons from a population of ten persons, six of whom are Democrats and four are Republicans. We write the names of the ten persons on ten slips of paper, fold them, and place them in a box. We then mix these slips of paper thoroughly and draw one. Let us assume that the selected slip of paper has the name of a Democrat. We return the selected slip of paper into the box, again mix the slips of paper thoroughly, and then draw another slip of paper. If we denote the selection of a Democrat on the first draw by A, then we ask: "What is the probability of the occurrence of B, B being the selection of a Democrat on the second draw?" It is obvious that the occurrence of the event A has no influence on the occurrence of the event B, which means that B is independent of A. So, we write

$$P(B|A) = P(B)$$

In other words, the probability of B, given that A has occurred, is equal to the probability of B. We derived earlier in formula (4-12) that

$$P(A)P(B|A) = P(B)P(A|B)$$

If $P(B|A) = P(B)$, then

$$P(A)P(B) = P(B)P(A|B)$$

Therefore,

$$P(A) = P(A|B)$$

which means that the occurrence of B has no influence on the occurrence of A and that A is independent of B. In other words, when B is independent of A, A is also independent of B. Now recall from formula (4-11) that

$$P(A \text{ and } B) = P(A)P(B|A)$$

Since A and B are independent of each other:

$$P(A \text{ and } B) = P(A)P(B)$$

Note that

$$P(A \text{ and } B) = P(B \text{ and } A)$$

and

$$P(A)P(B) = P(B)P(A)$$

It can be easily shown that when A, B, and C are independent of one another, then

(4-15) $P(A \text{ and } B \text{ and } C) = P(A)P(B)P(C)$

Formula (4-15) can be generalized to any number of events.

Example 4–12

We go back to our example and ask: What is the probability of selecting a Democrat on the first draw (A) and again a Democrat on the second draw (B), assuming the independence of A and B? In this case,

$$P(A \text{ and } B) = P(A)P(B)$$
$$= \tfrac{6}{10} \times \tfrac{6}{10} = \tfrac{36}{100} = .36$$

Example 4–13

To illustrate the concept of independence further, we again consider the example of the population of 90 voters, 50 of whom are registered Democrats and 40 are registered Republicans. We stated that 10 of the Democrats and 10 of the Republicans voted for the third-party candidate. We again select one person at random from this population and find that he is a Democrat. We ask the same question, that is: What is the probability that the selected person voted for the third-party candidate, given that he is a Democrat? Notationally, we wish to evaluate $P(T|D)$. Now, if voting for the third-party candidate and being a Democrat are independent, then $P(T|D) = P(T)$. Let us see if this is the case. We mentioned earlier that $P(T|D) = 1/5$. Since there are 20 persons voting for the third-party candidate in the population of 90, $P(T) = 2/9$. Thus, $P(T|D) \neq P(T)$. Hence, T and D are not independent.

Example 4-14

Suppose the governors of Connecticut and Nebraska introduced annual budgets before their respective state assemblies. Let us denote the approval of the proposed budget by the Connecticut State Assembly by A and the approval of the proposed budget by the Nebraska State Assembly by B. It seems reasonable to assume that A and B are independent, so $P(A \text{ and } B) = P(A)P(B)$. Unfortunately, this calculation is possible only by the use of subjective probability.

BINOMIAL TRIALS IN PROBABILITY

In Chapter 2 we discussed the binomial variable and derived its mean and variance. We now give a somewhat different interpretation of the binomial variable, relating it to probability. Consider an experiment in which only two outcomes are possible and both outcomes are independent of each other. Suppose that one of these outcomes is the occurrence of a certain event and the other outcome is the nonoccurrence of the same event. By convention, the occurrence of the event is called a success and its nonoccurrence is called a failure. The use of the terms *success* and *failure* does not imply that one of the outcomes is desirable and the other is not. A success has a certain probability, and we denote it by p. Then, the probability of a failure is $1 - p$, often written q, so that $p + q = 1$.

Let us now consider a specific experiment with a certain number of trials (say, three), each with two outcomes, success and failure. We call these trials *binomial* trials. In these three trials the following events are possible:

$$SSS \quad SSF \quad SFS \quad SFF \quad FSS \quad FSF \quad FFS \quad FFF$$

where S means a success and F means a failure. In order to know p and q, we have to know what is involved in the experiment. Let us assume that we are drawing one slip of paper at random from a box containing ten slips of paper with ten names, six of Democrats and four of Republicans. We have three trials; that is, we draw three times. After every draw, we replace the drawn slip so that the trials remain independent. Let us say the drawing of a Democrat's name in the experiment is a success and the drawing of a Republican's name is a failure. Then, $p = 6/10 = .6$ and $q = 4/10 = .4$. Note that if we denote the number of successes by k and the number of trials by n, then k may vary from 0 to n. In the present case, k may take any of these values: 0, 1, 2, 3. We express the probabilities of k as follows:

$$P(k = 0) = P(FFF)$$

$$P(k = 1) = P(SFF) + P(FSF) + P(FFS)$$

(the probabilities are added because $k = 1$ is considered a compound event consisting of three simple events)

$$P(k = 2) = P(SSF) + P(SFS) + P(FSS)$$

$$P(k = 3) = P(SSS)$$

But k may be also considered a random variable, or rather a binomial variable, which represents the number of successes, varying in the present case from zero to three. Since the three trials are independent, probabilities can be easily calculated. For example,

$$P(SFF) = \tfrac{6}{10} \times \tfrac{4}{10} \times \tfrac{4}{10} = (\tfrac{6}{10})(\tfrac{4}{10})^2$$

$$P(SSS) = \tfrac{6}{10} \times \tfrac{6}{10} \times \tfrac{6}{10} = (\tfrac{6}{10})^3$$

Using p and q, we can write

$$P(SFF) = pq^2$$

$$P(SSS) = p^3$$

In general, the probabilities in binomial trials may be written as

(4-16) $_p k_q (n-k)$

where k is the number of successes and n is the number of trials.

The probabilities of the different values of k can be calculated by adding the probabilities of the simple events as indicated above. However, in order to derive a convenient formula for the general case, consider $P(k = 2)$ in our example. This is a combination of three simple events. We ask: "In how many ways can $k = 2$ occur in $n = 3$?" This is written

$$\binom{n}{k} = \frac{n!}{k!(n-k)!}$$

and is discussed in Chapter 5. Here, $n!$ is called n *factorial* and is equal to $n(n-1)(n-2)\cdots 3\cdot 2\cdot 1$. Thus, $2! = 2\times 1$, $3! = 3\times 2\times 1$, and so on. Now, if we combine

$$\binom{n}{k} = \frac{n!}{k!(n-k)!}$$

with $_pk_q(n-k)$, then we can write

(4-17) $P(k) = \binom{n}{k}_pk_q(n-k)$

This is known as *binomial distribution*.

Example 4–15

Let us check formula (4-17) by calculating $P(k=2)$ in our example.[4]

$$P(k=2) = \binom{3}{2}(.6)^2(.4)^{3-2} = \frac{3!}{2!(3-2)!} \times .36 \times .4$$

$$= \frac{3\times 2\times 1}{(2\times 1)(1)} \times .36 \times .4 = 3 \times .36 \times .4 = .43$$

If we do not use the general formula, then

$$P(k = 2) = P(SSF) + P(SFS) + P(FSS)$$

$$= (.6)^2(.4) + (.6)^2(.4) + (.6)^2(.4)$$

$$= 3(.6)^2(.4) = .43$$

An extension of the binomial distribution is the *multinomial distribution*. In the multinomial distribution there are more than two outcomes, and with each outcome a certain probability is associated. In this distribution, if $x_1, x_2, ..., x_k$ represent the number of times outcomes $1, 2, ..., k$ occur, and $p_1, p_2, ..., p_k$ represent the probabilities of outcome 1, outcome 2, ..., outcome k, and $x_1 + x_2 + \cdots x_k = n$, then $x_1, x_2, ..., x_k$ jointly have multinomial distribution and the probability of $x_1, x_2, ..., x_k$ occurrences is

(4-18) $\dfrac{n!}{x_1!x_2!\cdots x_k!} p_1^{x_1}p_2^{x_2}\cdots p_k^{x_k}$

Example 4–16

If we change the earlier example of six Democrats and four Republicans to four Democrats, four Republicans and two Independents and by sampling with replacement want to find the probability of selecting one Democrat, one Republican, and one Independent in three draws, then

$$P(D, R, I) = \frac{3!}{1 \times 1 \times 1}(.4)(.4)(.2) = .19$$

SUMMARY

It is essential to understand the probability theory in order to comprehend the statistical models presented in this book. There are two main approaches to probability: subjective (or subjectivist) and objective (or objectivist). We emphasized objective approach because of the extensive treatment given it by statisticians and because of its importance in the understanding of statistical models. The objective approach to probability has two variations: a priori and relative frequency in the long run, and we emphasized the latter.

In the discussion of probability, certain terms—namely, simple events, compound events, sample points, sample space, set, complementary set, exclusive events, intersection of events, and union of events—were often used. These terms were defined.

The probability theory is based on certain basic postulates. These postulates concern simple events, compound events, exclusive events, and complementary events. In explaining these postulates, a uniform probability model was emphasized.

Sometimes we are interested in the probability of an event, given that another event has occurred. This is called conditional probability. Conditional probability was explained in the case of a uniform probability model as well as a nonuniform probability model. Formula (4-10) holds in both cases. A special case of the conditional probability (that is, Bayes' theorem) was also discussed.

If we have two events, neither of which depends on the other for its occurrence, we say they are independent of each other. Independence in probability was explained by relating it to conditional probability.

An experiment that has only two outcomes, both independent of each other, is said to have binomial trials. Binomial trials were discussed, emphasizing binomial variable and binomial distribution. The extension of the binomial distribution to multinomial distribution was also illustrated.

NOTES   Chapter 4

1. In fact, only those candidates who receive at least 10 percent of the votes in the first election can run in the second election. However, it is possible that if four candidates run, none receives less than 10 percent of the votes in the first election and all run again in the second election.

2. Although Bayes' theorem was developed in relation to the subjective approach to probability, it is equally applicable to the objective approach to probability.

3. Random sampling or, rather, simple random sampling is discussed in Chapter 5.

4. Tables are available to give $P(k)$ when n and p are given. We do not, however, reproduce such tables in the Appendix because in politics we seldom need to calculate $P(k)$.

REFERENCES   Chapter 4

Fraleigh, J. B. *Probability and Calculus: A Brief Introduction*. Reading, Mass.: Addison-Wesley, 1969.

Gangoli, R. A., and D. Ylvisaker. *Discrete Probability*. New York: Harcourt, 1967.

Hodges, J. S., and E. L. Lehmann. *Basic Concepts of Probability and Statistics*. San Francisco: Holden-Day, 1964.

Chapter 5

SAMPLING

Parametric statistical models are used to estimate the characteristics of a whole population while observing only a sample of the population. It should be quite clear that the quality of the sample from which inferences are made about the population is critical to the successful employment of a model. In this chapter we discuss how representative and bias-free samples are selected. We also discuss the idea of sampling distribution because it is essential to the understanding of sampling theory.

PROBABILITY SAMPLING

We emphasize probability sampling because of its extensive use in the study of politics. The basic idea of probability sampling is that we choose a sample on the basis of our knowledge of the probability of including each member of the population. The knowledge of these probabilities enables us to do two very important things: We can use probability models to analyze the sample data, and we can measure, and therefore control, random error due to sampling.

If we choose a sample without knowledge of the probability of including each member of the population in it, we have what is called a *nonprobability* sample. In nonprobability sampling, probability models cannot be used and random sampling error cannot be measured or controlled. Let us consider two examples of nonprobability sampling.

Example 5–1

Suppose we wanted to measure a population's reaction to a specific government policy. A nonprobability sampling technique would be to select "at random" a sample of some persons on a certain street. (This is *not* random sampling. Random sampling is a variation of probability sampling, and we shall discuss it at some length.) We cannot know the probability of each member of the population's being included in this sample because we do not know the probability of each being on the street from which we select the sample. The main reason for selecting a sample of some persons on a street is our convenience. A second example of nonprobability sampling occurs when we use our judgment to include certain items in a sample and to exclude others.

Example 5–2

Suppose we wanted to study election trends in a country during the last five elections and we wanted to concentrate on the elections to the lower house of the national legislature. For this purpose we select a sample of a certain size of the districts to be investigated. On the basis of our judgment we include in our sample only those districts that we consider representative of the entire country. In this case also, the probability of each member (that is, each district) of the population's being included in the sample is not known.

Nonprobability samples do not represent the population truly, and the inapplicability of probability models as well as the impossibility of measuring or controlling random sampling error makes them even less attractive for scientific studies. Therefore, only probability sampling will be discussed in the rest of the chapter.

Probability sampling has several variations, the most important of which is simple random sampling. Simple random sampling is the most commonly used method in sampling, and therefore we discuss it at length. We also discuss systematic sampling, stratified sampling, and cluster sampling, all of which are based on probability sampling.

SIMPLE RANDOM SAMPLING

Sampling is considered (simple) random if every possible sample of a certain size has an equal probability of being selected and if every member of the population has an equal probability of being included in every possible sample of equal size. Simple random sampling thus eliminates bias from sampling. In the preceding two examples of nonprobability sampling, a certain amount of bias is present. In Example 5-1, we included in our sample only some of those persons who happened to pass through a certain street at a certain time. The exclusion of every person who did not happen to pass through the selected street at the selected time (even some of those who passed through the selected street at the selected time are excluded) makes the sample biased. In Example 5-2, we included only those districts in our sample which we considered (because of our experience or perhaps familiarity) representative of the entire country. Our judgment about the variables to "represent" in the sample may have ignored some crucial factors or may have been linked to our biases about what we expected to find in the data. Thus, nonprobability sampling in this case also opened the sample to bias. The easiest way to eliminate this bias would be to use probability sampling and the easiest way of using probability sampling is simple random sampling.

Simple random sampling has several variations, the most important of which are ordered sampling, unordered sampling, sampling with replacement, and sampling without replacement. We now turn to these variations of simple random sampling.

Ordered Sampling

Let us consider an example of ordered sampling. Suppose we have a population of three items and we want to select a sample of size 2, in which the order of the items counts. If our population consists of A, B, and C, then the ordered samples are: AB, BA, BC, CB, AC, CA. Thus, a total of six samples are possible. The total number of the possible samples depends on the size of the population as well as on the size of the sample. If we consider the selection of a sample as a sequence of choices, then in the present example we have three choices: A, B, and C on the first selection; but on the second selection, we have only two choices. Hence, the total number of samples equals $3 \times 2 = 6$, the product of the number of choices. If we denote the population by N ($N = 3$ in our example), we can say that the total number of ordered samples of size 2 is $N(N-1)$. In case we want samples of size 3 from a population N ($N \geqslant 3$), then by the above reasoning (that is, we have N choices the first time we select an item, $N-1$ choices the second time we select an item, and $N-2$ choices the third time we select an item), we get $N(N-1)(N-2)$ ordered samples. If we denote our sample size by n, we can find the total number of ordered samples of size $n = 3$ from a population $N \geqslant 3$ as $N(N-1)(N-n+1)$, which is obviously equal to $N(N-1)(N-2)$. We can extend this argument for the general case and say that the total number of ordered samples of size n from a population N is

(5-1) $$N(N-1)(N-2) \cdots (N-n+1)$$

Note that in case the sample size is N, formula (5-1) becomes

$$N(N-1)(N-2) \cdots 3 \cdot 2 \cdot 1$$

which as explained in Chapter 4 is written $N!$ and is called N *factorial*.

For the total number of ordered samples of size n from the population N, the symbol used is $(N)_n$. Since the order is taken into consideration, $(N)_n$ is called the *number of permutations* of size n selected from N.

Unordered Sampling

In the field of politics we seldom study ordered samples, since it usually does not matter in which order the items are placed in the samples. For example, if we study a sample of voters or of legislators or of congressional districts, the order in which the voters or the legislators or the congressional districts are selected in the sample is usually of no concern to us. We call such samples "unordered" samples.

To illustrate unordered sampling, let us again consider the example in which $N = 3$ and we want to select unordered samples of size $n = 2$. If we identify our population as A, B, and C, the unordered samples available are AB, BC, CA. The reason for getting three unordered samples can be explained with the help of ordered samples. As shown for ordered sampling, we get six ordered samples of size 2 from a population of 3. In the example for ordered sampling, AB and BA are considered different samples, as are BC and CB, and CA and AC. Now each sample of size 2 can be ordered in 2! different ways. Hence, the number of unordered samples of size 2 from a population of 3 is

$$\frac{(3)_2}{2!} = \frac{6}{2} = 3$$

The symbol used for unordered samples is $\binom{N}{n}$, where N is population, n is the sample size, and the symbol is called the *binomial coefficient*. It is also called the *number of combinations* of size n selected from N.

By extending the present example of unordered samples of size 2 from a population of 3 to a general case, we can write

$$(5\text{-}2) \qquad \binom{N}{n} = \frac{(N)_n}{n!} = \frac{(N)(N-1)(N-2)\cdots(N-n+1)}{(n)(n-1)(n-2)\cdots 2\cdot 1}$$

By multiplying the numerator and the denominator by $(N-n)!$, we get an alternative formula:

$$(5\text{-}3) \qquad \binom{N}{n} = \frac{N!}{n!(N-n)!}$$

since $(N)(N-1)(N-2)\cdots(N-n+1)(N-n)! = N!$.

It can be shown that

$$(5\text{-}4) \qquad \binom{N}{N-n} = \frac{N!}{(N-n)!(N-N+n)!}$$

$$= \frac{N!}{(N-n)!(n)!} = \binom{N}{n}$$

We define $\binom{N}{0} = 1$, $0! = 1$. Therefore,

$$(5\text{-}5) \qquad \binom{N}{N} = \frac{N!}{(N!)(N-N)!} = \frac{N!}{N!} = 1$$

Note that, by the definition of simple random sampling, the probability of the selection of each ordered sample is $1/(N)_n$ and the probability of the selection of each unordered sample is $1/\binom{N}{n}$.

Example 5–3

Suppose we want to select an unordered sample of five elections from a population of ten elections. The number of possible unordered samples in this case is

$$\binom{10}{5} = \frac{10!}{5!(10-5)!} = \frac{10!}{5! \times 5!} = 252$$

Example 5–4

Suppose we want to study the attitudes of the defeated candidates in a certain election to a legislative assembly. For the sake of simplicity, let us assume that the total number of the defeated candidates is 100 and from this population we want to select an unordered sample of size 25. The number of possible unordered samples in this case is

$$\binom{N}{n} = \binom{100}{25} = \frac{100!}{25! \times 75!}$$

This number, as you can see, is very large indeed. In fact, for most research problems, the number of possible unordered samples is very large.

Sampling with or without Replacement

In the preceding discussion we considered only sampling without replacement; thus the same item did not appear more than once in a sample. If we replace the selected item after each draw, then the same item can obviously appear more than once in any particular sample. (This makes the draws independent of each other and the selection of an item on one draw does not affect the probability of the selection of the same or another item on the next draw.) Using the example with $N = 3$ and $n = 2$, if we consider replacement, then the number of ordered or unordered samples would increase by 3 and the additional samples would be AA, BB, and CC. In political research we are rarely, if ever, concerned with such cases, so in this discussion we do not emphasize sampling with replacement. In fact, as indicated earlier, we seldom need ordered samples in political research, so our main concern is with unordered sampling without replacement. The question now is: When we need an unordered sample (of a certain size) without replacement from a certain population, how do we select such a sample? We answer this question in subsequent sections.

Random Digits for Selecting Samples

A random sample is usually selected with the help of random digits. Although we are concerned with unordered samples without replacement, unordered samples with replacement and ordered samples with or without replacement also can be selected with the help of the same random digits. Table A-2 in the Appendix lists such random digits. Table A-2 has two important features: (1) the probability of each of the ten digits from 0 to 9 appearing in every place in the table is the same (that is, 1/10); and (2) the appearance of a digit in any given place in the table is independent of the appearance of the same or any other digit in any other place in the table. If we select a sample of a certain size with the help of this table it, satisfies two essential conditions of simple random sampling: (1) Each of the possible samples has the same probability of being selected; and (2) each of the items of the population has the same probability of being included in every sample.

We illustrate here how to use the table of random digits for drawing a random unordered sample without replacement. Consider again the earlier example (Example 5-3) of drawing unordered samples (without replacement) of size 5 from a population of ten elections. (We assume for simplicity that every election is equally important for the purpose of analysis.) For getting one such sample, we first number the elections consecutively from 01 to 10. We then use Table A-2, starting with any row or any column of random digits. Let us start with the fifth row. The first number of two digits that we get is 37 and the second number of two digits that we get is 57. We disregard these and any other numbers above 10. Also, we disregard a number if it already has been selected. (The same numbers appear more than once because tables of random digits are based on sampling with replacement.) Thus, the first number that we select is 03 and the second number that we select is 06. If we continue further, we select 05, 01, and 10. Thus, our unordered random sample consists of the first, third, fifth, sixth, and tenth elections. If we want one unordered random sample of 25 defeated candidates out of a population of 100 defeated candidates (see Example 5-4), we first number the 100 defeated candidates from 001 to 100 and then, starting with any row or any column and every time selecting three digits, get our random sample of 25 defeated candidates.

If we need several samples at the same time, it is a good idea to use a different row or a different column or even a different page for every different case. Thus, even if we remember the first digits of a row or a column, we would avoid this bias from entering into our samples.

Bowls or Containers for Selecting Samples

An alternative to the use of random digits is available. We number the items of the population consecutively and place them in capsules, or write them on slips of paper and fold the slips. We place the capsules or the slips of paper in a bowl or a container and then select one item at a time until we get the desired sample size. (Note that this is sampling *without* replacement. However, if the selected item is replaced every time, it then becomes sampling *with* replacement.) In doing this, we have to stir the capsules or the slips of paper thoroughly after every draw so that on each draw the probability of each of the remaining items being selected is the same. You may question that in such a case the probability of each item of the population being selected in a sample is not quite the same, since after every draw the probability of the selection of the remaining items increases. It can still be argued, however, that the probability of the selection of a particular item in a sample is the same, that is, n/N.

We give a statistical explanation for this. Suppose we want a sample of size 2 from a population of 3 (A, B, and C) and we sample without replacement, using a bowl. We want to find the probability of A's being included in the sample. Perhaps A will be selected on the first draw, in which case the probability of the selection of A is $1/3$. If A is not selected on the first draw, then it may be selected on the second draw, in which case the probability of the selection of A is, using formula (4-11), the multiplication rule, $2/3 \times 1/2 = 1/3$. Note that $2/3$ is the probability that A is not selected on the first draw and $1/2$ is the probability that A is selected on the second draw, given that it was not selected on the first draw. These two events (the selection of A on the first draw and the selection of A on the second draw) are exclusive, so the probability of the inclusion of A in the sample of size 2 is $1/3 + 1/3 = 2/3 = n/N$. If we were to sample with replacement, using a bowl, then the probability of the selection of A on the first draw or on the second draw is the same, that is, $1/3$. Therefore, by sampling with replacement, the probability of the inclusion of A in the sample of size 2 is $1/3 + 1/3 = 2/3$ (the two events are exclusive in this case also).

One of the best known uses of this method of drawing samples from containers is the draft lottery. However, random digits are more convenient to our use because we do not have to worry about getting containers and stirring the items.

SYSTEMATIC SAMPLING

When the two methods of simple random sampling (random digits and bowls or containers) appear cumbersome, systematic sampling may be used. By systematic sampling we can get a sample approximating a simple random sample. Systematic sampling is best explained with an example.

Example 5-5

Suppose we want a sample of 500 members of the American Political Science Association. The American Political Science Association has a membership of about 15,000 listed alphabetically in its *Biographical Directory*. We select every thirtieth individual from this *Biographical Directory* and thus get a sample of 500. We say "thirtieth individual" because $N = 15,000$ and $n = 500$; thus, N/n gives us an idea of the interval we seek between every two individuals. In order to decide who should be our first choice among the first 30 individuals, we use a random digits table. Thus, if the number found in the random digits table is 17, we start with the seventeenth individual and then select every thirtieth individual. Therefore, the main precaution to be taken in systematic sampling is that the list used must not contain individuals or items with certain characteristics at or within certain intervals. Thus, if the American Political Science Association arranged its list so that every fifth member was an international relations expert, our sample might exclude all the international relations experts, thereby making our sample biased.

STRATIFIED SAMPLING

Often we have populations that can be divided into two or more groups in such a manner that each group is relatively homogeneous with respect to a certain variable in which we may be interested. We call these groups "strata" and hereafter use the terms *groups* and *strata* interchangeably. Several examples of such populations can be given. The members of the American Political Science Association can be divided into several groups, each group representing a certain specialty or certain specialties in the field of politics. The student body of an undergraduate college can be divided into four groups, each group representing class standing. Voters can be divided into several groups, each group representing a certain race or a certain religion or a certain geographical region or a certain income level, to mention a few of the possibilities. In each of these examples we use some criterion to divide the population into groups. The criterion selected must be such that it makes the different groups relatively homogeneous with respect to a certain variable in which we may be interested. Thus, we may be interested in the annual income of the members of the American Political Science Association, and we use the criterion of specialty or specialties on the assumption that each group, based on this criterion, is relatively homogeneous with respect to annual income. Or, we may be interested in participation in the college activities, and we use the criterion of the college class on the assumption that each group, based on this criterion, is relatively homogeneous with respect to participation in the college activities. Or, we may be interested in voter turnout, and we may use the criterion of race on the assumption that the voters of different races are relatively homogeneous with respect to voter turnout.

We divide a population into strata in such a manner that each member of the population appears in only one of the strata. After we divide the population into strata by some criterion, we use simple random sampling or systematic sampling in each stratum. The sample selected in this manner is called a *stratified sample*.

Stratified sampling is of two types: proportional and disproportional. In proportional stratified sampling we select items from each stratum in such a manner that the proportion of the number of items selected from any particular stratum in the sample is the same as the proportion of the size of the stratum to the total population. Proportional stratified sampling thus gives a self-weighting sample.

Example 5–6

If we have a population of 100 persons, 60 of whom are high school graduates and 40 are college graduates, a proportional stratified sample of 10 would include 6 high school graduates and 4 college graduates. In other words, the proportion of 6 to 10 is the same as that of 60 to 100 and the proportion of 4 to 10 is the same as that of 40 to 100.

Notationally the case of proportional stratified sampling is written as follows:

$$(5\text{-}6) \qquad \frac{n_1}{n} = \frac{N_1}{N} \cdots \frac{n_k}{n} = \frac{N_k}{N}$$

where n_i (i ranges from 1 through k) is the number of items to be included in the sample from the ith stratum, n is the sample size, N_i (i ranges from 1 through k) is the total number of items in the ith stratum, k is the total number of the strata in the population, and N is the total population, so that $N = N_1 + N_2 + \cdots + N_k$.

If we select items for a sample from the different strata in such a manner that n_i/n does not equal N_i/N for every stratum, then we get a disproportional stratified sample. In Example 5-6, if we were to select four high school graduates and six college graduates, we would have a disproportional stratified sample.

The main advantages of the stratified sampling are two: First, a stratified sample is more representative of the population in case the population contains diverse strata; and second, the sample size needed for the same precision (we discuss the concept of sampling precision later in the chapter) is substantially smaller in the stratified sampling than in the nonstratified sampling. In fact, the more homogeneous the members of every stratum are, the smaller is the sample size needed. In other words, the variances (or standard deviations) of the different strata are the deciding factor in the selection of the sample size. When we say variances or standard deviations of the different strata, we mean, of course, the variance or the standard deviation of a certain variable in which we may be interested. In order to understand this intuitively consider a population with two strata, each with zero variance. If the variable to be considered is the years of education, then each of the two strata in the preceding example of 100 persons (60 high school graduates and 40 college graduates) has zero variance. In case we want to estimate μ, the population mean, we need a proportional stratified sample of only five—three from the group of high school graduates and two from the group of college graduates.

In this example the sample mean estimates the population mean perfectly. Note that the sample mean and the population mean are 13.6 years of education. Now, as a stratum becomes heterogeneous and its variance (or standard deviation) increases, the proportion of the sample needed from it also increases. The extreme case is of a population, which may have several strata, each very much heterogeneous. In such a case, there is no point in using stratified sampling; instead, simple random sampling can be used. We may, of course, have a population with some relatively homogeneous strata and others relatively heterogeneous strata. In such a case we should select more items from the strata, which are heterogeneous and have larger variances (or standard deviations), and less items from the strata, which are homogeneous and have smaller variances (or standard deviations). Obviously, disproportional rather than proportional sampling should be used in such cases.

If we do use disproportional stratified sampling based on the differences in the variances (or standard deviations) of the different strata, the question is: How do we decide the exact number of items to be selected from each stratum? The following formula is used for deciding the optimum allocation of items to each stratum:

$$(5\text{-}7) \qquad n_i = n\frac{N_i s_i}{N_1 s_1 + \cdots + N_k s_k}$$

where s_i is the actual standard deviation of the ith stratum and the rest of the terms are the same as defined above.

Formula (5-7) for optimum allocation is called Tschuprow–Neyman allocation and it minimizes the variance of $\bar{Y}_{est}$, where $\bar{Y}_{est}$ is an estimate of the population mean when stratified sampling is used. We can write $\bar{Y}_{est}$ as

$$(5\text{-}8) \qquad \bar{Y}_{est} = \frac{N_1}{N}\cdot\bar{Y}_1 + \cdots + \frac{N_k}{N}\cdot\bar{Y}_k$$

where $\bar{Y}_1$ is the mean of n_1 and so forth.

We may use formula (5-7) for optimum allocation when estimating the population mean. We illustrate its use with an example.

Example 5-7

Suppose we need a stratified sample of 100 students from an undergraduate college to estimate the average marijuana smoking in the past month. Further, suppose we have reasons to believe that marijuana smoking is much more prevalent among the students from the higher income families than among the students from the lower income families. If we have the information on family incomes of all students, we can divide them into four family groups. We assume that the variance of marijuana smoking in the total student body is greater than in each of the four income groups. That is, the members of each of the groups are more homogeneous in this respect than all the students considered together. Suppose we know the standard deviation of marijuana smoking in each group. The number of students and the standard deviation of marijuana smoking in each income group are given in Table 5-1.

Table 5-1

Marijuana Smoking and Annual Income Group

	Less than $10,000	$10,000–15,000	$15,000–20,000	Over $20,000
N_i	2000	1500	1000	500
s_i	1	3	4	2

Now, if we use proportional stratified sampling, we can easily calculate the number of students to be selected from each stratum. Since

$$\frac{n_1}{n} = \frac{N_1}{N} = \frac{2000}{5000} = \frac{2}{5}$$

then
$$n_1 = 40$$

Similarly,
$$n_2 = 30, \qquad n_3 = 20, \qquad n_4 = 10$$

But we are interested in disproportional stratified sampling because some of the strata are more homogeneous than others. Using formula (5-7), we compute the optimum allocation as follows:

$$
\begin{aligned}
n_1 &= n\frac{N_1 s_1}{N_1 s_1 + N_2 s_2 + N_3 s_3 + N_4 s_4} \\
&= 100\frac{(2000)\,1}{(2000)\,1 + (1500)\,3 + (1000)\,4 + (500)\,2} \\
&= \frac{2000}{115} \doteq 17
\end{aligned}
$$

Similarly,
$$n_2 \doteq 39, \qquad n_3 \doteq 35, \qquad n_4 \doteq 9$$

Strata 1 and 4 are more homogeneous than strata 2 and 3, so we select fewer students from the former than from the latter. Stratum 2 is more homogeneous than stratum 3, yet we select more students from stratum 2 than from stratum 3. Note, however, that in proportional sampling the number of students selected from stratum 2 is 50 percent more than from stratum 3, but in disproportional sampling the difference in the number of students selected from these two strata is much less.

In Example 5-7, we have assumed that s_i's are known. However, in actual practice they are not known and that makes it hard to make use of disproportional stratified sampling. We could calculate s_i for each stratum, but this would be obviously tedious and time consuming. Fortunately, we can sometimes rely upon reasonable guesses of s_i's.

So far we have not said anything about the cost of getting a sample. The general rule is to select a greater number of individuals from the strata for which sampling is relatively less expensive and to select fewer individuals from the strata for which sampling is relatively more expensive. This recommendation assumes that sampling costs are different in different strata and that the cost of sampling each individual in a particular stratum is the same.

CLUSTER SAMPLING

When we stratify the population, but select the sample only from some of the strata and not from each stratum, we call it *cluster* sampling.

However, in cluster sampling we do not stratify the population because we want to take into consideration the homogeneity of the different strata; rather, we stratify the population because the population may be so large that a single list of all items of the population may not be available, making it impossible to draw a simple random sample. Furthermore, preparing such a list may be so expensive that we do not want to consider the procedure. We often face such situations in politics when we want a sample from the population of an entire country, or from a region, or a state, or even a city. In such cases we divide the population into smaller units called clusters (note that we now use the term *clusters* for strata or groups) and then we select a certain number of clusters by simple random sampling or by systematic sampling. Thus, we may divide a state into election districts and then select a certain number of the election districts by simple random sampling or by systematic sampling. We designate the election districts as clusters.

At this stage we complete our sampling by including all the members (for example, voters) of the selected clusters in the sample (this is called *single-stage* cluster sampling) or we select a certain number of the members from each of the selected clusters by simple random sampling or by systematic sampling within the clusters. However, instead, we may subdivide the selected clusters into smaller clusters. Thus, we may subdivide the election districts into blocks. Then, from each of the selected election districts, we select a certain number of blocks by simple random sampling or by systematic sampling. We include all members (for example, voters) of the selected blocks (smaller clusters) in the sample or we select a certain number of the members by simple random sampling or by systematic sampling from each of the selected blocks. What we have described is called multistage cluster sampling because of the several stages involved in sampling. As to how many stages should be included in a particular sample depends on a number of factors involved, such as size of the population, number of clusters available, and cost.

While discussing stratified sampling we emphasized that it is highly desirable to have homogeneous strata. In case some of the strata are more homogeneous than others, then disproportional sampling was suggested. In cluster sampling on the other hand, we do not want the clusters to be homogeneous. Rather, we want them to be as heterogeneous as possible. Consider the situation when every cluster is different from every other cluster, but each is homogeneous. In such a case, if we select some of the clusters by simple random sampling or by systematic sampling and draw a sample from these clusters, the sample will not be representative of the population. On the other hand, if the clusters are quite heterogeneous and we select some of the clusters by simple random sampling or by systematic sampling in order to draw a sample from them, the sample will be representative of the population. However, since the clusters that we find in the real world are not always very heterogeneous, a sample selected by cluster sampling may not be so representative of the population as a sample selected by simple random sampling or by stratified sampling. We still may prefer cluster sampling if it reduces cost.

Cluster sampling is easier to use in a population with clusters of equal size than in a population with clusters of unequal size. Unfortunately, we often have to work with the latter type of population. Several methods have been devised to take this inequality of cluster sizes into account. Kish (1965, pp. 193–195), for example, regards *paired selection* as the most practical method for selecting clusters.

SAMPLING DISTRIBUTION

We now turn to the theory of sampling distribution based on simple random sampling. The idea behind sampling distribution is that we draw all possible samples of a certain size from a population and then find the probabilities of the different values of some statistic in those samples. The statistic under consideration is thus treated as a variable. The statistic whose sampling distribution is most commonly used is $\overline{X}$, the sample mean. It was mentioned in Chapter 3 that $\overline{X}$ is an unbiased estimator of μ, the population mean, and the idea of the sampling distribution of sample means was introduced. Let us explore in detail the sampling distribution of sample means. In actual practice it would be too costly to construct a sampling distribution of sample means, that is, to calculate $\overline{X}$ for all possible samples. Instead, we estimate the population mean and test the hypotheses concerning it on the basis of a single sample. However, such estimation and hypothesis testing are based on the assumption that a sampling distribution of sample means exists. In addition to sample means, sample proportions are also frequently used, so we discuss the sampling distribution of sample proportions also.

Sampling Distribution of Sample Means

In order to illustrate the sampling distribution of sample means, we use an example similar to the one in Table 3-6.

Example 5–8

Suppose we have a population of six equal-sized election districts with varying rates of voter turnout, as shown in Table 5-2. We want to consider all possible samples of size 2. All possible samples here means all possible ordered samples with replacement. This ensures independent trials, which, incidentally, is an important assumption of the Central Limit theorem. However, the sampling distribution of sample means may be also illustrated if we consider, as shown in Table 5-3, all possible unordered samples without replacement. (We have emphasized earlier that in common practice we use unordered samples without replacement.) Of course we shall have to use the *finite population correction*, as explained in Chapter 3. But if the sampling is done with replacement, the population becomes infinitely large; therefore, this correction is not needed.

Table 5-2

Voter Turnout in Six Districts

District	Voter Turnout
X_1	.9
X_2	.8
X_3	.7
X_4	.6
X_5	.5
X_6	.4

Table 5-3

All Possible Unordered Samples without Replacement

Sample number*	Sample values	Sample mean, $\bar{X}$
1	.9, .8	.85
2	.9, .7	.80
3	.9, .6	.75
4	.9, .5	.70
5	.9, .4	.65
6	.8, .7	.75
7	.8, .6	.70
8	.8, .5	.65
9	.8, .4	.60
10	.7, .6	.65
11	.7, .5	.60
12	.7, .4	.55
13	.6, .5	.55
14	.6, .4	.50
15	.5, .4	.45

*The total number of samples is 15 because $\binom{6}{2} = \dfrac{6!}{2!(4!)} = 15$

Table   5-4

Sampling Distribution of Sample Means

Sample mean, $\overline{X}$	Number of samples with a particular mean, f	$P(\overline{X})$
.85	1	1/15
.80	1	1/15
.75	2	2/15
.70	2	2/15
.65	3	3/15
.60	2	2/15
.55	2	2/15
.50	1	1/15
.45	1	1/15

Note that each of the 15 samples has the same probability (1/15) of being selected; thus, the mean of each of the samples also has the same probability (1/15). However, some of the values of the means in Table 5-3 occur more than once, so the probabilities of those means must be greater than 1/15. For example, the mean .75 occurs twice, so its probability is 2/15; and the mean .65 occurs three times, so its probability is 3/15. The sampling distribution of sample means shows such probabilities of all possible sample mean values. These probabilities are shown in Table 5-4. Figure 5-1 is presented to illustrate further the sampling distribution of the sample means in our data.

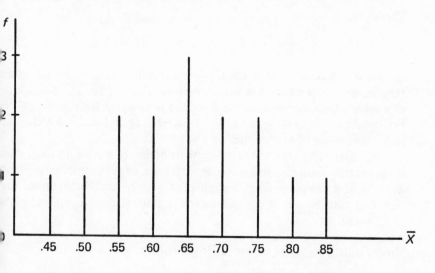

FIGURE 5-1

In this sampling distribution,

$$\overline{X} \text{ (mean of } \overline{X}) = \frac{9.75}{15} = .65$$

If we calculate μ, the population mean, of the population of six election districts, then

$$\mu = \frac{3.9}{6} = .65$$

Therefore, $\overline{X} = \mu$. Note that

$$E(\overline{X}) = \overline{X} = \mu = .65$$

We gave an intuitive proof of $E(\overline{X}) = \mu$ in Chapter 3. The discussion here further confirms that result.

If we use the *finite population correction*, the variance and the standard deviation of this distribution are as follows:

$$(5\text{-}9) \qquad \sigma\bar{x}^2 = \frac{\sigma^2}{n} \cdot \frac{N-n}{N-1}$$

$$(5\text{-}10) \qquad \sigma\bar{x} = \frac{\sigma}{(n)^{1/2}} \cdot \left(\frac{N-n}{N-1}\right)^{1/2}$$

In our population of six election districts,

$$\sigma^2 = \frac{\sum_{i=1}^{N}(X_i-\mu)^2}{N} = \frac{.16}{6} = .03 \qquad \text{and} \qquad \sigma = .17$$

Therefore,

$$\sigma\bar{x}^2 = \frac{.03}{2} \cdot \frac{6-2}{6-1} = .01 \qquad \text{and} \qquad \sigma\bar{x} = .1$$

In case σ is unknown, as is usually the case when we consider only one sample, we use its estimate in the calculation of $\sigma\bar{x}^2$ or $\sigma\bar{x}$. The estimation of σ (or σ^2) from one sample was discussed in Chapter 3. $\sigma\bar{x}$ is also called the *standard error of the mean* and is considered again later in this chapter in the discussion of sample size.

An interesting aspect of sampling distribution of sample means is that it approaches normal distribution as n (sample size) becomes large, that is, $\geqslant 30$. If a sample is from a population with normal distribution, the sampling distribution of sample means is normal despite the sample's being small.

Sampling Distribution of Sample Proportions

We now discuss the sampling distribution of sample proportions, a concept introduced in Chapter 3. Recall that the population proportion is symbolized as π and the sample proportion as p. Suppose we are interested in the proportion of the districts in which the voter turnout is .6 or less. Then, in Example 5-8, $\pi = .5$. In order to find the sampling distribution of p in this example, we write in Table 5-5 all possible unordered samples of size 2, sample values, and the sample proportion (p) of districts with voter turnout less than or equal to .6. This table is similar to Table 5-3.

Table 5-5

All Possible Unordered Samples without Replacement

Sample number	Sample values	Sample proportion, p
1	.9, .8	0
2	.9, .7	0
3	.9, .6	.5
4	.9, .5	.5
5	.9, .4	.5
6	.8, .7	0
7	.8, .6	.5
8	.8, .5	.5
9	.8, .4	.5
10	.7, .6	.5
11	.7, .5	.5
12	.7, .4	.5
13	.6, .5	1.0
14	.6, .4	1.0
15	.5, .4	1.0

The sampling distribution of p is shown in Table 5-6 and in Figure 5-2.

Table 5-6

Sampling Distribution of Sample Proportions

Sample proportion, p (of districts with voter turnout ≤ .6)	Number of samples with a particular proportion, f	P(p)
0	3	3/15
.5	9	9/15
1.0	3	3/15

In this sampling distribution,

$$\bar{p} \text{ (mean of } p) = \frac{7.5}{15} = .5$$

Note that $E(p) = .5$. We mentioned earlier that $\pi = .5$; therefore

$$E(p) = \bar{p} = \pi = .5$$

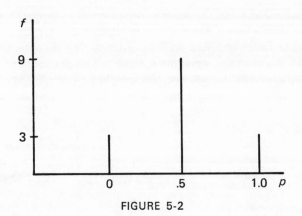

FIGURE 5-2

We stated in Chapter 3 that p is an unbiased estimator of π. The preceding discussion supports that statement.

The variance and the standard deviation of this distribution, using the *finite population correction*, are

$$(5\text{-}11) \qquad \sigma p^2 = \frac{\pi(1-\pi)}{n} \cdot \frac{N-n}{N-1}$$

$$(5\text{-}12) \qquad \sigma p = \left(\frac{\pi(1-\pi)}{n}\right)^{\!\frac{1}{2}} \cdot \left(\frac{N-n}{N-1}\right)^{\!\frac{1}{2}}$$

In case π is unknown, as is usually the case when we consider only one sample, we use $(p(1-p))/n$ for $(\pi(1-\pi))/n$.

From (5-11),

$$\sigma p^2 = \frac{\pi(1-\pi)}{n} \cdot \frac{N-n}{N-1} = \frac{.5 \times .5}{2} \cdot \frac{4}{5} = .1$$

and from (5-12), $\sigma p = .3$. σp is also called the standard error of the sample proportion; it is considered again later in the chapter in the discussion of the sample size.

As is the case with the sampling distribution of sample means, the sampling distribution of sample proportions also approaches normal distribution when n is large.

RANDOM SAMPLING ERROR AND SAMPLE SIZE

We encounter two types of errors in sampling: random sampling error (also referred to as probability sampling error or variable error) and bias. As discussed earlier, simple random sampling eliminates bias. However, random sampling error usually cannot be eliminated from simple random sampling, but it can be measured and controlled. This error is the difference between our estimate from a sample and the real value of the estimated parameter in the population. Thus, if our estimate of the mean voter turnout from a sample is .75 and the real value of this mean in the population is .65, then the random sampling error is .10. In other words, in this case the random sampling error equals $\bar{X} - \mu$. Similarly, in estimating population proportion from a sample, the random sampling error equals $p - \pi$.

The amount of random sampling error depends on the sample size and on the heterogeneity (or homogeneity) of the population. Thus, a larger sample (in relation to the population) will have smaller random sampling error than will a smaller sample (in relation to the population). Also, given a specific sample size, the more heterogeneous a population is, the greater will be the random sampling error. (Stratified sampling reduces this error in a heterogeneous population with relatively homogeneous strata.)

Example 5–9

Consider again the members of the American Political Science Association listed in its *Biographical Directory* and suppose that we want to estimate the members' mean annual income from a simple random sample drawn from this directory. Further suppose that we want to keep the random sampling error within $100. By introducing this error, we are saying in effect how precise we want our estimate to be. Our question is: How large a sample should we select in order to assure us 95 percent confidence of our estimate lying within this error? In order to answer this question, and assuming that $\bar{X}$ is normally distributed, we construct the following statistic:

$$(5\text{-}13) \qquad Z(\bar{X}) = \frac{\bar{X} - \mu}{\sigma\bar{x}} = \frac{e}{\sigma\bar{x}} = \frac{e}{\sigma/(n)^{\frac{1}{2}}}$$

ignoring the *finite population correction*. Then

$$(5\text{-}14) \qquad e = Z(\bar{X})\left(\frac{\sigma}{(n)^{\frac{1}{2}}}\right)$$

It can be clearly seen that e increases as σ increases, and it decreases as n increases. To continue with our discussion of the sample size required, we write this equation as

$$(5\text{-}15) \qquad n = \frac{Z^2(\bar{X})\sigma^2}{e^2} = \frac{(1.96)^2\sigma^2}{(100)^2}$$

in the present example. The main problem here is that σ, the population standard deviation, may not be known. For illustration, however, suppose that we know the population standard deviation to be $3000. Then

$$n = \frac{(1.96)^2 \times (3000)^2}{(100)^2} \doteq 3460$$

This sample is obviously very large. If we want a smaller sample, we shall have to increase our random sampling error or decrease our confidence level, or do both.

Example 5–10

Suppose that we want to estimate the proportion of the members of the American Political Science Association listed in its *Biographical Directory* who earn $15,000 or more annually, and we want to decide the sample size, keeping in mind that we want a 95 percent confidence of the error's being within 3 percent. Then, assuming p to be normally distributed, we construct the following statistic:

$$(5\text{-}16) \qquad Z(p) = \frac{p - \pi}{\sigma p} = \frac{e}{\sigma p} = \frac{e}{(\pi(1-\pi)/n)^{\frac{1}{2}}}$$

Therefore

$$(5\text{-}17) \qquad e = Z(p)\left(\frac{\pi(1-\pi)}{n}\right)^{\frac{1}{2}}$$

and

$$(5\text{-}18) \qquad n = \frac{Z^2(p)\pi(1-\pi)}{e^2} = \frac{(1.96)^2\pi(1-\pi)}{.0009}$$

in the present example. A rule of the thumb is to assume that $\pi = 1/2$ so that $\pi(1-\pi) = 1/4$. This is the maximum value of $\pi(1-\pi)$, so we are assured of a large enough sample. Now, if we work out equation (5-18), then

$$n = \frac{(1.96)^2 \times \frac{1}{4}}{.0009} \doteq 1070$$

SUMMARY

A parametric statistical model uses a sample to draw inferences about the whole population. The quality of the sample, therefore, is very important for the successful employment of a parametric statistical model. The quality of the sample depends upon whether it is bias-free and representative of the population. Probability sampling assures us bias-free and representative samples. In probability sampling, the probability of each member of a population's being included in a sample is known, probability models can be used, and random sampling error can be controlled and measured.

Probability sampling has several variations, the most important of which is simple random sampling. In simple random sampling every possible sample of a certain size has an equal probability of being selected and every member of the population has an equal probability of being included in every sample.

Simple random sampling also has several variations, the most important of which are ordered sampling, unordered sampling, sampling with replacement, and sampling without replacement. In ordered sampling, the order of the items is taken into consideration. In unordered sampling, the order of the items is not taken into consideration. In sampling with replacement, the same item may appear more than once in a sample. In sampling without replacement, the same item does not appear more than once in a sample. In political research we generally use unordered samples without replacement.

Two methods are used for drawing a simple random sample: random digits and bowls or containers. Both methods were discussed.

Besides simple random sampling, the variations of probability sampling are systematic sampling, stratified sampling, and cluster sampling. A sample selected systematically approximates a simple random sample. Stratified sampling is used when the population contains two or more groups (strata) that are homogeneous with respect to a certain variable in which we may be interested. Stratified sampling is of two types: proportional and disproportional. Both types were discussed. In cluster sampling we also take into account the different groups in the population, but the clusters (groups) should be heterogeneous rather than homogeneous.

Sampling distributions of sample means and sample proportions were explained because of their importance in the sampling theory.

The relationship among random sampling error, sample size, and population heterogeneity was discussed toward the end of the chapter. This relationship is such that the sample size depends on how much random sampling error we are prepared to tolerate and on how heterogeneous (or homogeneous) the population is.

REFERENCES   Chapter 5

Cochran, W. E. *Sampling Techniques*. New York: Wiley, 1963.

Ferber, R. *Market Research*. New York: McGraw-Hill, 1949.

Kish, L. *Survey Sampling*. New York: Wiley, 1965, pp. 182–212.

Chapter 6

HYPOTHESIS TESTING

A two-step process is required in testing for the existence of a relationship between quantifiable variables through the use of statistical models. First, we measure the difference between the variables with a sample of observations, and second, we apply the mathematics of probability to determine whether the measured difference is real, or only due to random errors to be expected in sampling. The theory of hypothesis testing deals with the construction of decision rules for the second step. In Chapter 1 we said that the main advantage of parametric statistical models over other data analytic techniques is that we can measure the reliability of the results drawn from the model. Measures of reliability enable us to make a decision rule, in *advance* of testing a hypothesis, for the acceptance or rejection of a hypothesis, depending on conditions in the data. Let us illustrate the need and use for such a decision rule.

In Chapter 1 we presented a hypothesis drawn from a theory as an illustration of the use of cognitive models in research. The hypothesis is that persons with a business interest, I, were more likely to vote for the Republican party, R, than were persons without a business interest. This hypothesis was expressed as a linear equation:

(6-1) $R = a + bI$

We defined the parameter a as the net Republican vote and designated b as the slope of the line graphing the functional relationship of R and I. Assuming that we have operationalized R and I for a sample data set, we face this question: How do we decide whether the sample data support or conflict with our hypothesis? Suppose we decide that if b turns out to be positive, we accept the hypothesis, and if it does not, we reject the hypothesis. Suppose b turns out to be positive; should we accept the hypothesis? Not yet! We want some measure of *how sure* we can be that b is indeed positive. That is to say, we want to know how likely we are to be wrong in concluding from our *sample* data that the b in the *population* is positive. If the sample b turns out to be positive but there are four chances in ten that it is actually zero or negative in the population, then we surely would not conclude that b is really positive. Hence, our original decision rule (accept the hypothesis if $b > 0$ and reject it otherwise) is insufficient. A more appropriate decision rule would be: Accept the hypothesis if $P(b \leqslant 0) < q$, where q is some predetermined limit decided arbitrarily by the researcher. The rule reads: Accept the hypothesis if the probability that b is less than or equal to zero ($P(b \leqslant 0)$) is less than a predetermined limit (q). This rule includes both the original decision rule (the sign of b) and a measure of the reliability of the information from the sample (the probability that b is zero or less). Such decision rules are clearly critical for the appropriate use of statistical models.

There is another important aspect of this decision rule. We have deliberately chosen to express q as the chance that b in the population actually is zero or less. That is, we have expressed the decision rule in terms of the chance that we could be *wrong* in concluding that there is a relationship between R and I. The form of this expression is not purely arbitrary. As we shall soon see, the form of the decision rule depends on the kind of mistake the researcher wants to avoid, but it is always expressed in the probability of being wrong. An equally valid rule would be: Reject the hypothesis if $P(b > 0) < q$. The first rule is expressed in terms of the chance that we conclude that R and I are not related when in fact they are; and the second rule is expressed in terms of the chance that we conclude that R and I are related when in fact they are not. Which form is used depends on the purpose of the test, but every statistical test requires the construction of a formal decision rule, and all are based on the same set of principles.

The first task of this chapter is to present this set of principles, called the *theory of hypothesis testing*. Then we introduce three types of statistical tests that illustrate the application of decision rules. The first type of test is used to compare data within a sample. Second, we present tests of hypotheses about a sample estimate; and third, we present tests for comparing data from two samples.[1]

ELEMENTARY CONCEPTS

The foregoing illustration serves to introduce four important concepts of hypothesis testing: the *null hypothesis, significance level, type I errors,* and *type II errors.*

The *null hypothesis* is the hypothesis we would reject if the proposition we are testing is true. Suppose we were to test the hypothesis expressed above as $b > 0$. If this were true, its opposite, that is, $b \leqslant 0$, would be false. This hypothesis, $b \leqslant 0$, is called the null hypothesis because it postulates no relationship as hypothesized. If we reject it, then we conclude that the original proposition is true. There are two reasons for testing the null hypothesis rather than the substantive proposition. One reason, introduced in Chapter 1, is philosophical: Logical positivists point out that it is not possible to prove that a hypothesis is true; it is only possible to prove that it is not false. The mathematical reason for testing the null hypothesis is that it is not possible to maximize the probability of being right; it is only possible to minimize the probability of being wrong. This is further discussed below. The null hypothesis always is stated in terms of an equality: Some parameter is equal to zero, or one parameter is equal to another (or the difference between them is zero). Thus, the null hypothesis from our example must be $b = 0$ rather than $b \leqslant 0$. This means that the null hypothesis (denoted H_o) indicates that there is no relationship between R and I. The null hypothesis is symbolized as

$$(6\text{-}2) \qquad H_o: b = 0$$

If we reject the null hypothesis, then the proposition we are testing is *not falsified*. Because we cannot falsify the inference with the data we have analyzed, we tentatively accept the proposition as true. Symbolically, the proposition we are accepting is stated as

$$(6\text{-}3) \qquad H_1: b > 0$$

This proposition is called the *alternate hypothesis*. Rejection of the null hypothesis implies acceptance of the alternate hypothesis.

Example 6–1

You have been asked to plan a congressional campaign in a nonpresidential year and you decide that you will need to have a reliable estimate of the likely rate of voter turnout in each of the 300 precincts in the congressional district. The best estimate, you decide, would be the turnout rate for Congress in the previous nonpresidential election year. You shudder at the thought of calculating 300 percentages, but fortunately someone comes along and tells you that data from the state assembly election held the preceding year are available, already percentaged. You decide that it would be a grave error if you concluded that the turnout rates were unequal when they were in fact the same. So, just to make sure that you are not making such an error, you decide to perform a statistical test. The null hypothesis for such a test would be

$$H_o: T_a = T_c$$

where T_a is the turnout rate for state assembly and T_c is the turnout rate for Congress in the previous off-year election. The value of T_a is already calculated, and T_c can be calculated from summary statistics for the district. If the data suggest that you cannot reject the null hypothesis, then the assembly election results can be used.

The decision rule in Example 6-1, as in the example in our introductory comments, is incomplete. Both turnout rates, we assume, are normally distributed random variables. Thus, we cannot conclude with certainty that T_a and T_c are or are not equal. We can make a statement only about their *probable* relationship, based on our sample of knowledge of the characteristics of each distribution. Therefore, an essential component of our decision rule should be the degree of certainty we require in order to accept or reject the null hypothesis.

The degree of certainty stipulated in a decision rule is called the *confidence level*. The confidence level tells us how sure we can be of our results, given the information we have about the sampling distribution of T_a and T_c. Suppose that we set the confidence level at .95; then we would conclude that $T_a \neq T_c$ if our data indicate that $T_a \neq T_c$ will be true in 95 samples of 100 chosen from the population. The confidence level is sometimes mistakenly taken to be the probability that some hypothesis is true. This is an invalid interpretation. The point made by logical positivists is well taken: We cannot prove that a hypothesis is true; we can only prove that the data at hand show that it is not false. The confidence level is not the measure of certainty we seek (momentarily we shall see that it is not a useless measure).

Since the probability of being right is philosophically unacceptable, we construct a measure of the probability of being wrong! It is simply this: $(1 - \text{confidence level}) = $ *significance level*. If we use a significance level of $.05 = (1 - .95)$ in testing the hypothesis, our decision rule is this: Accept $T_a \neq T_c$, the alternate hypothesis, if the sample data indicate that there is less than 1 chance in 20 that the hypothesis is false. In the introductory illustration, the significance level is represented by q. The meaning of the significance level is this: It is the probability of falsely rejecting the null hypothesis and therefore falsely accepting the alternate hypothesis. Using the .05 level of significance means that you are willing to accept the alternate hypothesis as true if there is less than 1 chance in 20 that the null hypothesis is true.

Nothing we have said thus far has pointed to using a specific significance level. This is not possible because the choice of a significance level, an acceptable probability of being wrong, is a purely arbitrary decision on the part of the researcher. The .05 level is most commonly used, but it is not necessarily the "best" level.

Two types of error are useful for conceptualizing the problem of hypothesis testing. So that we cannot be accused of using jargon in reporting their names, we shall label the first a *Type I error* and the second a *Type II error*. They are sometimes called alpha and beta errors, respectively. The Type I error is committed when one falsely rejects the null hypothesis. The significance level is interpretable as the probability of making a Type I error. The Type II error is committed when one falsely rejects the alternate hypothesis. These errors are illustrated diagrammatically in Figure 6-1. If a conclusion from a decision rule agrees with the true state of the population, then we are correct; if not, we have made either a Type I or a Type II error. As Figure 6-1 illustrates, if we conclude

True State of the Population

		Null hypothesis prevails	Alternate hypothesis prevails
Conclusions from the Sample	Null hypothesis prevails	Correct decision	Type II error
	Alternate hypothesis prevails	Type I error	Correct decision

FIGURE 6-1

that the alternate hypothesis prevails (that is, reject the null hypothesis) when in the true state of the population the null hypothesis prevails, then we have made a Type I error. If we conclude that the null hypothesis prevails when in fact the alternate hypothesis is the true state of the population, then a Type II error has been committed.

Type I errors are the most important for hypothesis testing. As stated before, this importance is due to the philosophical view of hypothesis testing: We can falsify but we cannot verify. The importance of the choice of the null hypothesis is now clearer. We must choose as the null hypothesis the state of nature we wish to be most sure does not exist. This can be stated another way: We set up the null hypothesis so that we can minimize the risk of making the worst kind of error. Example 6-1 serves as a good illustration.

Determining the null hypothesis boils down to this question: Which would be a worse error, (1) calculating 300 percentages unnecessarily, or (2) incorrectly estimating the rate of voter turnout? If (1) is the most important error to avoid, then we set up our null hypothesis as in Example 6-1. This error would occur if we falsely concluded that $T_a \neq T_c$. These

True States of Population

	$H_0 : T_a = T_c$	$H_1 : T_a \neq T_c$
Conclusions from sample $H_0 : T_a = T_c$	correct	Type II
$H_1 : T_a \neq T_c$	Type I	correct

FIGURE 6-2

conditions are represented in Figure 6-2. If, on the other hand, we wished to avoid error (2), concluding that $T_a = T_c$ when in fact they are not equal, we would set up our decision rule as in Figure 6-3. From these two interpretations of the problem in Example 6-1, we can see the importance of

True State of the Population

	$H_0 : T_a \neq T_c$	$H_1 : T_a = T_c$
Conclusions from sample $H_0 : T_a \neq T_c$	correct	Type II
$H_1 : T_a = T_c$	Type I	correct

FIGURE 6-3

properly setting up the statistical test. It is also evident that the question of the appropriateness of a null hypothesis is one that is answered by the researcher and not by the statistical model he employs.

Before illustrating some uses of hypothesis testing, let us briefly summarize the basic features of a situation in which a hypothesis is tested. Our problem is that we have only a sample of data from a population. We wish to employ a statistical model in order to reach some conclusion about the true state of the population. We construct a null hypothesis about the true state of the population and then define a statistical decision rule that specifies the conditions in the sample which will lead us to accept or reject the hypothesis. The null hypothesis is stated as the condition in the population which we least want to find. The decision rule is stated in terms of the probability that we would be wrong if we rejected the null hypothesis. Consider the illustration in the introduction to this chapter. We least want to find that $b = 0$, and so that $H_o: b = 0$. Our decision rule is (if b is positive) to accept $b > 0$ if

(6-4) $P(b = 0) \leqslant q$

where q is the significance level. We reject the null hypothesis (and accept the alternate hypothesis) if the probability that we are wrong is less than some specified lower limit (q).

SINGLE-SAMPLE HYPOTHESIS TESTS

Three basic classes of hypothesis tests will be discussed in the remainder of this chapter. The explanations of these tests should provide sufficient illustration of the concepts we have just introduced, as well as introduce some valuable research tools. First, we shall present a model for tests of data within a sample. Second, we present models for testing hypotheses about a sample statistic. Third, we show some models for testing hypotheses that compare two or more samples. The latter models entail the introduction of a modification of the normal distribution.

The first model of interest to us is used to deal with a class of problems within a sample of data. Suppose that we have a sample of values for the variable X and decide that it is reasonable to assume that $X: N(\mu, \sigma)$. From the sample we can calculate estimates for the population parameters μ and σ. We encounter a new sample mean $\overline{Y}$, which is greater than $\overline{X}$, and we wish to determine whether $\overline{Y}$ came from the same population from which we drew the sample of X. We want to avoid the error of concluding that $\overline{Y}$ came from a population of larger values of X, if in fact it is merely a large value of the observed distribution. That is, we wish to avoid making the Type I error of falsely rejecting the null hypothesis, $H_o: \overline{Y} = \overline{X}$. The risk we are willing to take—that we have made a Type I error—is 1 chance in 20 (that is, .05 level of significance). Our decision rule states that if there is 1 chance in 20 or less that $H_o: \overline{Y} = \overline{X}$ is true, then we reject the null hypothesis.

Now we can employ the concepts presented in Chapter 3 and translate the decision rule into a workable problem. The null hypothesis states that $\overline{Y}$ came from the same population as $\overline{X}$; therefore, it can be standardized with the standard deviation of $\overline{X}$, $\sigma/\sqrt{n}$. (Recall from Chapter 3 the result from the Central Limit theorem, namely, that the variance of a distribution of sample means is equal to $1/n$ times the population variance σ^2. Therefore the standard deviation of a distribution of sample means is equal to $\sqrt{(1/n)\sigma^2} = \sigma/\sqrt{n}$.) Since the Central Limit theorem tells us that a distribution of sample means is normal, we can use Table A-1 in the Appendix to test the hypothesis. Our model is

$$(6\text{-}5) \qquad Z(\overline{Y}) = \frac{(\overline{Y} - \mu)}{\sigma/\sqrt{n}}$$

We use $\overline{X}$ as an estimate of μ and find $Z(\overline{Y}) = (\overline{Y} - \overline{X})/(\sigma/\sqrt{n})$. We can now state the decision rule in terms of a Z score. We look up the Z score for the abscissa that divides the area under the normal curve into two segments: .95 to the left and .05 to the right. The area under the normal curve to the right of $Z = 1.645$ is 5 percent of the total area. If $Z(\bar{Y}) \geqslant$ 1.645, we reject the null hypothesis. If $Z(\bar{Y}) < 1.645$, we accept the null hypothesis. The decision rule is shown in Figure 6-4. Our rule is to reject

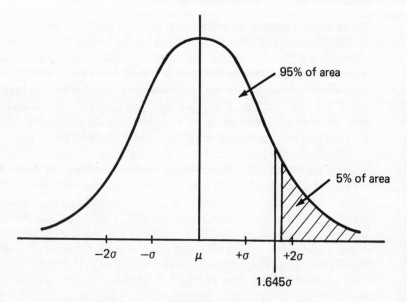

FIGURE 6-4

the null hypothesis if the new value $\bar{Y}$ is $1.645(\sigma/\sqrt{n})$ or more away from the old value $\bar{X}$.

Example 6–2

Suppose the data from Example 6-1 were $T_a = .8$, $T_c = .82$, and $\sigma^2 = .0225$. You decide on a significance level of .05. You wish to avoid concluding that $T_a \neq T_c$ when the true state of nature is $T_a = T_c$. That is, you wish to avoid calculating 300 percentages unnecessarily. The null hypothesis is $H_o: T_a = T_c$. The test will determine whether the difference between T_a and T_c could be due to sampling error, given σ^2. You calculate the 300 percentages if T_c is significantly larger than T_a, that is, if $Z(T_c)$ is greater than 1.645. Thus,

$$Z(T_c) = \frac{.82 - .8}{\sqrt{.0225/300}} = \frac{.02}{.00866} = 2.31$$

It turns out that you have to calculate the 300 percentages.

The model for proportions is analogous to the model just presented. The main difference, of course, is the method of estimating σ and, therefore, the standardization of the known sample value and the new sample data. We know that the variance of the distribution of population proportions is $(\pi(1-\pi))/N$, where π is the population proportion. The sample proportion p is an unbiased estimate of π and $(p(1-p))/n$ is an estimate of the variance of π. The standard deviation is, of course, $((p(1-p))/n)^{1/2}$. Now we can construct a model analogous to the one presented in (6-5):

(6-6) $$Z(p) = \frac{p-\pi}{(p(1-p))/n}$$

Of course the finite population correction, $(N-n)/(N-1)$, should be used to calculate σ when p is being estimated from a small population.

Example 6–3

It's the third week in October and the congressional campaign you have managed has gone quite well. Weekly polls to this point show that your candidate has been ahead 55 to 45. You have withheld contingency funds to cover unforeseen eventualities at the end of the campaign, and your opponent has just accused your candidate of beating his wife. There is one more poll in the field, and if it continues to show that your candidate is ahead 55 to 45, you intend to use the money to help set up a Washington office; if the poll indicates that the outcome of the election is in doubt, you will use the money in an intensive effort on your candidate's behalf (for example, distributing pictures of your candidate looking lovingly at his unscathed wife). The final poll results come in and they show your candidate ahead 51 to 49. You want to avoid the error of concluding that the proportion of the sample supporting your candidate is $\pi = .55$ when the true π is $\pi < .55$; that is, your candidate is in trouble. The null hypothesis, therefore, would be $\pi < .55$, but you can convert this to an equality: H_o: $\pi = .50$ by hypothesizing the worst possible conditions. Given a sample of 625, you estimate the standard error of π, as

$$\left(\frac{p(1-p)}{n}\right)^{1/2} = \left(\frac{(.5)^2}{625}\right)^{1/2} = (.0004)^{1/2} = .02$$

Using a significance level of .05, your decision rule is—if $Z(.5) \leqslant -1.645$—to spend the contingency fund on the campaign; if $Z(.5) > -1.645$, you save the money for the Washington office. You decide this by computing

$$\frac{(p-\pi)}{(p(1-p)/n)^{1/2}} = \frac{.5-.55}{.02} = \frac{-.05}{.2} = -2.5$$

$$Z(p) = -2.5$$

You conclude that the new results are significantly different from the previous survey results, and therefore the contingency fund should be used in the campaign.

The problems we have considered thus far have dealt with situations in which we desired to know if the mean of a sample was different from another sample mean in one direction only. That is, we sought to determine whether one value was significantly larger than another. Such a test is called a *one-tail test* because it concerns only one tail of a frequency distribution. Commonly, however, problems are encountered in which a *two-tail test* is required. In such a case we must construct a decision rule that specifies an interval of values of $\bar{X}$ for which H_o will be accepted and all others for which H_o will be rejected. Such an interval is called a *confidence interval*, and it is very easily determined once a significance level is decided upon. The general type of problem to which a two-tail test is appropriate would be as follows: Suppose that we have a set of observations for an experimental variable under controlled conditions. From these data, μ and σ are estimated. Then, experimental conditions are altered (a treatment is effected) and a series of samples of observations of the treated variable are taken. By establishing a confidence interval about the mean of the variable, we can determine which altered conditions (treatments) significantly increased or significantly decreased the value of the variable.

Suppose the significance level for testing the null hypothesis is set at .05. This leads us to $1 - .05 = .95$ confidence interval. Assuming that the interval will be symmetrical about μ, the mean of the normally distributed variable X, .95, is divided, with .475 of the area under the normal curve to the right of μ and .475 to the left of μ. Looking at the Table A-1 (Appendix), we find that the Z score for the abscissa at .475 is equal to 1.96. This means that .475 of the area under the curve describing a normally distributed variable lies between the mean and 1.96 standard deviations to the right of the mean. Since the distribution is symmetrical, we surmise that .95 of the area under the normal curve lies in an area bounded by ± 1.96 standard deviations about μ. We then plug in estimates for μ and σ and solve for the values of $\bar{X}$ in the distribution of sample means, which defines the limits of the .95 confidence interval. (See Figure 6-5.) The interval will range from

$$(6\text{-}7) \qquad \mu - 1.96\frac{\sigma}{(n)^{\frac{1}{2}}} \qquad \text{to} \qquad \mu + 1.96\frac{\sigma}{(n)^{\frac{1}{2}}}$$

or, more generally stated,

$$(6\text{-}8) \qquad \mu \pm Z\frac{\sigma}{(n)^{\frac{1}{2}}}$$

where Z is the Z score for the desired significance level.

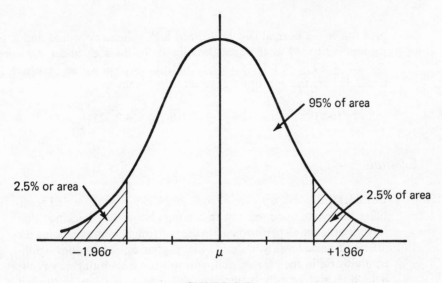

FIGURE 6-5

A special case of the determination of a confidence interval would prevail·when we were more concerned about making one kind of error than another. If, for example, we were four times as concerned about making an error toward lower values than toward higher values in a .95 confidence interval, the critical .05 area could be distributed to the tails accordingly. Toward low values, the Z score would indicate the abscissa bounding .46 of the area under the curve to the left of μ (leaving .04 of the

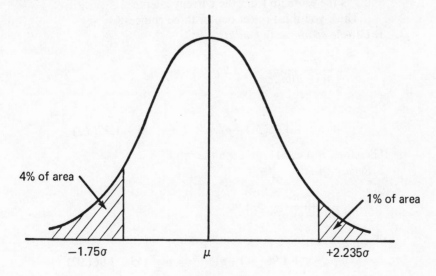

FIGURE 6-6

area under the normal curve); toward high values, we would find Z corresponding to .49 of the area (leaving .01 of the area under the normal curve). (See Figure 6-6.) Such a confidence interval would be where 1.75 and 2.325 are the appropriate values from Table A-1.

$$(6\text{-}9) \qquad \mu - 1.75 \frac{\sigma}{(n)^{1/2}} \qquad \text{to} \qquad \mu + 2.325 \frac{\sigma}{(n)^{1/2}}$$

Example 6–4

Consider the problem presented in Example 6-3, with the added possibility that your opponent's wife-beating charge may backfire; that is, your candidate's performance in the polls might improve. Using the .05 significance level, you decide that if your candidate does significantly worse in the current poll, you will use the contingency fund; if he does significantly better, you will reduce spending in the last couple of weeks of the campaign in order to save more money for the Washington office. If there is no change, you continue spending at the present level. To keep yourself honest, you make a decision rule in advance of receiving the data:

$$\pi = .55$$

$$\left(\frac{p(1-p)}{n}\right)^{1/2} = .02$$

and p is the estimate from the current sample

Thus, you must select one of three choices:

1. *Use the contingency fund if*

$$\frac{p-\pi}{(p(1-p)/n)^{1/2}} < -1.96$$

or, if

$$p < \pi - 1.96(p(1-p)/n)^{1/2} = p < .55 - 1.96(.02)$$

Therefore, if $p < .511$, you use the fund.

2. *Reduce spending if*

$$\frac{p-\pi}{(p(1-p)/n)^{1/2}} > 1.96$$

or if

$$p > \pi + 1.96 (p(1-p)/n)^{1/2} = p > .55 + 1.96(.02)$$

Therefore, if $p > .589$, you reduce spending.

3. *Continue present spending if*

$$\pi - 1.96(p(1-p)/n)^{1/2} \leqslant \pi + 1.96(p(1-p)/n)^{1/2}$$

That is, you continue spending if $.511 \leqslant p \leqslant .589$.

TESTS FOR SAMPLE ESTIMATES

In Chapter 3 we mentioned interval estimation as an alternative to point estimation. A point estimate is a method of calculating a single value for a parameter. An interval estimate indicates a range of possible values for a parameter. Interval estimates are most valuable when μ and σ are being used as descriptive statistics; rarely would they be of value as parameters in a statistical model.

Constructing confidence intervals for estimates of population parameters is easy to comprehend when you become aware of the assumption that each estimate ($\bar{X}$ or σ) is considered to be the mean of a distribution of estimates. The distributions are normal, of course; thus, they can be described when we know the parameters of their distributions. The mean of the distribution is the point estimate and the abscissa of this distribution is measured in units of standard error (perfectly analogous to the standard deviation of a population of X).

The interval estimate for μ, employing $\bar{X}$, follows directly from our discussion of *two-tail* tests. From the Central Limit theorem we know that $\bar{X}$ is $N(\mu, (\sigma/(n)^{1/2}))$; that is, $\sigma/(n)^{1/2}$ is the standard error of $\bar{X}$. Expression (6-10) is a .95 confidence interval for μ. That is, in the sampling distribution of $\bar{X}$, 95 percent of the means of samples are likely to fall within $\pm 1.96(\sigma/(n)^{1/2})$ of $\bar{X}$. An asymmetrical confidence interval for $\bar{X}$ would be constructed analogous to (6-9):

$$(6\text{-}10) \qquad \bar{X} \pm 1.96 \frac{\sigma}{(n)^{1/2}}$$

The distribution of σ is ignored in most treatments of statistical models, but since the dispersion of a variable frequently is important in establishing relationships among variables, we include its description. The standard error of the standard deviation for large n is stated without explanation of its derivation:

$$(6\text{-}11) \qquad \sigma_\sigma = \left(\frac{\sigma}{(2n)^{1/2}}\right)\left(1 + \frac{\beta_2 - 3}{2}\right)$$

where σ_σ means the standard error of the estimated population standard deviation and β_2 is the fourth moment measure about the mean (defined in Chapter 3). Since, for normal distributions, $\beta_2 = 3$, a reasonable approximation is

$$(6\text{-}12) \qquad \hat{\sigma}_\sigma = \frac{\sigma}{(2n)^{1/2}}$$

Assuming that the standard deviation is $N(\sigma, (\sigma/(2n)^{1/2}))$, we can calculate a confidence interval using the Table A-1 (Appendix). A .95 confidence interval for σ would be

$$(6\text{-}13) \qquad \sigma \pm 1.96 \frac{\sigma}{(2n)^{1/2}}$$

Our ability to describe the distribution of σ completely makes it a somewhat more versatile statistic.

Example 6-5

In Example 3-5, you compared the dispersions of strength of Republican vote in Atlantic and Union Counties, New Jersey. You found the standard deviation of the dispersion of this variable among municipalities in each county. For Atlantic County, $\sigma_a = .0233$; for Union County, $\sigma_u = .0457$. Now you wish to decide whether the dispersion of the distribution of Republican strength in Atlantic County is significantly different from the dispersion of the respective distribution for Union County. The null hypothesis of the test is $H_o: \sigma_a = \sigma_u$. If you construct a .95 confidence interval for σ_a, and if σ_u falls outside the interval, you will reject H_o. Given that there are 23 municipalities in Atlantic County,

$$\hat{\sigma}_{\sigma_a} = \frac{.0233}{(2(23))^{1/2}} = \frac{.0233}{6.78233} = .00343$$

The .95 confidence interval about σ_a is $.0233 - 1.96(.00343)$ to $.0233 + 1.96(.00343)$, or .01658 to .03002. Therefore, $\sigma_u = .0457$ is clearly outside the interval, so you reject the null hypothesis and conclude that the dispersions are significantly different.

TESTS COMPARING SAMPLES

Thus far we have dealt with tests of hypotheses involving two means and a single estimate of the variance. What happens, you might legitimately ask, when two or more estimates of the variance are available? How can we take into account the added information of extra values for σ^2 (and σ)? These problems are faced in a model for testing the difference in means of samples. The test is designed to discover whether two samples came from the same population. Two models can be used for this test. The first one is based on the normal distribution. It builds naturally on the relationships we have already developed, and requires only that you understand how to pool the variance from two or more samples. When pooling variance has been mastered, the model should be quite familiar. The second model is specifically appropriate for performing the same test on small samples. It should be intuitively obvious that the smaller the sample, the less reliable are the estimates calculated from the sample. To overcome the problem, Gosset developed a distribution that varies its shape according to sample size, but for large samples ($n \geqslant 30$) it approximates the normal distribution. This distribution is called the t-distribution and it is a one-parameter distribution. As with the normal distribution, the use of the t-distribution is simplified by the presentation of a table of critical values of t as Table A-3 (Appendix).

LARGE SAMPLE TESTS

The general form of the problem we are concerned with here is this: Given two samples and therefore two means (estimates of μ) and two variances (estimates of σ^2), we wish to determine whether the samples came from the same population. Specifically, we want to determine if the means of the two samples are significantly different. To perform the test, we have to combine the data from the two samples into a single distribution. This is done by constructing a distribution of the differences between X_1 and X_2, and then finding the parameters of the distribution of $(X_1 - X_2)$. The mean of this distribution is easy to find: The mean of a distribution of differences between variables is equal to the difference between the means of the variables. Thus, $(\mu_1 - \mu_2)$ is the mean of the distribution of $(X_1 - X_2)$. The derivation of the $\text{Var}(X_1 - X_2)$ is a little more subtle, however:

(6-14)

$$
\text{Var}(X_1 - X_2) = \frac{\sum [(X_1 - X_2) - (\mu_1 - \mu_2)]^2}{N}
$$

$$
= \frac{[(X_1 - \mu_1) - (X_2 - \mu_2)]^2}{N}
$$

$$
= \frac{\sum [(X_1 - \mu_1)^2 + (X_2 - \mu_2)^2 - 2(X_1 - \mu_1)(X_2 - \mu_2)]}{N}
$$

$$
= \frac{\sum (X_1 - \mu_1)^2}{N} + \frac{\sum (X_2 - \mu_2)^2}{N}
$$

$$
- \frac{2\sum (X_1 - \mu_1)(X_2 - \mu_2)}{N}
$$

where $\sum (X_1 - \mu_1)(X_2 - \mu_2) = 0$ if X_1 and X_2 are independent random variables. This term is called the covariance of X_1 and X_2 and is written $\mathrm{Cov}(X_1, X_2)$.

$$(6\text{-}15) \qquad \mathrm{Var}(X_1 - X_2) = \mathrm{Var}(X_1) + \mathrm{Var}(X_2)$$

$$(6\text{-}16) \qquad \sigma_{X_1 - X_2} = \sqrt{\sigma_{X_1}^2 + \sigma_{X_2}^2}$$

This proof is valid, of course, when we are dealing with estimates of the variable as well as with the population variance, as above.

Assuming that X_1 and X_2 are normally distributed, another question arises: Would the distribution of the difference between two normally distributed variables be normally distributed? Not necessarily, but our test concerns a difference in *means*. From the Central Limit theorem we know that a distribution of the means of a set of samples from the same population is normally distributed, regardless of the shape of the distribution of the population for large N. The variance of that distribution of sample means is σ^2/n, where σ^2 is the population variance. Therefore, from the Central Limit theorem and (6-16), the variance of the distribution of the difference in sample means is

$$(6\text{-}17) \qquad \mathrm{Var}(\overline{X}_1 - \overline{X}_2) = \frac{\sigma_1^2}{n_1} + \frac{\sigma_2^2}{n_2}$$

when n_1 and n_2 are sample sizes.

Now we are able to present the model for testing the difference between the means for large n. The null hypothesis is that the difference is zero, that is, that the samples came from the same population. The means $\overline{X}_1$ and $\overline{X}_2$ are estimates of μ_1 and μ_2. The null hypothesis states that $H_o: \mu_1 = \mu_2$.

$$(6\text{-}18) \qquad \frac{(\overline{X}_1 - \overline{X}_2) - (\mu_1 - \mu_2)}{((\sigma_1^2/n_1) + (\sigma_2^2/n_2))^{1/2}}$$

Since $\mu_1 - \mu_2 = 0$,

$$(6\text{-}19) \qquad \frac{\overline{X}_1 - \overline{X}_2}{((\sigma_1^2/n_1) + (\sigma_2^2/n_2))^{1/2}}$$

Expressions (6-18) and (6-19) represent the general form of the test. It is possible to simplify this test somewhat if it can be established that $\sigma_{\overline{X}_1}^2$ is not significantly different from $\sigma_{\overline{X}_2}^2$. The F ratio, a test described in Chapter 8, can be used to establish this.

When $\sigma_1^2 = \sigma_2^2$, the denominator of (6-18) is changed to

$$(6\text{-}20) \qquad \hat{\sigma} \left(\frac{1}{n_1} + \frac{1}{n_2} \right)^{1/2} = \hat{\sigma} \left(\frac{n_1 + n_2}{n_1 n_2} \right)^{1/2}$$

The method of arriving at a value for $\hat{\sigma}$ is the method of pooling variances.

Since each estimate contains information about the true σ^2, it is important that we take into account both estimates, σ_1^2 and σ_2^2, in calculating the estimate of the variance of the population. We presume that larger samples produce better estimates of parameters than do smaller samples, so in calculating the estimate of σ^2 for the population ($\hat{\sigma}^2$), we should differentially weight σ_1^2 and σ_2^2 according to the relative amount of information in each of the samples that produced them. As a measure of this information we use the denominator of the ratio

$$\sigma_1^2 = \frac{\sum (X_1 - \overline{X}_1)^2}{n_1 - 1}$$

The estimate of σ^2 is

(6-21)

$$\hat{\sigma}^2 = \frac{(n_1 - 1)\sigma_1^2}{(n_1 - 1) + (n_2 - 1)} + \frac{(n_2 - 1)\sigma_2^2}{(n_2 - 1) + (n_1 - 1)}$$

$$= \frac{(n_1 - 1)\left(\sum\limits^{n_1}(X_1 - \overline{X}_1)^2/(n_1 - 1)\right) + (n_2 - 1)\left(\sum\limits^{n_2}(X_2 - \overline{X}_2)^2/(n_2 - 1)\right)}{n_1 + n_2 - 2}$$

$$= \frac{\sum\limits^{n_1}(X_1 - \overline{X}_1)^2 + \sum\limits^{n_2}(X_2 - \overline{X}_2)^2}{n_1 + n_2 - 2}$$

As (6-21) shows, the pooled variance for the two samples is the total sum of squared deviations for both samples divided by the sum of the sample sizes minus 2 (the number of samples). This formula can be made more simple for the purposes of computations by introducing a new term, the sample variance S^2. Let

$$S_i^2 = \frac{\sum (X_i - \overline{X}_i)^2}{n_i}$$

(note the difference in the denominator). Then

(6-22) $$S_i^2 = \frac{\sum (X_i - \overline{X}_i)^2}{n_i} = \frac{\sum (X_i - \overline{X}_i)^2}{n_i - 1}\left(\frac{n_i - 1}{n_i}\right)$$

$$= \sigma_i^2\left(\frac{n_i - 1}{n_i}\right)$$

Given the values for the σ_i^2, they can be multiplied by $(n-1)/n$ and plugged into (6-23) for more convenient computation:

(6-23) $$\hat{\sigma}^2 = \frac{n_1 S_1^2 + n_2 S_2^2}{n_1 + n_2 - 2}$$

This formula can be generalized to any number of samples:

$$(6\text{-}24) \qquad \frac{n_1 S_1^2 + n_2 S_2^2 + \cdots n_k S_k^2}{n_1 + n_2 + \cdots n_k - k}$$

Thus, we have a general formula for pooling variances. All we need to do is to select a significance level, and we can construct a decision rule for the null hypothesis, $\mu_1 = \mu_2$.

In general,

$$(6\text{-}25) \qquad Z(\overline{X}_1 - \overline{X}_2) = \frac{(\overline{X}_1 - \overline{X}_2)}{((\sigma_1^2/n_1) + (\sigma_2^2/n_2))^{\frac{1}{2}}}$$

And if $\sigma_1 = \sigma_2$, the denominator of this formula can be simplified[2]:

$$(6\text{-}26) \qquad Z(\overline{X}_1 - \overline{X}_2) = \frac{(\overline{X}_1 - \overline{X}_2)}{\hat{\sigma}((n_1 + n_2)/n_1 n_2)^{\frac{1}{2}}}$$

where $\hat{\sigma}$ is found by taking a weighted average of σ_1 and σ_2 (pooling variances).

Basically, the test just outlined assumes that we have two estimates of the mean, each with a standard error:

$$\overline{X}_1, \frac{\sigma_1}{(n_1)^{\frac{1}{2}}} \qquad \text{and} \qquad \overline{X}_2, \frac{\sigma_2}{(n_2)^{\frac{1}{2}}}$$

We then find the mean and variance of the distribution of the difference between those two variables, as indicated by the derivation from (6-14) to (6-16). This derivation provides the basic information we need to apply the results of the Central Limit theorem.

Example 6–6

New Jersey county government is called the Board of Chosen Freeholders. This name was given the board in the prerevolutionary period when only freeholders (land owners) were eligible to serve. They were called "Chosen" because they were not elected, but chosen by the governor. The contemporary Board, consisting of three to nine members, depending on county size, is elected and members serve three-year staggered terms. The boards are elected at large; some counties always have three vacancies to fill. This means that each voter votes for three persons for Freeholder, and the three with the most votes are elected. Would-be reformers in New Jersey argue that this ballot form[3] is too complicated for many voters, who simply give up somewhere before they get to their third choice for

Freeholder. You have tried to measure voter participation for different ballot positions by calculating the percentage of votes used (PVU). This measure is the ratio of the ballots cast for the first-ballot position to the total number of voters who went to the polls; likewise for the second- and third-ballot positions. The basic unit of analysis is a single municipality. Based on the PVU, you create two new variables: PVU for the first position minus PVU for the second position is the "drop-off for position 2" (X_1). PVU for the first position minus PVU for the third position is the "drop-off for position 3" (X_2). You estimate μ_1 and μ_2 with $\overline{X}_1$ and $\overline{X}_2$, respectively.

$$\overline{X}_1 = .0006 \quad \sigma_1^2 = .0053824 \quad \sigma_1 = .0232 \quad n_1 = 201$$

$$\overline{X}_2 = .0137 \quad \sigma_2^2 = .00131044 \quad \sigma_2 = .0362 \quad n_2 = 201$$

You wish to decide whether the drop-off for position 3 is significantly larger than the drop-off for position 2. For a test of the difference in means, you establish the null hypothesis

$$H_o: \mu_1 = \mu_2 \quad \text{or} \quad H_o: (\mu_1 - \mu_2) - (\overline{X}_1 - \overline{X}_2) = 0$$

Next you must find the pooled standard deviation $\sigma_{\overline{X}_1 - \overline{X}_2}$. By using an F test (explained in Chapter 8), you establish that $\sigma_1 \neq \sigma_2$; thus the computationally more difficult pooling procedure is used:

$$\sigma_{\overline{X}_1 - \overline{X}_2} \left(\frac{\sigma_1^2}{n_1} + \frac{\sigma_2^2}{n_2} \right)^{\frac{1}{2}} = \left(\frac{.0053824 + .00131044}{201} \right)^{\frac{1}{2}}$$

$$= (.00000919)^{\frac{1}{2}} = .00302$$

At the .05 level you reject the null hypothesis if $Z(\overline{X}_1 - \overline{X}_2) \leqslant -1.96$. The test statistic is

$$Z(\overline{X}_1 - \overline{X}_2) = \frac{(\mu_1 - \mu_2) - (\overline{X}_1 - \overline{X}_2)}{\sigma_{\overline{X}_1 - \overline{X}_2}}$$

$$= \frac{.0006 - .0137}{.00302} = -4.34$$

Therefore, you can reject the null hypothesis that $H_o: \mu_1 = \mu_2$ and add the weight of evidence to the ideals of the reformers. The implication here is that the ballot form discriminates against some voters. The next step for the reformers should be to identify population groups that are being discriminated against, so that the ballot form can be taken to court.

Example 6–7

Suppose that σ_1 and σ_2 were not significantly different. You want to find $\sigma_{\bar{X}_1 - \bar{X}_2}$ by the weighted average method:

$$(6\text{-}27) \qquad \hat{\sigma}^2 = \frac{n_1 S_1^2 + n_2 S_2^2}{n_1 + n_2 - 2}$$

$$S_1^2 = \frac{n_1 - 1}{n_1} \sigma_1^2 = \frac{200}{201}(.0232) = .02308$$

$$S_2^2 = \frac{n_2 - 1}{n_2} \sigma_2^2 = \frac{200}{201}(.0362) = .03602$$

$$\hat{\sigma} = \frac{201(.02308) + 201(.03602)}{201 + 201 - 2}$$

$$= \frac{11.8791}{400} = .0297$$

You weight $\sigma_{\bar{X}_1}$ and $\sigma_{\bar{X}_2}$ by their relative sample size to get $\hat{\sigma}_{\bar{X}_1 - \bar{X}_2}$. Since $n_1 = n_2$, the weighted variance is simply the average of $\sigma_{\bar{X}_1}$ and $\sigma_{\bar{X}_2}$:

$$\frac{.0232 + .0362}{2} = .0297$$

Now continue with the same test outlined in Example 6-6. You know that

$$\sigma_{\bar{X}_1 - \bar{X}_2} = \left(\frac{\sigma_1^2}{n_1} + \frac{\sigma_2^2}{n_2}\right)^{1/2}$$

and if $\sigma_1 = \sigma_2$, then

$$\sigma_{\bar{X}_1 - \bar{X}_2} = \hat{\sigma}\left(\frac{1}{n_1} + \frac{1}{n_2}\right)^{1/2} = \hat{\sigma}\left(\frac{n_1 + n_2}{n_1 n_2}\right)^{1/2}$$

$$= .0297\left(\frac{201 + 201}{201^2}\right)^{1/2} = .0297(.09975) = .00296$$

Compared to the method used in Example 6-6, $(.00302 - .00296 = .00006)$, the results of Example 6-7 are not *very* different, but they *are* different. Had $Z(\bar{X}_1 - \bar{X}_2)$ been closer to the critical level set in the decision rule, the difference might have been important.

TESTS FOR SMALL SAMPLES

The smaller the sample, the more likely that estimates calculated from the sample will be inaccurate. This means that small samples from normally distributed populations are less likely to be characteristic of the population than are large samples. For these reasons and others, statisticians are reluctant to make the same assumptions about small samples ($n < 30$) that they can comfortably make about larger samples. To overcome the problems of small samples, a one-parameter distribution was developed and was found to approximate reasonably the distribution of the means of small samples from a normally distributed population. This distribution, the t-distribution, enables us to test the means of small samples; thus it is quite useful to the political scientist who may find himself dealing with the political characteristics of 20 counties, 25 cities, or other multiples. The one parameter of the t-distribution is *degrees of freedom*.

Degrees of freedom, in reference to an estimate, is a measure of the amount of information that has gone into the calculation of the statistic. The number of degrees of freedom of a statistic is the number of independent bits of information contributing to the value of the statistic. The concept of degrees of freedom is so essential that it nearly defies verbal explanation. But like most such concepts, it is quite simple. We present two illustrations of the basic idea.

Say that we have a 3 by 3 matrix for which we know only the marginal totals. Suppose that for some strange reason we wanted to find the minimum number of cells in the matrix which would have to be filled in before we knew all values in the matrix. We know all the n_i and n_j. It should be obvious from Figure 6-7 that we can know all nine cells of the matrix by knowing only cells a, b, d, and e. If we know less than four values, we will not be able to fill in the matrix completely. Of course it is possible to know four values and not be able to fill in the matrix (for example, a, b, c, and d), but it is not possible to complete the matrix with less than four cells known. We see that for a 3 by 3 matrix there are four cells that may vary completely independently; their values do not depend on any of the other cells. We have established that a 3 by 3 matrix has 4 degrees of freedom. In general a matrix has $(r-1)(c-1)$ degrees of freedom, where r equals the number of rows and c equals the number of columns. In the present illustration, $(3-1)(3-1) = 4$.

As a second illustration, suppose that we have calculated an estimate of σ^2 from a distribution of X. Given the value of σ^2, how many independent bits of information have gone into the calculation? Suppose, for the sake of the illustration, that X has only five observations. Note that $\overline{X}$ and n are constants. The formula for estimating σ^2, using $\overline{X}$ as an estimate of μ, is

(6-28)

$$\sigma^2 = \frac{\sum(X - \overline{X})^2}{n-1}$$

$$= \frac{(X_1 - \overline{X})^2 + (X_2 - \overline{X})^2 + (X_3 - \overline{X}) + (X_4 - \overline{X})^2 + (X_5 - \overline{X})^2}{n-1}$$

Column
Totals

a	b	c	N_1
d	e	f	N_2
g	h	i	N_3

Row
Totals N_1 N_2 N_3 N

FIGURE 6-7

Given that we know the value of σ^2, how many values of X may vary freely before all values of X are determined? The answer is: All but one value of X may vary freely, that is, $n-1$. If X_1 through X_4 take on any extreme values, we can always find a value for X_5 that will produce σ^2. Looked at in another way, the value of the estimate for σ^2 is determined by $n-1$ independent bits of information; σ^2 has $n-1$ degrees of freedom.

A test of the difference between means of small samples, using the t-distribution, can be used most easily if the variances of the means are *not* significantly different. The method for pooling variances for the t-test is identical to that already discussed (remembering to employ the finite population correction when necessary). After a discussion of the case where $\sigma_1^2 = \sigma_2^2$, we shall briefly show why the t-test is not defined for $\sigma_1^2 \neq \sigma_2^2$ and state, without explanation, one method for dealing with such cases.

Like the normal distribution function, the t-distribution function is a specific mathematical formula. It is based on a normal distribution, through the χ^2 distribution (see Chapter 7). In particular, we construct a random variable t that is a function of $X: X_1 X_2 \cdots X_n$, $X: N(\mu, \sigma)$. Each value of t can be found as follows:

$$(6\text{-}29) \qquad t_i = \frac{X_i^*}{(u/(n-1))^{\frac{1}{2}}}$$

where X^* is the standardized normal variable X,

(6-30) $X_i^* = \dfrac{X_i - \mu}{\sigma}$

and u is defined without explanation as the χ^2 value of the variable X with $n-1$ degrees of freedom,

(6-31) $u = \sum \left(\dfrac{X_i - \mu}{\sigma}\right)^2$

The whole expression for t is

(6-32) $t_i = \dfrac{(X_i - \mu)/\sigma}{\left(\sum((X_i - \mu)/\sigma)^2/(n-1)\right)^{1/2}}$

Note that we can simplify this expression by removing $1/\sigma$ from the numerator and $(1/\sigma^2)^{1/2}$ from the denominator. This is an important simplification because σ is the population standard deviation. Thus, we have

(6-33) $t_i = \dfrac{X_i - \mu}{\left(\sum(X_i - \mu)^2/(n-1)\right)^{1/2}}$

It turns out that the denominator is the formula for calculating an unbiased estimate of σ. The values of t are found easily by using $\overline{X}$ as an estimate of μ.

Now, in order to make use of this new random variable t, we must know its exact distribution. This is found by first stating the distribution function in terms of a standardized normal variable (the denominator) and a χ^2 distribution with $n-1$ degrees of freedom (the numerator). These two determinant distributions enable us to produce a third determinant distribution. Complex mathematical techniques simplify this density function, given as

(6-34) $F(t) = \dfrac{((v-1)/2)!}{(v\pi((k-2)/2)!)^{1/2}} \dfrac{1}{(1+(t^2/v))^{(v+1)/2}}$

What this formula means to us is that if we know only v, the degrees of freedom, we can completely describe the distribution of t. And t, of course, is a function of an $X: N(\mu, \sigma)$. The resulting distribution is unimodal and symmetrical like the normal distribution, but for smaller n (and consequently smaller v) the distribution is less peaked (it is more platykurtic) and the tails of the t-distribution are longer. (See Figure 6-8.) These features allow us to cope with extreme values in the small samples without having as large a likelihood of error. Furthermore, the smaller the n, the more the distribution flattens out; conversely, as n approaches ∞, the t-distribution approaches the normal distribution (t is close enough to Z at $n = 30$ so that for $n > 30$ the normal distribution is adequate). The fact that the

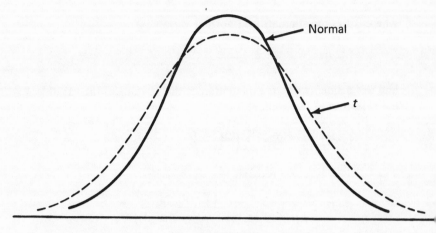

FIGURE 6-8

t-distribution is an exact distribution for each v enables us to present Table A-3 (Appendix), which reduces your workload considerably.

We set up decision rules for the t-test exactly as we would set up Z test. We seek a critical value of t exactly as we would seek a critical value of Z. Table A-3, however, is set up somewhat differently because it contains three pieces of information: t, degrees of freedom, and significance level, whereas the Z table (Table A-1) contains only Z and significance level. The t-table is set up with preselected significance levels in columns and degrees of freedom in rows. When you decide on a significance level (say, .05 in a two-tail test), read down to the row for $n-1$ degrees of freedom. The value where the column and row cross is the critical value of t for that level of significance and degrees of freedom.

Example 6–8

Suppose you are conducting a single sample test on a sample of 16 observations and you want to use a one-tail test at the .025 level of significance. The .025 column of Table A-3 is the appropriate column. Read down to $(n-1) = (16-1) = 15$ degrees of freedom. The critical value of t is found to be 2.131. The probability of getting a value of t greater than 2.131, given 15 degrees of freedom, is .025. If you used the .05 level in a one-tail test and $n = 30$ ($df = 29$), then the critical value of t is 1.699.

We began this discussion to lead to a test for the difference of means of small samples. The test for small samples is closely analogous to the test for large samples; again, $[(\overline{X}_1 - \mu_1) - (\overline{X}_2 - \mu_2)]$ is normally distributed, as the Central Limit theorem states, so it is legitimate to calculate the statistic t for its distribution. The transformation of $\overline{X}$ is given as

$$(6\text{-}35) \qquad t(\overline{X}) = \frac{(\overline{X}-\mu)/(\sigma/\sqrt{n})}{((1/(n-1))\sum((X-\mu)/\sigma)^2)^{\frac{1}{2}}}$$

$$= ((1/n)\sum(x-\mu)^2/(n-1))^{\frac{1}{2}}$$

which is distributed t with $n-1$ degrees of freedom and where

$$((1/n)\sum(x-\mu)^2/(n-1))^{\frac{1}{2}}$$

is the standard deviation of the distribution of the difference of sample means. For the case where $\sigma_{\overline{X}_1}$ is not significantly different from $\sigma_{\overline{X}_2}$, simplifications are possible, and the statistic we seek turns out as expected. $\hat{\sigma}$ is the pooled variance for the two samples as presented in (6-21) to (6-24):

$$(6\text{-}36) \qquad t_{\overline{X}_1-\overline{X}_2} = \frac{\overline{X}_1-\overline{X}_2}{\hat{\sigma}_{\overline{X}_1-\overline{X}_2}}\left(\frac{n_1+n_2}{n_1 n_2}\right)^{\frac{1}{2}}$$

which is distributed t with n_1+n_2-2 degrees of freedom. This statistic enables us to perform tests between the means of small samples.

Example 6–9

In Example 3-6 you compared the dispersion of the distribution of Democratic strength in Middlesex and Mercer counties, New Jersey. Using the information in that example, test for the difference in the mean Democratic strength between the counties. To perform the test, first pool the variance of the two distributions:

Mercer County:

$$\sigma^2 = .0079, \qquad n_1 = 13, \qquad \overline{X}_1 = .52$$

Middlesex County:

$$\sigma^2 = .0289, \qquad n_2 = 25, \qquad \overline{X}_2 = .501$$

$$S_1^2 = .0079\left(\frac{13-1}{13}\right) = .0073$$

$$S_2^2 = .0289\left(\frac{25-1}{25}\right) = .0277$$

$$\hat{\sigma}^2 = \frac{n_1 S_1^2 + n_2 S_2^2}{n_1 + n_2 - 2} = \frac{13(.0073) + 25(.0277)}{13 + 25 - 2} = .022$$

$$\hat{\sigma} = \sqrt{.022} = .148$$

$$\hat{\sigma}_{\bar{X}_1 - \bar{X}_2} = (.148)\left(\frac{13 + 25}{(13)(25)}\right)^{\frac{1}{2}} = .016$$

The null hypothesis of the test is

$$H_o: (\mu_1 - \mu_2) - (\bar{X}_1 - \bar{X}_2) = 0$$

Since $(\mu_1 - \mu_2) = 0$, $H_o: (\bar{X}_1 = \bar{X}_2)$. Choosing .05 as the significance level, reject $H_o: (\bar{X}_1 = \bar{X}_2)$ if the chances of its being true are less than or equal to .05. In terms of t, you should reject the null hypothesis if $t_{\bar{X}_1 - \bar{X}_2} \geqslant 2.03$ (degrees of freedom = 36):

$$t_{\bar{X}_1 - \bar{X}_2} = \frac{.52 - .501}{.016} = 1.19$$

Therefore you cannot reject the null hypothesis and you conclude that the means of Democratic strength in Mercer and Middlesex counties are not significantly different.

We stated that the t-test is difficult to use as a test between means if $\sigma_1 \neq \sigma_2$ because, in deriving the simple ratio for the t-test—from (6-32) to (6-33)—the *population* standard deviation σ cancels out when $\sigma_1 = \sigma_2$. The reason it cancels out is that $\sqrt{(\sigma_1^2/n_1) + (\sigma_2^2/n_2)}$ can be expressed as $\sigma\sqrt{(1/n_1) + (1/n_2)}$ and the denominator contains σ. But if $\sigma_1 \neq \sigma_2$, the population standard deviation cannot be removed from under the square root sign and so σ does not cancel out. If we substitute the sample estimate for the population standard deviation, we create other problems. A method has been suggested to overcome all these problems. A reasonable approximation of the distribution of the statistic t is available for this case, $\sigma_1 \neq \sigma_2$. One must calculate t as usual, using the weighted formula for $\hat{\sigma}^2$ in (6-23), and estimate the number of degrees of freedom as follows:

(6-37)
Degrees of freedom

$$= \frac{(\hat{\sigma}_1^2/n_1 + \hat{\sigma}_2^2/n_2)^2}{(\hat{\sigma}_1^2/n_1)^2(1/(n_1 + 1)) + (\hat{\sigma}_2^2/n_2)^2(1/(n_2 + 1))} - 2$$

The degrees of freedom of the t-statistic are taken as the nearest whole number.

Example 6–10

Suppose the variances of the distributions of Democratic strength for Mercer and Middlesex counties had been significantly different (we checked; they were not significantly different, although it was close). Then

$$t_{\bar{X}_1 - \bar{X}_2} = \frac{\bar{X}_1 - \bar{X}_2}{((\sigma_1^2/n_1) + (\sigma_2^2/n_2))^{1/2}}$$

$$= \frac{.52 - .501}{((.0079/13) + (.0289/25))^{1/2}} = \frac{.019}{(.00061 + .00116)^{1/2}}$$

$$= \frac{.019}{.042} = .45$$

and

Degrees of freedom

$$= \frac{[(.0079/13) + (.0289/25)]^2}{(.0079/13)^2 (1/14) + (.0289/25)^2 (1/26)} - 2$$

$$\doteq 47$$

The t-distribution should be used when calculating a confidence interval for $\bar{X}$ derived from a small sample ($n < 30$). Its use is analogous to the use of the Z transformation, since t-values are expressed in standard units as well. Once you have decided what size confidence interval you want to calculate, knowing the degrees of freedom, find the value of t that includes the appropriate proportion of the area under the curve. Suppose you wanted to calculate a .95 confidence interval for $\bar{X}$ with 15 degrees of freedom. Reading down in the .025 column (.025 in each tail leaves .95 in between) to row 15, $t = 2.131$. That means that $\bar{X} \pm 2.121\hat{\sigma}$ bounds 95 percent of the area under the t-distribution function curve. By simply plugging in values for σ, the confidence interval can be readily calculated. Asymmetrical confidence intervals can be calculated analogous to the model presented for the normal distribution, substituting t for Z.

SUMMARY OF TESTS ON SAMPLE MEANS

The apropriateness of a test for the difference of sample means is determined by three things: (1) the character of the data; (2) the sample size; and (3) the amount of information we have about the variables. This information is presented here in summary form.

Tests for the Difference between Samples

	Test statistic	Comments
A. Normally distributed variables, large samples σ_1 and σ_2 known: $\sigma_1 = \sigma_2$ or $\sigma_1 \neq \sigma_2$	$(\bar{X}_1 - \bar{X}_2)/(\sigma\sqrt{n}) = Z(\bar{X}_1 - \bar{X}_2)$ (6–26)	σ, the population standard deviation is a weighted average of σ_1 and σ_2. (6–23).
σ_1 and σ_2 unknown: $\sigma_1 = \sigma_2$ or $\sigma_1 \neq \sigma_2$	Same as above (6–26) except that $\hat{\sigma}$ replaces σ	$\hat{\sigma}$, the estimated population standard deviation is derived from $\hat{\sigma}_1$ and $\hat{\sigma}_2$ by the weighted average method (6–23).
B. Normally distributed, small samples σ_1 and σ_2 known, $\sigma_1 = \sigma_2$. σ_1 and σ_2 unknown, $\hat{\sigma}_1 = \hat{\sigma}_2$.	Same as large samples t-distribution, $(\bar{X}_1 - \bar{X}_2/(\hat{\sigma}\sqrt{n}))$, $(n-1)$ df. (6–35 or 6–36)	population standard deviation is known $\hat{\sigma}$ is derived from $\hat{\sigma}_1$ and $\hat{\sigma}_2$ by the weighted average method. (6–23)
σ_1 and σ_2 unknown, $\hat{\sigma}_1 \neq \hat{\sigma}_2$.	Same except df estimated as in (6–37)	
C. Variables not normally distributed, large samples All cases are the same as the normally distributed variables.		
D. Variables not normally distributed, small samples All cases are indeterminate; no tests have been presented		

NOTES   Chapter 6

1. At a less elementary level a number of other topics are covered under the subject of hypothesis testing. Modern decision theory, the O.C. curve, power of a test, and experimental design are examples. For an elementary discussion, see Yamane (1967).

2. To say that two statistics are equal is not to say that they are exactly equal. Precisely, one means that the two are not significantly different; thus the need for a method of pooling the different (but not significantly different) estimates of the same parameter.

3. Data in this example are from a study of the New Jersey ballot form conducted at the Eagleton Institute of Politics. Sara McLean gathered and analyzed the data presented here.

REFERENCES   Chapter 6

Chernoff, Herman, and Lincoln E. Moses. *Elementary Decision Theory.* New York: Wiley, 1959.

Gosset, W. H. *Students' Collected Papers*, edited by E. S. Pearson and John Wishard, with Cambridge. Published for the Biometrika Trustees at the University Press, 1958.

Lehmann, Erich L. *Testing Statistical Hypotheses.* New York: Wiley, 1959.

Yamane, Taro. *Statistics, An Introductory Analysis.* New York: Harper & Row, 2d ed. 1967. (See especially chaps. 8 and 9.)

Chapter 7

CHI-SQUARE

In the introduction to Chapter 6 we said that hypothesis testing was a two-stage operation. We measure the differences between variables from a sample of observations and then decide whether the differences are real or due only to sampling error. After outlining the theory of hypothesis testing, we illustrated the theory with some elementary models, specifically tests on the means of samples. In this chapter we present a tool of measurement which is more sophisticated than tests on means. This tool is the chi-square (symbolized χ^2) test. The χ^2 test is performed on one or on two variables. χ^2 has a distribution similar to the t-distribution in that we need know only the degrees of freedom to know the distribution completely. Since the distribution is determinant, we can calculate the likelihood of getting specific values of χ^2 for varying degrees of freedom and thereby use the magnitude of the χ^2 statistic to test hypotheses. The null hypothesis of the test in case of one variable is: The observed frequencies (of the variable) do not differ significantly from the expected frequencies (of the variable). The null hypothesis of the test in case of two variables is: No relationship exists between the two variables under consideration. We state a decision rule in terms of a critical value of χ^2. If the computed χ^2 equals or exceeds this value, then we reject the null hypothesis; if the computed χ^2 is less than this value, then we accept the null hypothesis.

Of the many types of questions we face in politics, three are very common:

1. Are the observed data significantly different from what we expect, our expectations being based on past experience?
2. Are the variables under consideration independent of each other?
3. Are the variables under consideration related in such a manner that the data or samples containing them could be considered to be from the same population?

As an example of (1) we may want to know if the votes of the members of the U.S. Senate on a particular issue are significantly different from our expectations, our expectations being based on the past record of the votes of the U.S. Senate. As an example of (2) we may want to know if political participation and income are independent of each other. And as an example of (3) we may want to know if living in different regions of the U.S. and views on the civil rights are related in such a manner that samples of views from two or more regions could be considered to be from the same population.

Chi-square can be used to answer such questions. It is a relatively easy statistic to work with, and if we know the formula and have the data, the data can be very easily plugged into the formula and we will have some findings to talk about. However, as we emphasize throughout this book, it is important to know the assumptions and mechanics of a statistical test before it is put to use. χ^2 is a special type of distribution, and our first job is to explain the properties of this distribution. Therefore, we first explain what χ^2 is about, or rather we review the underlying assumptions of this model. We then discuss the use of χ^2 as a goodness-of-fit test and as a test of independence.

CHI-SQUARE AS A DISTRIBUTION

Suppose that we have k normally distributed independent variables in a population: $X_1, X_2, \ldots X_k$. Further suppose that the mean of each X_i is μ_i and the variance of each X_i is σ_i^2. If $\mu_1 = \mu_2 = \cdots = \mu_k = 0$, and $\sigma_1 = \sigma_2 = \cdots = \sigma_k = 1$, then $X_1^2 + X_2^2 + \cdots + X_k^2$ has a χ^2 distribution with k degrees of freedom. When we have k normally distributed independent variables, but the mean of each is not zero and the standard deviation of each is not 1, we standardize them in the following manner:

$$X_1^* = \frac{X_1 - \mu_1}{\sigma_1}$$

$$X_2^* = \frac{X_2 - \mu_2}{\sigma_2}$$

$$\vdots$$

$$X_k^* = \frac{X_k - \mu_k}{\sigma_k}$$

The asterisk denotes a standardized variable. Each of these standardized variables has 0 mean and standard deviation 1. Now, $X_1^{*2} + X_2^{*2} + \cdots + X_k^{*2}$ has a χ^2 distribution with k degrees of freedom. Most of the time, however, we deal with situations in which we have less than k degrees of freedom.

Note that μ and σ are the population parameters of X. In common practice, however, we deal with samples and use an approximation of the

χ^2 distribution. Karl Pearson showed that when n is very large, the multinomial distribution approaches a χ^2 distribution. In order to understand this approximation of χ^2, consider the data in Table 7-1.

Table 7-1

Observed and Expected Voting on a Bill

	With the party	Not with the party	Abstained
Observed	48	25	27
Expected	60	20	20

The data in Table 7-1 represent the observed and the expected voting on a bill in a legislative assembly of 100 members and 2 political parties. The expected voting is based upon how the legislators have voted on the average in the past. Now, if we write $x_1 = 48$, $x_2 = 25$, $x_3 = 27$, and $p_1 = 3/5$, $p_2 = 1/5$, $p_3 = 1/5$, then (as discussed in Chapter 4) x_1, x_2, and x_3 jointly have a multinomial distribution with

$$P(x_1, x_2, x_3) = \frac{n!}{x_1! \, x_2! \, x_3!} (p_1)^{x_1} (p_2)^{x_2} (p_3)^{x_3}$$

Karl Pearson showed that when n is very large,

$$\sum_{i=1}^{k} \frac{(x_i - np_i)^2}{np_i}$$

approaches a χ^2 distribution with $k - 1$ degrees of freedom. The formula

$$(7\text{-}1) \qquad \chi^2 = \sum_{i=1}^{k} \frac{(x_i - np_i)^2}{np_i}$$

is usually written

$$(7\text{-}2) \qquad \chi^2 = \sum_{i=1}^{k} \frac{(o_i - e_i)^2}{e_i}$$

Thus, in Table 7-1,

$$\chi^2 = \sum_{i=1}^{3} \frac{(o_i - e_i)^2}{e_i}$$

$$= \frac{(48 - 60)^2}{60} + \frac{(25 - 20)^2}{20} + \frac{(27 - 20)^2}{20}$$

$$= \frac{144}{60} + \frac{25}{20} + \frac{49}{20} = \frac{366}{60} = 6.1$$

If we work out the sum, we get one number, which is the χ^2 value. The whole idea behind this calculation is to know the discrepancy between the observed and the expected frequencies. In fact, we want to know whether the discrepancy that we find between the observed and the expected frequencies is due to sampling variations or not. We do this by using a χ^2 table for which we need information about degrees of freedom. We shall explain the use of this table presently. Note that χ^2 is a measure of discrepancy, as well as a distribution.

The shape of the χ^2 distribution depends on the degrees of freedom. Figure 7-1 shows the shape of χ^2 for different degrees of freedom. By

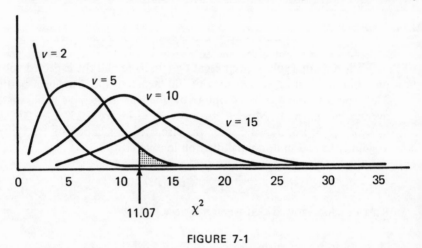

FIGURE 7-1

degrees of freedom we mean here the number of cells whose values can be freely changed. Thus, in Table 7-1, we can freely change the values of two of the cells. Once the values of two of the cells are determined, the third cell is not free to change, for the total has to add up to 100. In general, for such tables, the degrees of freedom (usually written v) equal k (number of cells) -1. In contingency tables (tables with rows and columns), the degrees of freedom equal $(r-1)(c-1)$, where r is the number of rows and c is the number of columns. In this case also, the reasoning is the same. We know the total cell frequencies of each row and the total cell frequencies of each column. These are called *marginals*. The information about marginals leaves only $(r-1)(c-1)$ cells to be determined freely.

Figure 7-1 indicates probabilities of getting the values of χ^2 for 2, 5, 10, and 15 degrees of freedom. Note that a certain portion of the curve for 5 degrees of freedom is shaded. This shaded area is 5 percent of the curve for 5 degrees of freedom. In other words,

$$\frac{\text{Area of shaded curve}}{\text{Total area of the curve}} = 5\%$$

Such calculation of the area of the part of a curve is done with the help of integral calculus. Fortunately, statisticians have calculated the areas of the parts of such curves for different values of χ^2 with different degrees of freedom. Table A-4 (Appendix) is a typical listing of χ^2 distribution. For getting familiar with this table, locate the cell that gives the value of χ^2 as 11.07. The column identifies the probability as .05 and the row identifies the degrees of freedom as 5. We show this in Figure 7-1 also. In Figure 7-1, look at the value of χ^2 given as 11.07 and the shaded area of the curve (for 5 degrees of freedom) to the right of 11.07. In other words, the shaded area of the curve represents the probability shown in Table A-4, given 5 degrees of freedom and a χ^2 value of 11.07. What all this means is that the probability of getting a value of χ^2 equal to or greater than 11.07 is .05, provided the sampling is random.

The four curves given in Figure 7-1 indicate that as the value of χ^2 increases, the area of the curve to the right decreases. This means that the probability of getting larger values of χ^2 is smaller than the probability of getting smaller values of χ^2. We can also say that, since the probability of getting larger values of χ^2 is smaller, such values of χ^2 are less likely to occur as a result of sampling fluctuations. We explain later in this chapter that larger values of χ^2 make us reject our null hypotheses. Such larger values of χ^2 are called *significant*.

Perhaps you have noticed by this time that the values of χ^2 are always positive and that the curves (as in Figure 7-1) are skewed to the right. However, as the number of degrees of freedom increases, this skewness decreases so much that the curve begins to look more like a normal curve. In fact, if we have a situation with more than 30 degrees of freedom, we can make use of normal distribution.[1]

Assumptions of the Chi-Square Distribution

The χ^2 distribution is based on certain assumptions. These assumptions are as follows: normally distributed independent variables, random sampling, a large sample size, nominal scale measurement of the variable or the variables considered, and a limitation on the minimum number required of the expected frequencies in each cell.

The assumption regarding normally distributed independent variables is the most fundamental of all the assumptions. As mentioned in the introduction to this section, we assume that we have k normally distributed independent variables, $X_1, X_2, ..., X_k$, each with zero mean and unit standard deviation, and that the sum of the squares of these variables has a χ^2 distribution with k degrees of freedom.

Random sampling does not require much elaboration here, since this was discussed in Chapter 5. We want to emphasize, however, that the discussion of the probabilities of the different values of χ^2 requires this assumption of normally distributed independent variables.

Sample size is considered sufficiently large for the purpose of χ^2 if it is at least 50. A large sample size makes the χ^2 approximation possible.

The assumption regarding the nominal scale measurement of variables is mentioned because χ^2 is best suited for analyzing such data. Although χ^2 may be used for the ordinal and the interval data, it is better to use some other model for them.

The last assumption pertains to the minimum number required of the expected frequencies in each cell. This minimum number must be equal to or greater than 5. The method for approximating χ^2 assumes that the expected frequencies in each cell be equal to or greater than 5. Later in this chapter we discuss a method for dealing with cases when the expected frequencies in one or more of the cells are less than 5.

CHI-SQUARE AS A TEST

Goodness-of-Fit-Test

The first test of χ^2 to be discussed is called the goodness-of-fit test and is performed on one variable. The main purpose of this test is to decide whether the observed frequencies of a variable are significantly different from its expected frequencies. The null hypothesis of this test is that the observed frequencies do not differ significantly from the expected frequencies. If the computed value of χ^2 is equal to or greater than some value (in Table A-4) specified by the appropriate degrees of freedom and significance level (usually .05), then we reject the null hypothesis; otherwise, we accept the null hypothesis.

We now present two examples of the use of the goodness-of-fit test.

Example 7-1

For the first example, use the data presented in Table 7-1. Using the formula (7-2), calculate χ^2 for Table 7-1 as 6.1. In Table A-4 (Appendix) the value of χ^2 for 2 degrees of freedom is 5.99 for $P = .05$. Any value of $\chi^2 \geqslant 5.99$ (as in the present case) is significant, so reject the null hypothesis. This means that the observed data are significantly different from the expected data. In other words, the assembly members did not vote as they were expected to.

Example 7-2

For the second example, consider the data presented in Table 7-2, which relate to the occupations of 100 members of a legislative assem-

Table   7-2

Observed and Expected Occupations of Assembly Members

	Law	Business	Agriculture	Journalism	Teaching	Other
Observed	45	15	20	10	5	5
Expected	50	20	15	5	5	5

bly of size 100. Note that the expected frequencies indicate the average frequencies based on the past experience. Calculate χ^2 as follows:

$$\chi^2 = \sum_{i=1}^{6} \frac{(o_i - e_i)^2}{e_i}$$

$$= \frac{(45-50)^2}{50} + \frac{(15-20)^2}{20} + \frac{(20-15)^2}{15} + \frac{(10-5)^2}{5}$$

$$+ \frac{(5-5)^2}{5} + \frac{(5-5)^2}{5}$$

$$= \frac{25}{50} + \frac{25}{20} + \frac{25}{15} + \frac{25}{5} + 0 + 0 = 8.4$$

In this case you have 5 degrees of freedom, and in Table A-4 (Appendix) the value of χ^2 for .05 significance level and 5 degrees of freedom is given as 11.07. This means that the value of $\chi^2 = 8.4$ is not significant, so accept the null hypothesis. In other words, the observed distribution of occupations among assembly members is not significantly different from what you expected.

Test of Independence

The second test of χ^2 to be considered is called the test of independence. By this test we find out whether two variables are independent of each other. Often a third category of test is mentioned, the test of *homogeneity* (see Yamane, 1967, p. 636). However, the test of independence and the test of homogeneity are essentially the same and can be treated together as shown by Table 7-3.

We can use the χ^2 test of independence to find whether the two variables in Table 7-3, type of town and voting, are independent. The null hypothesis in this case is that voting and the type of town are independent. An alternative expression of this hypothesis is that the samples of two towns came from the same population; that is, with respect to voting behavior, the two towns are homogeneous. This is where we derive the

Table 7-3

Type of Town and Voting

Voting	Type of town		Total
	Town A	Town B	
Voted	30 (25)	20 (25)	50
Did not vote	20 (25)	30 (25)	50
Total	50	50	100

name "test of homogeneity." When the null hypothesis is expressed in this manner the implication is that there is no relationship between the type of town and voting.

In a contingency table the expected frequencies are easily calculated. If the two variables in Table 7-3 are unrelated, which is our null hypothesis, then in the upper left-hand cell the expected frequencies would be $(50 \times 50)/100 = 25$. If voting behavior and town are independent, then we would expect the number of voters to be distributed between towns in proportion to the proportion of the sample drawn from each town. To find the expected frequency of voters in town A, we take the proportion of voters in the whole sample (50/100), multiply it by the proportion of the sample taken from town A (50/100), and multiply this product by the total sample size (100). We get $(50/100) \cdot (50/100) \cdot 100$, which becomes $(50 \cdot 50)/100$ through cancellation. Thus the expected frequencies in this cell are 25. Half the sample came from town A; therefore, half the voters would be expected to be in that sample. The expected frequencies for the other cells are calculated similarly.

The standard procedure of calculating expected frequencies is to find the product of the marginal totals corresponding to a particular cell and then, dividing by n, the total number of observations. Thus, the expected frequencies are the same in each of the remaining three cells in Table 7-3 (that is, 25). The expected frequencies are written in parentheses next to the observed frequencies in Table 7-3 as well as in the subsequent tables.

The calculation of the expected frequencies can be understood also with the help of the rules of probability and expectation. Let us denote the row 1 by r_1, column 1 by c_1, and the cell containing both (upper left-hand cell) by a. Then

$$P(a) = P(r_1 \cap c_1) = P(r_1) P(c_1)$$

since under the null hypothesis rows and columns are independent, and

$$P(a) = \frac{\sum r_1}{n} \times \frac{\sum c_1}{n} = \frac{50}{100} \times \frac{50}{100} = \frac{1}{4}$$

Therefore,

$$E(a) = P(a) \times n = \tfrac{1}{4} \times 100 = 25$$

The expected frequencies of the other cells can be calculated using the same rules of probability and expectation.

Example 7–3

Now calculate χ^2 for the data of Table 7-3.

$$\chi^2 = \sum \frac{(o_i - e_i)^2}{e_i}$$

$$= \frac{(30-25)^2}{25} + \frac{(20-25)^2}{25} + \frac{(20-25)^2}{25} + \frac{(30-25)^2}{25}$$

$$= \frac{25}{25} + \frac{25}{25} + \frac{25}{25} + \frac{25}{25} = 4$$

Since $\chi^2 = 4$ for 1 degree of freedom $[(r-1)(c-1) = 1]$ is significant at .05 level, so reject the null hypothesis that there is no relationship between type of town and voting or that the samples of town A and town B came from the same population.

Yates' Continuity Correction

F. Yates showed that in cases with only one degree of freedom, the χ^2 approximation is improved by using the following formula:

$$(7\text{-}3) \qquad \chi^2 = \sum_{i=1}^{k} \frac{(|o_i - e_i| - 0.5)^2}{e_i}$$

The obvious result of this correction is to make χ^2 smaller; thus the null hypothesis is less likely to be rejected. We can verify this by repeating Example 7-3, but using formula (7-3) to recalculate χ^2:

$$\chi^2 = \sum \frac{(|o_i - e_i| - 0.5)^2}{e_i}$$

$$= \frac{(4.5)^2 + (4.5)^2 + (4.5)^2 + (4.5)^2}{25} = 3.2$$

This value of χ^2 for 1 degree of freedom is not significant at .05 level, so formula (7-3) leads us to accept the null hypothesis.

However, if the sample is quite large or if the expected frequencies are quite large, Yates' continuity correction does not have much effect on the value of χ^2.

Tables 7-4 and 7-5 contain the data for two more examples that show further uses of χ^2.

Table   7-4

Membership in the Legislature and Age
Membership in the Legislature

Age	Lower House	Upper House	Total
Below 30	10 (8)	0 (2)	10
31–40	40 (40)	10 (10)	50
41–50	150 (144)	30 (36)	180
51+	200 (208)	60 (52)	260
Total	400	100	500

Table   7-5

Party Identification and Education

Education	Party identification			Total
	Democrat	Republican	Independent	
Less than high school	30 (23.7)	20 (22.1)	10 (14.2)	60
High school	25 (23.7)	20 (22.1)	15 (14.2)	60
College	20 (27.6)	30 (25.8)	20 (16.6)	70
Total	75	70	45	190

Table 7-4 contains data on the number of legislators in the lower or the upper house of a legislature and their ages. In Table 7-5 the data relate to party identification and education. The degrees of freedom for Tables 7-4 and 7-5 are, using the formula $(r-1)(c-1)$, 3 and 4, respectively.

Let us derive an alternative method for calculating χ^2:

$$\chi^2 = \sum \frac{(o_i - e_i)^2}{e_i} = \sum \frac{o_i^2 + e_i^2 - 2o_i e_i}{e_i}$$

$$= \sum \left(\frac{o_i^2}{e_i} + e_i - 2o_i \right) = \sum \frac{o_i^2}{e_i} + \sum e_i - 2\sum o_i$$

and, since $\sum e_i = n$ and $\sum o_i = n$,

(7-4) $$\chi^2 = \sum \frac{o_i^2}{e_i} + n - 2n$$

$$= \sum \frac{o_i^2}{e_i} - n$$

χ^2 calculated in either manner is the same. Which formula to use depends on the data; the main consideration should be to reduce the tediousness of computation.

Example 7–4

Now calculate χ^2 by formula (7-4). For the data in Table 7-4,

$$\chi^2 = \sum \frac{o_i^2}{e_i} - n$$

$$= 12.5 + 0.0 + 40.0 + 10.0 + 156.3$$

$$+ 25.0 + 192.3 + 69.2 - n$$

$$= 505.3 - 500 = 5.3$$

For 3 degrees of freedom, $\chi^2 = 5.3$ is not significant at .05 level, so accept the null hypothesis that the membership in the lower or the upper house and age are independent.

Example 7–5

For the data in Table 7-5,

$$\chi^2 = \sum \frac{o_i^2}{e_i} - n$$

$$= 18.1 + 38.0 + 7.0 + 18.1 + 26.4 + 15.8$$

$$+ 34.9 + 14.5 + 24.1 - n$$

$$= 196.9 - 190 = 6.9$$

For 4 degrees of freedom, $\chi^2 = 6.9$ is not significant at .05 level, so in this case also accept the null hypothesis that party identification and education are independent.

Combination of Cells

We mentioned in the discussion of the assumptions of the χ^2 distribution that the expected frequencies in each cell must be at least 5. If we have less than 5 expected frequencies in one or more cells (and we have more than 1 degree of freedom), we should combine two or more cells so that no cell contains less than 5 expected frequencies.[2] This can be done in the goodness-of-fit test as well as in the test of independence. For illustration, consider the data in Table 7-6. The expected frequencies in two of the cells in Table 7-6 are less than 5, so we combine cells and make Table 7-7.

Table   7-6

College Year and Participation in Peaceful Demonstrations

	College year				
Participation in peaceful demonstrations	Freshman	Sophomore	Junior	Senior	Total
Regular	2 (4.4)	3 (4.4)	7 (5.6)	9 (6.6)	21
Occasional	7 (9.1)	9 (9.1)	11 (11.3)	16 (13.6)	43
Never	11 (6.5)	8 (6.5)	7 (8.2)	5 (9.8)	31
Total	20	20	25	30	95

Table   7-7

College Year and Participation in Peaceful Demonstrations

	College year			
Participation in peaceful demonstrations	Freshman and sophomore	Junior	Senior	Total
Regular	5 (8.8)	7 (5.6)	9 (6.6)	21
Occasional	16 (18.2)	11 (11.2)	16 (13.6)	43
Never	19 (13.0)	7 (8.2)	5 (9.8)	31
Total	40	25	30	95

Example 7–6

Now calculate χ^2, which is

$$\sum \frac{o_i^2}{e_i} - n = 2.8 + 8.8 + 12.3 + 14.1 + 10.8 + 18.8$$

$$+ 27.8 + 6.0 + 2.6 - 95$$

$$= 118.1 - 95 = 23.1$$

For 4 degrees of freedom, $\chi^2 = 23.1$ is significant at .05 level, so reject the null hypothesis that college year and participation in peaceful demonstrations are unrelated.

Pooling Data or Adding χ^2

If we have similar data in different tables, we can pool them and form a single table. Also in such cases, we can add the different values of χ^2.

Example 7-7

Tables 7-8, 7-9, and 7-10 contain similar data. By pooling the data of these tables, form Table 7-11.

Table   7-8

Party Identification and Voting

	Party identification		
Voting	Democrat	Republican	Total
Voted	30 (35)	40 (35)	70
Did not vote	20 (15)	10 (15)	30
Total	50	50	100

Table   7-9

Party Identification and Voting

	Party identification		
Voting	Democrat	Republican	Total
Voted	35 (37.5)	40 (37.5)	75
Did not vote	15 (12.5)	10 (12.5)	25
Total	50	50	100

Table 7-10

Party Identification and Voting

Voting	Party identification		Total
	Democrat	Republican	
Voted	25 (30)	35 (30)	60
Did not vote	25 (20)	15 (20)	40
Total	50	50	100

Table 7-11

Party Identification and Voting

Voting	Party identification		Total
	Democrat	Republican	
Voted	90 (102.5)	115 (102.5)	205
Did not vote	60 (47.5)	35 (47.5)	95
Total	150	150	300

For Tables 7-8, 7-9, 7-10, and 7-11 χ^2 is 4.0, 0.8, 3.4, and 8.8, respectively, using Yates' continuity correction, formula (7-3). Consider the first three tables: χ^2 is significant at .05 level only in one case, Table 7-8. However, when the data are pooled in Table 7-11, $\chi^2 = 8.8$ becomes significant at .05 level. Significant χ^2 in these examples means that party identification and voting are related.

When you add the different values of χ^2, you also add the degrees of freedom. Yates' continuity correction is not used in this case. If you do not use the correction, the χ^2 for Tables 7-8, 7-9, and 7-10 is 4.8, 1.4, and 4.2, respectively. The added χ^2 is 10.4 and the added degrees of freedom are 3. At .05 significance level, this value of χ^2 is significant.

SUMMARY

Chi-square was presented in this chapter as a distribution and as a test. It is the χ^2 as a test that is often used. The essential point to remember, however, is that the χ^2 tests are based on the χ^2 distribution. In presenting the χ^2 distribution its importance in the population as well as in samples was explained. Since we generally deal with samples, the importance of the χ^2 distribution in samples was emphasized. In using the χ^2 distribution in samples, Pearson's contribution, expressed by formula (7-1), that when n is very large, a multinomial distribution approaches a χ^2 distribution was explained. We made the following assumptions about the χ^2 distribution:

1. Normally distributed independent variables
2. Random sampling
3. A large sample size
4. Nominal scale measurement of the variable or variables considered
5. A limitation on the minimum number required of the expected frequencies in each cell.

Two tests of χ^2 were presented: goodness-of-fit test and test of independence. The goodness-of-fit test is used to examine the observed frequencies of a variable to determine whether they differ significantly from its expected frequencies. The test of independence shows whether two variables are independent. Often a third test of χ^2, the test of homogeneity, is mentioned. It was argued that the test of homogeneity is only an alternative way of expressing the test of independence. The use of the χ^2 tests was illustrated with several examples. In illustrating the use of these tests, Yates' continuity correction, combination of cells, pooling data, and adding χ^2 were also explained.

NOTES   Chapter 7

1. If there are more than 30 degrees of freedom, $\sqrt{2\chi^2}$ has approximately normal distribution with mean $\sqrt{2v-1}$ and unit standard deviation.

2. When a sample is small in a 2 by 2 table and the expected frequencies in one or more of the cells are less than 5, another test, called Fisher's exact test, can be used. (Obviously, we cannot combine cells in a 2 by 2 table.) Fisher's exact test has a limited use in the study of politics. For a discussion of this test see Anderson and Zelditch (1968).

REFERENCES   Chapter 7

Anderson, T. A., and Morris Zelditch, Jr. *A Basic Course in Statistics.* New York: Holt, Rinehart and Winston, 1968, pp. 264–269.

Graybill, F. A., and A. M. Mood. *Introduction to the Theory of Statistics.* New York: McGraw-Hill, 1950.

Maxwell, A. E. *Analyzing Qualitative Data.* London: Methuen, 1961.

Yamane, T. *Statistics: An Introductory Analysis.* New York: Harper & Row, 1967.

Yule, G. U., and M. G. Kendall. *An Introduction to the Theory of Statistics.* London: Griffin, 1950.

Chapter 8

TESTS OF THE ASSOCIATION
OF DISTRIBUTIONS

In this chapter we introduce a new distribution function, which is, of course, a function of distributions already presented. This distribution, the F distribution, is very valuable in testing hypotheses in a variety of statistical models. We also introduce sets of statistical models to which this new distribution is fruitfully applied. As your knowledge of statistics broadens, you will discover many other uses for the F distribution. In Chapter 9, we show the uses of the F distribution in testing hypotheses about regression models.

The first new model we introduce is the correlation coefficient, a statistic that is used to measure the degree of association of two or more distributions. The second model, analysis of variance, is used for two purposes: to test hypotheses about the means of a number of samples simultaneously, or as a measure of the association of two variables. In the latter case, analysis of variance may be used as a substitute for correlation when some of the rather strict assumptions of correlation are not met.

Thus far we have dealt with statistical tests that tested hypotheses definitively: Either the results were significant or they were not. The correlation coefficient and analysis of variance add a new tool to your bag of statistical tests. With these techniques you can measure the *degree* of relationship between two or more distributions. Instead of focusing primarily on the means of distributions, as in hypothesis testing, these techniques focus on the variances of distributions. The correlation coefficient is a measure of how much two or more normally distributed variables vary. Analysis of variance tells how much of the variance of a normally distributed variable can be accounted for by a variable that is measured only by a nominal scale. We begin with a discussion of the F ratio and show its utility in testing hypotheses about the equality of variances. Next we explain the correlation coefficient and lead into a discussion of analysis of variance where the F ratio is applied to these two sets of statistical models.

THE F RATIO

The F ratio was developed by Fisher (1948) whose initial it bears, as a versatile distribution that enables tests of a number of hypotheses concerning sample variance.

In Chapter 7 it was stated that the χ^2 distribution is a determinant distribution with one parameter, degrees of freedom; that is, the statistic χ^2 has a density function that can be found by knowing only its degrees of freedom. The F ratio is a simple extension of the χ^2 distribution: It is the ratio of two independent χ^2 values divided by their respective degrees of freedom. Since F is a function of two determinant distributions, it, too, is determinant. As you might expect, the likelihood of any value of F is determinable if we know only two parameters: the degrees of freedom of the numerator χ^2 value and the degrees of freedom of the denominator χ^2 value. The density function of F is given by

(8-1)

$$\frac{((d_1 + d_2 - 2)/2)!}{((d_1 - 2)/2)!((d_2 - 2)/2)!} \left(\frac{d_1}{d_2}\right)^{d/2} \frac{F^{(d_1 - 2)/2}}{\left(1 + \frac{d_1 F}{d_2}\right)^{(d_1 + d_2)/2}}$$

where d_1 is the degrees of freedom of the numerator χ^2 value, and d_2 is the degrees of freedom of the denominator χ^2 value.

The F ratio is generally denoted $F_{(n_1 - 1)(n_2 - 1)}$, where $(n_1 - 1)$ is the degrees of freedom of the numerator and $(n_2 - 1)$ is the degrees of freedom of the denominator.

$$F_{(n_1 - 1)(n_2 - 1)} = \frac{((\sum X_1 - \overline{X}_1)/\sigma)^2/(n_1 - 1)}{((\sum X_2 - \overline{X}_2)/\sigma)^2/(n_2 - 1)}$$

where X_1 consists of n_1 observations and X_2 consists of n_2 observations. Note that σ is the true population standard deviation. The null hypothesis of the F test is that X_1 and X_2 are from the same population; thus, σ cancels out. The cancellation makes the F ratio a more familiar statistic.

(8-2) $$F_{(n_1 - 1), (n_2 - 1)} = \frac{\sum (X_1 - \overline{X}_1)^2/(n_1 - 1)}{\sum (X_2 - \overline{X}_2)^2/(n_2 - 1)}$$

The F ratio turns out to be the ratio of two unbiased estimators of σ^2. Indeed, one of the commonly used names of the F ratio is the "variance ratio." Using this distribution, we can test hypotheses about the variance of two samples. The value of F runs from zero to infinity, and it is possible to perform two-tail tests on variance ratios. Practically speaking, most tests are one-tail tests, and they are designed to discover if the difference between two estimates of σ^2 are significantly large (that is, not due to chance). Formally stated, the null hypothesis of a test for the equality of variances is

H_o: $\sigma_1^2 = \sigma_2^2$. If F is larger than could be expected by chance, given $(n_1 - 1)$ and $(n_2 - 1)$ degrees of freedom, we reject the null hypothesis. In setting up the F ratio to test for the equality of variance, the larger σ^2 is always used as the numerator; thus, $F \geqslant 1.0$.

Example 8–1

In Example 6-6, you tested a hypothesis that compared the means of two samples of drop-off in rates of voter participation for different ballot positions in multiple candidate races. The two estimates of σ^2 presented were $\sigma_1^2 = .0053824$ and $\sigma_2^2 = .00131044$, $n_1 - 1 = 200$, $n_2 - 1 = 200$, expressed as

$$\frac{\sigma_1^2}{\sigma_2^2} = \frac{.0053824}{.00131044} = 4.107$$

Refer to Table A-5, "F Distribution," in the Appendix and find the appropriate column for the degrees of freedom in the numerator (200) and the appropriate row for the degrees of freedom in the denominator (200). The lightface type indicates 1.26 and the boldface type indicates 1.39. These numbers are the critical values of F for the .05 and .01 level of significance, respectively. The 1.26 in light type means that for $n_1 - 1 = 200$ and $n_2 - 1 = 200$, $P(F \geqslant 1.26) = .05$. That is, the probability of getting a value of F greater than or equal to 1.26 is .05. The value 1.39 means $P(F \geqslant 1.39) = .01$. Clearly, the σ_1^2 is significantly larger than σ_2^2.

As we stated earlier, two-tail tests using the F ratio are not commonly used, but the method for discovering the .05 and .01 critical values of F in the left tail is not complicated. A two-step process is required.

1. Invert the normal F ratio (that is, put the large σ^2 as the denominator and the smaller σ^2 as the numerator).
2. Look up the critical value of F corresponding to the new arrangement of degrees of freedom. The left-tail critical value of F is the reciprocal of the value found in Table A-5.[1]

The method of finding left-tail critical values is illustrated in Example 8-2 as an exercise. Note that left-tail points are irrelevant when the F ratio is used to test for the equality of variances, since $F \geqslant 1$. Left-tail points are useful, however, in other connections. As you will see later in this chapter, the values of F are not restricted to $F \geqslant 1$ in tests on the correlation coefficient or on some tests on the analysis of variance model.

Example 8-2

You want to compare the role of the United States in foreign trade in different developing areas. (Data from Rai, 1969.) Specifically, you want to see if the proportion of trade of 16 Latin American countries with the United States is significantly different from that of 44 Asian, African, and Middle Eastern countries with the United States. This proportion of trade is found by adding each country's imports from and exports to the United States and dividing by the country's total imports and exports. All trade is measured in standard dollars.

Use a test for the difference in the means of the two samples. Since the samples are small, use a t-test. Therefore, it is important to know whether the variances of the two distributions are significantly different. If they are, then you must use the more tedious method of pooling the variances and estimating the degrees of freedom as shown in Chapter 6. Now construct .95 and .99 confidence intervals for F.

The null hypothesis is H_o: $\sigma_1^2 = \sigma_2^2$, where σ_1^2 is the variance of the distribution of Latin American trade with the United States and σ_2^2 is the variance of the other distribution: $\sigma_1^2 = .0220$, $\sigma_2^2 = .0096$. The critical values for F for the right-tail points, given $(n_1 - 1) = 16 - 1 = 15$ and $(n_2 - 1) = (44 - 1) = 43$, are

$$P(F \geqslant 1.93) = .05 \quad \text{and} \quad P(F \geqslant 2.55) = .01$$

You find these values by seeking the column corresponding to 15 degrees of freedom and the row corresponding to 43 degrees of freedom (this is done by interpolating between columns 14 and 16 and rows 44 and 42). For left-tail points, invert the ratio of σ_1^2 and σ_2^2 and seek the appropriate values of F. These are 2.19 for the .05 level and 3.09 for the .01 level. Next, take the inverse of these values: $1/2.19 = .4566$, $1/3.09 = .3236$. Then

$$P(F < .4566) = .05 \quad P(F < .3236) = .01$$

The .95 confidence interval for $F_{15,43}$ is given by

$$P(.4566 \leqslant F_{15,43} \leqslant 1.93) = .95$$

The .99 confidence interval for $F_{15,43}$ is given by

$$P(.3236 \leqslant F_{15,43} \leqslant 2.55) = .99$$

With these confidence intervals to guide you, calculate the F ratio of the variances of the two samples:

$$F = \frac{\sigma_1^2}{\sigma_2^2} = \frac{.0220}{.0096} = 2.2916$$

The value of F falls in the right tail between the critical values for the .05 and .01 levels of significance. You conclude that the variances are significantly different at the .05 level, but not significantly different at the .01 level.

With this basic introduction of the F ratio let us turn to an explanation of the correlation coefficient.

CORRELATION

Frequently when we discuss a relationship between variables, we say that one variable is correlated with another. What we mean is that the values of one variable are systematically related to the values of another. If it is the case that high values of one variable are associated with high values of another, then the variables are positively correlated. Alternatively, if high values of one variable are associated with low values of the other, the variables are said to be negatively correlated. When variables are uncorrelated, there is no systematic relationship among their values. The problem we face in this section is the development of a technique to measure the degree of "correlation" between variables.

Suppose we had the following set of observations for two variables, X and Y in Table 8-1. By casual observation we can see that X and Y are

Table   8-1

Observations for Two Variables

Observation	Variable X	Variable Y
1	$X_1 = -2$	$Y_1 = -3$
2	$X_2 = -1$	$Y_2 = -2$
3	$X_3 = 3$	$Y_3 = 4$
4	$X_4 = 4$	$Y_4 = 6$

positively associated, but we graph X and Y on a rectangular coordinate system in Figure 8-1 for a more careful inspection. The problem is to measure this association. Note in Figure 8-1 that the line approximating the relationship between X and Y runs from quadrant I to quadrant III, suggesting that one measure of association might be the sum of the products of X and Y, $\sum XY$. Products of coordinates in quadrants I and III are positive, and products of coordinates in quadrants II and IV are negative; thus in this example, all products would be positive and the sum would be positive. In summing products, the sum will be positive if there are more positive products than negative products. If there are more points in quadrants II and IV than in I and III, the sum will be negative. And if points

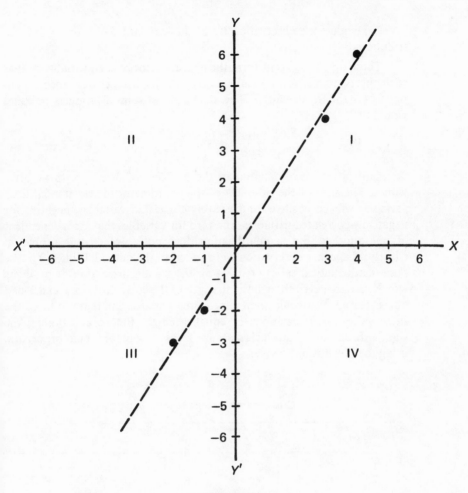

FIGURE 8-1

are evenly distributed among quadrants (that is, there is no relationship between variables) the sum will be zero.

There are two important weaknesses in the sum of products measure. First, the sum will be a function of the size of the index numbers representing the variable. Second, two variables could be positively associated but at the same time have a negative sum of products if all their values fall in quadrants II or IV. Part of the problem will be solved if both variables are measured in the same units. Fortunately, we have at hand a transformation, presented in Chapter 3, which can standardize the measurement of all variables. It is a two-step procedure:

1. Subtract the mean of the variable from each observation; that is, $(X - \mu_X)$ and $(Y - \mu_Y)$.

2. Divide each observation by σ, the standard deviation of the distribution.

These operations transform the measurement of each variable so that each observation is now measured in terms of its distance from the mean in units of standard deviation. The standardized sum-of-products measure would be

$$(8\text{-}3) \qquad \frac{\sum (X - \mu_X)(Y - \mu_Y)}{\sigma_X \sigma_Y}$$

Standardization clearly eliminates the problem of dealing with negative values. The sum of the products of the coordinates of two standardized variables will be positive for positively correlated variables, negative for negatively correlated variables, and zero for variables that are independent of one another. But standardization does not solve all our problems. Clearly, if another observation were added to the data in Table 8-2 in the same mathematical series ($Y = X + 5$), the standardized sum of products would increase, even though the strength of the correlation of X and Y had not increased. We would want a measure of association that produced the same value for associations of equal strength. Before abandoning the standardized sum-of-products measure, let us explore some of its properties, using the illustrations above.

Table 8-2

Crossproducts of Standardized Variables

Observation	X	Y	X*	Y*	X*Y*
1	$X_1 = -4$	$Y_1 = 1$	-1.34	-1.34	+1.99
2	$X_2 = -3$	$Y_2 = 2$	- .45	- .45	+ .20
3	$X_3 = -2$	$Y_3 = 3$	+ .45	+ .45	+ .20
4	$X_4 = -1$	$Y_4 = 4$	+1.34	+1.34	+1.89

$$\sum X^* Y^* = 4.28$$

$\bar{X} = -2.5 \qquad \sigma_X = 1.12$
$\bar{Y} = +2.5 \qquad \sigma_Y = 1.12$

We know that $Y = X + 5$. The denominator of (8-3) is $\sigma_X \sigma_Y$:

$$(8\text{-}4) \qquad \sigma_X^2 = \frac{\sum (X - \mu_X)^2}{N}$$

for the population. Substituting for X, that is, $(Y - 5)$, we get

$$(8\text{-}5) \qquad \sigma_X^2 = \frac{\sum [(Y - 5) - (\mu_Y - 5)]^2}{N} = \frac{\sum (Y - \mu_Y)^2}{N}$$

We have found that when X is a linear function of Y, $\sigma_X^2 = \sigma_Y^2$; thus, $\sigma_X = \sigma_Y$ and the denominator of (8-3) is $\sigma_X \sigma_Y = \sigma_X^2 = \sigma_Y^2$. Now we look at the numerator of (8-3) and substitute $(Y-5)$ for X again:

$$(8\text{-}6) \qquad \sum [(Y-5) - (\mu_Y - 5)] [Y - \mu_Y] = \sum (Y - \mu_Y)^2$$

Therefore, when X is a linear function of Y,

$$(8\text{-}7) \qquad \sum (X - \mu_X)(Y - \mu_Y) = \sum (Y - \mu_Y)^2 = \sum (X - \mu_X)^2$$

We have discovered that under these conditions the numerator of (8-3) is the numerator of the variance of X (or Y) except that when X and Y are negatively associated, (8-7) will have a negative sign. Consider the function $X = -Y$, where X is a negative linear function of Y.

$$(8\text{-}8) \qquad \sum (X - \bar{Y})(Y - \bar{Y}) = \sum [-Y - (-\bar{Y})](Y - \bar{Y})$$
$$= \sum (-1)(Y - \bar{Y})(Y - \bar{Y})$$
$$= -\sum (Y - \bar{Y})^2$$

Now we are in a position to construct a measure of correlation that meets all our objections thus far. If we multiply the numerator of (8-3) by $1/N$, we have an index that equals $+1$ if the two variables are related by a positive linear function, and -1 if the variables are related by a negative linear function. This statistic, the *correlation coefficient*, is defined for a *population* as follows:

$$(8\text{-}9) \qquad \rho = \frac{1}{N} \frac{\sum (X - \mu_X)(Y - \mu_Y)}{\sigma_X \sigma_Y}$$

It is evident that this expression is the same as

$$(8\text{-}10) \qquad \rho = \frac{E[(X - \mu_X)(Y - \mu_Y)]}{\sigma_X \sigma_Y}$$

Expression (8-10) is the formal definition of the population correlation coefficient. We can place one more restriction on ρ, which will give it some very useful properties. If we know the distributions of both X and Y, the distribution of ρ is determinate. The most convenient (and behaviorally realistic) assumption to make is that X and Y are normally distributed, and of course this assumption also enables us to test hypotheses about the statistic.

Next, we must present a method of estimating ρ, since (8-9) is the expression for the *population*. The derivation is very simple. First we must use estimates for μ and σ. If we must estimate σ_X and σ_Y, then the denominator of the estimate of these parameters will be $n-1$, where n is the sample size. The extension of our discussion above is straightforward:

$$(8\text{-}11) \qquad r = \frac{(1/(n-1)) \sum (X - \bar{X})(Y - \bar{Y})}{\hat{\sigma}_X \hat{\sigma}_Y}$$

Now this expression can be simplified because we can cancel out $1/(n-1)$ in the following calculation:

$$(8\text{-}12) \qquad r = \frac{(1/(n-1))\sum(X-\bar{X})(Y-\bar{Y})}{((1/(n-1))\sum(X-\bar{X}))^{1/2}((1/(n-1))\sum(Y-\bar{Y}))^{1/2}}$$

$$(8\text{-}13) \qquad r = \frac{\sum(X-\bar{X})(Y-\bar{Y})}{(\sum(X-\bar{X}))^{1/2}(\sum(Y-\bar{Y}))^{1/2}}$$

For the purpose of calculation, (8-13) can be simplified:

$$(8\text{-}14) \qquad r = \frac{\sum XY - n\bar{Y}\bar{X}}{((\sum X^2 - n\bar{X}^2)(\sum Y^2 - n\bar{Y}^2))^{1/2}}$$

$$= \frac{n\sum XY - \sum X \sum Y}{((n\sum X^2 - (\sum X)^2)(n\sum Y^2 - (\sum Y)^2))^{1/2}}$$

Formula (8-14) is a computationally convenient form of r.

Let us review the assumptions that underlie the correlation coefficient:

1. X and Y form a bivariate normal distribution.

2. If X and Y are related, the relationship is linear. This should be clear from the discussion of equations (8-4) through (8-8).

3. Both variables are measured by at least an interval scale.

4. X and Y are independent; this means that the null hypothesis of a test is $H_o: r_{XY} = 0$. If X and Y are not independent, then r takes on some value approaching either -1 or $+1$.

It should be emphasized that r may approach -1 or $+1$ if *any* of these four assumptions are not met. To avoid such a misinterpretation, each of the first three assumptions should be explored prior to using the statistic. Assumption (1) can easily be checked by methods outlined in Chapter 3. Assumption (2) can be checked by plotting data on a rectangular coordinate system (such a plot is called a *scatter diagram*; see Figure 8-2). The researcher should be aware of assumption (3) by observation. When assumptions (1) through (3) have been found to be true, we interpret the value of r as a measure of the independence or, positively stated, the association of X and Y. When r approaches $+1$ or -1, and assumptions (1), (2), and (3) are true, r indicates that X and Y are not independent.

If assumptions (1), (2), and (3) have been checked and found to be reasonable, what exactly does it mean to say that we are measuring the degree of association or the degree of independence of two variables? By inspecting the formulas for the correlation coefficient, either (8-12) or (8-14), we can see that the variables X and Y are treated symmetrically Therefore,

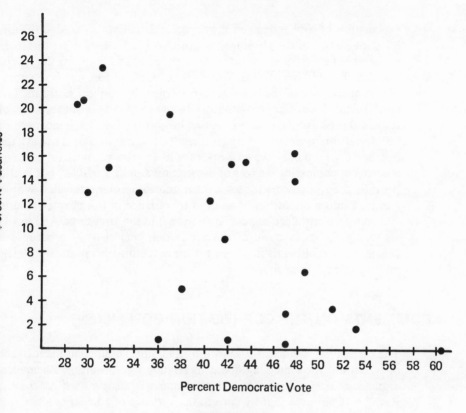

FIGURE 8-2

there is no presumption in the correlation coefficient that either is an independent or a dependent variable. Furthermore, it is difficult to find a verbal interpretation for the correlation coefficient. Standardized normal variables, $Z(X)$, tests on small samples, $t(X)$, and χ^2 can be verbally interpreted in terms of a probability distribution. Because of the ambiguity of r, it is not so useful as an absolute measure as it is as a relative measure. That is, we can compare correlation coefficients with each other, but not with some objective standard, as we can with some other statistics. The correlation coefficient permits only statements about the relative degrees of association of distributions.

If the correlation coefficient is such an elusive statistic, why are we spending valuable time trying to understand it and why is it so widely used in political science research? To defend our fellow political scientists first, we return to an argument presented in Chapter 1. Occasionally, when no explanation of a phenomenon presents itself, we must refine our perceptions of the object of study. The correlation coefficient is sometimes used as a means of searching for patterns in data. The flash of insight that comes as an explanation of a phenomenon may require extensive knowledge of how different aspects of the phenomenon are associated. Many other instances of the use of correlation coefficients rely on comparison among degrees of association to test hypotheses. These applications, we feel, justify the widespread acceptance of the correlation coefficient by political scientists. But recall further from Chapter 1 that we recommended against these uses of statistical models by the novice. How, then, do we justify the inclusion of this discussion in an elementary level text? Of course we would not ask the question if we did not have an answer for it. The statistic is useful per se as a means of comparing degrees of association among variables, but it also provides the groundwork for some other, more important statistics. We use r to lead into a discussion of analysis of variance in this chapter, and in Chapter 9 we introduce regression analysis into the discussion. And finally we justify the explanation of the correlation coefficient here because it provides a useful heuristic device for understanding bivariate and, later, multivariate relationships.

COMMENTS ON THE CORRELATION COEFFICIENT

The correlation coefficient is known by a number of different names, each of which tells us something about its relationship to other mathematical arguments in statistics. One common name is *standardized covariance*. Recall in Chapter 6 that we derived the variance of a linear combination of X and Y:

(8-15)

$$\text{Var}(X+Y) = \frac{\sum[(X+Y)-(\mu_X+\mu_Y)]^2}{N}$$

$$= \frac{\sum(X-\mu_X)^2}{N} + \frac{\sum(Y-\mu_Y)^2}{N} + \frac{2\sum[(X-\mu_X)(Y-\mu_Y)]}{N}$$

so that

(8-16) $\text{Var}(X+Y) = \text{Var}(X) + \text{Var}(Y) + 2\text{Cov}(X,Y)$

As you can see, the covariance of (X,Y) is the numerator of (8-9). The covariance is standardized by dividing it by the product of the standard deviations of X and Y. Thus, r is the standardized covariance of (X,Y):

(8-17) $\rho = \dfrac{\text{Cov}(X,Y)}{\sigma_X \sigma_Y}$

Another common name for the common correlation coefficient is the *product-moment* correlation coefficient. This name is easily understood also

Recall from Chapter 3 the definition of the kth moment about the mean of a distribution:

$$k\text{th moment} = \frac{\Sigma(X-\mu_X)^k}{N}$$

The numerator of (8-9) is $1/N$ times the product of the first moments about the mean of X and Y.

Example 8–3

Political parties in New Jersey are most thoroughly organized at the county level. This is partially the result of legal restrictions, but is due more to the availability of patronage from local government. The county committee of each party consists of one committeeman and one committeewoman from each election district in the county (this is behaviorally true, but not legally prescribed). Committee posts are filled by election at each party's primary. Given the nature of parties and elections, you would expect that there would be an association between a party's electoral strength and its ability to fill committee vacancies. We say that there is an association between these variables because we lack a clear theory that classifies the variables in a causal ordering. The problem is that if an association exists, then there are too many possible explanations. We list three:

1. Everybody likes a winner, so when one party consistently wins, people compete for formal positions in the party.

2. A party consistently wins because it is able to fill committee vacancies for exogenous reasons, and more party workers produce more votes.

3. A consistently winning party can fill vacancies with persons in patronage jobs, and the committee posts are attractive to others as routes to patronage jobs.

Any one or a combination of these explanations might in fact be accurate. For now, let us explore the association of party strength and committee vacancies. Having checked assumption (1) in the preceding section by mathematical techniques and assumption (3) by observation, now we explore assumption (2), the linearity of the relationship between X and Y. To do this, construct a scatter diagram, as in Figure 8-2.

From Figure 8-2 it is seen that there is a rough pattern to the bivariate distribution of X and Y. The relationship seems to be negative, but it is difficult to make a judgment about linearity. To try

Table 8-3

Democratic Proportion of Vote for Assembly, 1969, and Proportion of Vacancies in Democratic County Committee, 1969, by County, New Jersey.

County	Assembly vote (X)	Committee vacancies (Y)
Atlantic	.359	.011
Bergen	.387	.054
Burlington	.420	.152
Camden	.419	.013
Cape May	.321	.152
Cumberland	.372	.196
Essex	.469	.033
Gloucester	.436	.155
Hudson	.605	0
Hunterdon	.294	.205
Mercer	.511	.037
Middlesex	.487	.063
Monmouth	.419	.093
Morris	.342	.128
Ocean	.294	.206
Passaic	.472	.004
Salem	.402	.125
Somerset	.312	.236
Sussex	.478	.140
Union	.478	.163
Warren	.537	.026

to improve the "picture" of the data, standardize X and Y and present the scatter diagram (Figure 8-3) of the standardized variables. Now the pattern in the data can be seen much more clearly. The relationship seems to be roughly linear, extending from quadrant II to quadrant IV; thus it is negative, as expected. All that remains is the calculation of r to tell the degree of association. The following values are needed to calculate r:

$$\sum X = 2.191$$

$$\sum Y = 8.814$$

$$\sum X^2 = .3459$$

$$\sum Y^2 = 3.838874$$

$$\sum XY = .83663$$

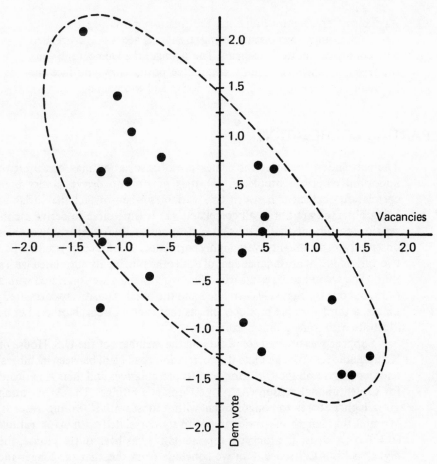

FIGURE 8-3

Then

$$r = \frac{\sum XY - \sum X \sum Y}{([n\sum X^2 - (\sum X)^2][n\sum Y^2 - (\sum Y)^2])^{\frac{1}{2}}}$$

$$= \frac{21(.83663) - (2.191)(8.814)}{([21(.345958) - (2.191)^2][21(3.838874) - (8.814)^2])^{\frac{1}{2}}}$$

$$= \frac{17.56923 - 19.311474}{((2.464637)(2.929758))^{\frac{1}{2}}}$$

$$= \frac{-1.742244}{(7.22079)^{\frac{1}{2}}}$$

$$= -.65$$

As the scatter diagram indicates, the relationship is negative, with $r = -.65$. County Democratic voting strength is negatively correlated with county committee vacancies. The stronger the Democratic vote, the fewer vacancies in county committee posts. Now you face the problem of choosing an explanation for this phenomenon.

PARTIAL CORRELATION

The correlation coefficient as a measure of association may obscure two important empirical problems. (1) It is possible to derive a very high correlation coefficient between two variables when in fact the variables being observed are not at all correlated. (2) It is possible to derive a correlation coefficient that results in a near-zero value when the variables observed are, in actuality, very highly correlated. The first case results when two variables that are independent of each other are highly correlated with a third. The second case results when the two variables are correlated with a third, but one is negatively correlated and the other is positively correlated; that is, a third variable produces effects that cancel out each other. Let us illustrate with some political examples.

Suppose we gathered some data on the members of the U.S. House of Representatives. We calculate the correlation coefficient between members' length of service in the U.S. House of Representatives and their Americans for Constitutional Action (ACA) performance ratings. The ACA rating gives higher scores to congressmen with "conservative" voting records. We find that length of service is positively correlated with ACA ratings ($r = +.6$); that is, the longer a representative has been in the House, the higher is his ACA score. Can we conclude from this that the longer the tenure of a House representative, the more conservative he becomes? No, we cannot. The real reason for this pattern follows from the fact that members with longest tenure come from the most homogeneous congressional districts, that is, one-party districts. Most one-party districts are located in the Midwest and in the southern areas of the United States, in which the voters are proud of their conservatism. Thus, if we "control" for region, the correlation disappears. This situation is called *spurious correlation* (see Simon, 1954, and Blalock, 1964).[2] Region is identified as an intervening variable.

The second case is that of a weak correlation coefficient that shows up in a simple correlation when there really is a strong association. Suppose that the correlation coefficient between income and Democratic voting is calculated for a set of election districts and the degree of association is found as $r = -.3$. The lore of political science tells us that for this pair of variables, r should be substantially stronger than $-.3$. Rather than conclude that income is not strongly related to Democratic voting, we note the fact that within our sample of election districts there are classes of blue-collar workers who have higher incomes than some classes of white-collar workers and professionals. For example, there are plumbers who make more than teachers, skilled craftsmen make more than clerks, etc. Now, if it is the case for plumbers, teachers, skilled craftsmen, clerks, etc., that job type does more than income to shape their political values, then we should control for the effects of job type on the relationship between income and Democratic voting. To explore this more complex relationship, we find the correlation coefficients for district income and percentage blue-collar workers in the district at $r = -.4$. The fact that r is relatively weak suggests that many of the districts in the sample contain highly paid blue-collar workers. Next we calculate the correlation coefficient for Democratic vote and percent blue-collar worker and find $r = .8$. Apparently, occupational class, by being negatively correlated with one variable and positively correlated with the other, is suppressing the relationship between income and Democratic voting.

The sources of the problems just illustrated are clearly not mathematical. We hypothesized on the basis of exogenous information that the simple correlation coefficients were misleading. In the first case, it does not "make sense" to conclude that tenure in a legislature would affect a legislator's political convictions. In the second case, we come to expect a strong negative relationship between income and Democratic voting. The source of the decision to pursue the simple correlation further was the judgment of the researcher and therefore a very arbitrary decision. We cannot use statistical models to make such decisions; they are useful only to test validity of decisions after they have been made.

In both cases we had difficulty interpreting a simple correlation coefficient because we hypothesized that a third variable interfered with the simple relationship. In order to find the true relationship between two variables, it is clear that we would have to control for the effects of the third variable on the relationship between the original two. A method exists for calculating the correlation coefficient between two variables while controlling for a third variable (or a fourth or more). By this method we can calculate the *partial correlation coefficient* between two variables while controlling for the effects of others. Let us turn to an intuitive explanation of partial correlation.

The statistic r measures the covariance of two distributions; that is, the degree to which two standardized distributions vary from each other. When each of the standardized values of X, (X^*) equals the respective standardized values of Y, (Y^*), the two distributions coincide perfectly and $r = 1$. When, for all i, $X_i^* = -Y_i^*$, then $r = -1$. When two distributions perfectly coincide, they have equal means and variances. When variables are standardized, as they are for r, their *means* are equal; thus, r is a measure of the closeness of the *variances* of two distributions. We say that r is a measure of how much the variance of one distribution "accounts for" the variance of another. When we control for the effect of a third variable on a simple correlation, we literally subtract the effect of the third variable on the variance of the original two variables. That is, we literally change the values of the original variables by subtracting the portion of each observation accounted for by the third variable. This transforms the two original variables into two new variables. Then we calculate a correlation coefficient that measures the degree of association between the new variables. The new correlation coefficient is the partial correlation coefficient; it is the net degree of correlation between two variables after the effects of intervening variables have been factored out.

A partial correlation is denoted as $r_{13.2}$ when we are expressing the net correlation between variables 1 and 3 and controlling for 2. Variables for which the net correlation is being expressed are identified by the pair of numbers to the left of the dot in the subscript, and control variables are identified to the right of the dot. The symbol $r_{47.135}$ indicates the partial correlation between variables 4 and 7, with control for variables 1, 3, and 5.

For the three-variable case, the formula for the partial correlation coefficient turns out to be

$$(8\text{-}18) \qquad r_{ij \cdot k} = \frac{r_{ij} - (r_{ik})(r_{jk})}{([1 - r_{ik}{}^2][1 - r_{jk}{}^2])^{1/2}}$$

This means the partial correlation between variables i and j, controlling for k.

Example 8–4

Calculate the partial correlation coefficients for the two preceding illustrations. First, calculate the partial r for ACA voting and tenure, controlling for region. For convenience, number the variables 1, 2, and 3, respectively: $r_{12} = .6$, $r_{13} = .7$, $r_{23} = .9$. Compute:

$$
\begin{aligned}
r_{12.3} &= \frac{r_{12} - r_{13} r_{23}}{((1 - r_{13}^2)(1 - r_{23}^2))^{1/2}} \\
&= \frac{-.6 - (-.7)(-.9)}{((1 - (-.7)^2)(1 - .9^2))^{1/2}} \\
&= \frac{.03}{.983} \doteq .03
\end{aligned}
$$

When you take into account the effects of the third variable on the first two, the simple correlation r_{12} "washes out."

In the second illustration, a simple correlation of $r_{12} = -.3$ for income (1) and Democratic voting (2) was found. After percent blue-collar workers was introduced, $r_{13} = -.4$ and $r_{23} = +.8$ were found.

The partial $r_{12.3}$ is found as follows:

$$r_{12.3} = \frac{-.3 - (+.4)(.9)}{([1-(-.4)^2][1-.9^2])^{\frac{1}{2}}}$$

$$= \frac{-.66}{1.02} \doteq -.65$$

By controlling for class of worker, it is possible to more than double the correlation coefficient between income and Democratic voting and find results that are intuitively satisfying.

The number of control variables determines the nomenclature partial correlation coefficients. A zero-order partial has no control variables, a first-order partial has one control variable, a second-order partial has two control variables, etc. As we stated earlier, there is no mathematical restriction on the number of variables that can be used as control variables. Calculations, however, become quite tedious as the number increases. The formula for calculating a second-order partial is

$$(8\text{-}19) \qquad r_{ij \cdot kl} = \frac{r_{ij \cdot k} - (r_{jl \cdot k})(r_{il \cdot k})}{((1 - r_{jl \cdot k}^2)(1 - r_{il \cdot k}^2))^{\frac{1}{2}}}$$

To calculate the second-order partials, one must calculate the first-order partials. Note that the sequence of calculating first-order partials is irrelevant. We could equally well partial-out variable l first as well as variable k; thus, k and l are interchangeable in (8-19). Higher-order partials are calculated in an analogous fashion. The control variables are partialled out one at a time, in any order. For example, suppose we wished to control for a fifth variable, m:

$$(8\text{-}20) \qquad r_{ij \cdot klm} = \frac{r_{ij \cdot kl} - (r_{im \cdot kl})(r_{jm \cdot kl})}{((1 - r_{jm \cdot kl}^2)(1 - r_{im \cdot kl}^2))^{\frac{1}{2}}}$$

The notation gets a little tricky, but the result is quite general. Each time a variable is factored out, the variables i and j are transformed. The correlation coefficient for the transformed variables is denoted $r_{ij \cdot kl}$. To partial out m, we simply follow the procedure for a three-variable case, with m as the control variable.

A coefficient of multiple correlation is available. It is used to calculate the degree of association between a single dependent variable and a set of independent variables. Symbolized R, the multiple correlation coefficient is most useful as a measure of the quality of a multiple regression model, and so R receives extensive treatment in Chapter 9. For the time being, let us define R as the sum of the partials between each independent variable, and the dependent variable controlling for all others. In the case of three variables, where 1 denotes the dependent variable, $R_{123} = r_{12.3} + r_{13.2}$.

A significance test is available for the statistics r and R, but it is not generally used because the correlation coefficient per se is difficult to interpret. Frequently substituted for a significance test on the correlation coefficient is the F ratio. This test is explained after the presentation of the analysis of variance model.

ANALYSIS OF VARIANCE

Analysis of variance was developed as a technique for analyzing a particular type of problem. It is widely used in agricultural research to analyze data from controlled experiments in which fields are treated or not treated according to an experimental design. The crop output of the fields (the dependent variable) is measured and then there is an attempt to discover if the variance in output can be attributed to experimental treatments. The basic idea of analysis of variance is to divide the variance of the dependent variable into a component that can be attributed to the treatments and a component that is due to random factors. It is not necessary, however, to conduct a controlled experiment in order to use analysis of variance. Consider a political example. In a sample of election districts we have reason to believe that the rate of turnout is due in part to the level of office (local, county, state) that is being elected. The distribution of turnout rates for all offices is the dependent variable, and the attribute of interest is the level of office. We attempt to account for differential turnout rates by the attribute level of office (this example is considered below). Level of office is measured in a nominal scale, and the dependent variable is measured by a ratio scale.

This problem is a simple one for analysis of variance, and the versatility of this technique enables a large variety of modifications on the basic model. Analysis of variance models are constructed according to three criteria. First is the number of qualitative variables or attributes used to subdivide the dependent variable. When the variable is subdivided by one attribute, we construct a one-way analysis of variance model; two attributes entail a two-way analysis of variance, etc. In political science research it would be quite unusual to encounter a situation where three or more attributes could be used successfully to study a variable. Therefore, only two-way analysis of variance models are presented here. The second important characteristic determining the structure of an analysis of variance model is the number of observations per cell in the matrix cross-classifying attributes and variable. In political science, both single observation and multiple observation data are likely to be encountered; thus we consider both cases here. Third analysis of variance models is classified as fixed effects models or random effects models. This distinction is useful to consider in the design of controlled experiments, and therefore is not likely to be an interesting topic for political scientists.[3] The models considered here are fixed effects models.

In political science, where the bulk of our research is *post hoc*, analysis of variance can be used to deal with two classes of problems. First, it can be used to test for the difference in means in a number of samples simultaneously. Second, analysis of variance can be used in lieu of correlation to measure the degree of association between two or more variables when only one variable meets the assumptions of correlation. Specifically, to execute an analysis of variance test, it is necessary that only the dependent variable be normally distributed and measured by an interval scale. The other variables may be distributed in any way and measured in a nominal scale. However, the dependent variable must be normally distributed for each value or category of the second variable.

Let us turn now to analysis of variance in the two-variable case, called *one-way* analysis of variance. We explain the model by illustration of the preceding political problem. We wish to account for the fact that voters participate in some elections but not in others. One possible argument is that voter participation is directly related to the visibility of the office being filled. The more visible an office, the easier it is for a voter to make a choice. We find participation rates for 11 election districts in one municipality for municipal, county, and state elections. Our theory would hold that participation rates increase in the order in which the offices are listed. The rate of participation is measured by the ratio of the actual number of votes cast to the number of voters who come to the polls. The data are presented in Table 8-4.

Table 8-4

Voter Participation Rates by Level of Office for Eleven Election Districts

District	State (X_1)	County (X_2)	Municipal (X_3)
1	.962	.955	.932
2	.956	.938	.913
3	.951	.947	.924
4	.965	.938	.911
5	.965	.955	.928
6	.956	.923	.919
7	.942	.944	.919
8	.954	.951	.924
9	.961	.935	.919
10	.969	.968	.940
11	.975	.934	.940
	$\sum X_1 = 10.556$	$\sum X_2 = 10.388$	$\sum X_3 = 10.169$
	$\sum X_1^2 = 10.130754$	$\sum X_2^2 = 9.811618$	$\sum X_3^2 = 9.401733$
	$\bar{X}_1 = .9496363$	$\bar{X}_2 = .9443636$	$\bar{X}_3 = .9244545$
	$S_1^2 = .0008326$	$S_2^2 = .0015686$	$S_3^2 = .0009548$

First we look at analysis of variance as a method for testing hypotheses about the means of samples. The grand mean $(\overline{\overline{X}})$ of the variable X (that is, variable X_1, variable X_2, and variable X_3) is given as

(8-21)

$$\overline{\overline{X}} = \frac{\sum\limits_{i=1}^{n}\sum\limits_{j=1}^{3} X_{ij}}{\sum\limits_{j=1}^{3} m_j} = \frac{10.556 + 10.16 + 10.388}{11 + 11 + 11} = .942818$$

where there are ($m = 11$) observations per group. The unbiased estimate of the variance of X can be found with the weighted average technique presented in Chapter 6. We combine the three bits of information we have about σ^2 from the three subsamples of X. This can be done because the three estimates are assumed to come from the same population (that is, null hypothesis).

(8-22)

$$\frac{m_1 S_1^2 + m_2 S_2^2 + m_3 S_3^2}{m_1 + m_2 + m_3 - 3}$$

$$\hat{\sigma}^2 = \frac{11(.0008326) + 11(.009548) + 11(.0018686)}{11 + 11 + 11 - 3}$$

$$= .0012305$$

This estimate is called the *within-group variance* because it relies totally on information from within each subsample.

If we assume that the samples were drawn from the same population, then $\mu_1 = \mu_2 = \mu_3$. This is the null hypothesis of the test for the difference in means, $H_o: \mu_1 = \mu_2 = \mu_3$. Of course we use $\overline{X}_1$, $\overline{X}_2$, and $\overline{X}_3$ as estimates of these population parameters. Now, if the null hypothesis is true, an alternative method for estimating σ^2 exists, based on the Central Limit theorem. Recall that the Central Limit theorem tells us that an unbiased estimate of the variance of a distribution of sample means is σ^2/n. If μ_1, μ_2, and μ_3 are drawn from the same population, we can use this result to construct an alternative method for estimating the variance. We know that

$$\sigma^2 = n\sigma_{\overline{X}}^2$$

and we have an estimate of $\sigma_{\overline{X}}^2$ from each of the three samples. Therefore, we can make use of all $k = 3$ estimates by averaging them and dividing by the degrees of freedom, $k = 1$:

(8-23) $$\sigma^2 = \frac{\sum m(\overline{X}_j - \overline{\overline{X}})^2}{k-1} = \frac{m\sum(\overline{X}_j - \overline{\overline{X}})^2}{k-1}$$

or

(8-24)

$$\sigma^2 = \frac{1}{k-1} m[(\overline{X}_1 - \overline{\overline{X}})^2 + (\overline{X}_2 - \overline{\overline{X}})^2 + (\overline{X}_3 - \overline{\overline{X}})^2] = \frac{1}{2}.0068475$$

so that

$$\hat{\sigma}^2 = .003423$$

If the null hypothesis is true, then the second method of estimating σ^2 will produce a value close to the value produced by the first method. If the null hypothesis is false, then the second method (the between-group variance) will always produce an estimate of σ^2 that is larger than the estimate by the first method (the within-group variance). This is true because, if there is no significant difference among group means, the between-group estimate will be just another estimate of the population variance and hence equal to the within-group variance. The between-group variance produces estimates that exceed the estimates of the within-group variance as the distances between the subgroup means increase.

Now a question arises: How do we test the null hypothesis? Well, since the between-group variance is always larger than the within-group variance, we can construct a variance ratio of between-group to within-group and execute an F test:

$$(8\text{-}25) \qquad F = \frac{\left(m\sum_j (\bar{X}_j - \bar{X})^2\right)\Big/(k-1)}{\left(\sum_i \sum_j (X_{ij} - \bar{X}_j)^2\right)\Big/(k(m-1))}$$

Using the estimate produced in (8-24), we get

$$F = \frac{.003423}{.0012305} = 2.7817$$

The critical values of $F_{2,30}$ are

$$P(F_{2,30} > 3.32) = .05$$

$$P(F_{2,30} > 5.39) = .01$$

Given $F = 2.78$, we cannot reject the null hypothesis that $\mu_1 = \mu_2 = \mu_3$. Should we then conclude that level of office is not related to rate of voter participation? Perhaps not. In this example we defined level of office by size of constituency and we assumed that the larger the constituency, the more important the office to voters. We think that the data reasonably represent voter participation rates, but the sample is probably too small to account for the magnitude of the differences in turnout rates. Rather than abandon an attempt to explain voter participation by level of office, we would choose a larger sample of election districts. Then, perhaps, the analysis of variance model would produce significant results.

The second important use of analysis of variance is to tell us how much we can learn about the total distribution of the dependent variable, given only the subgroups into which we have divided it. In the illustration we have been using, analysis of variance will tell us how much we can know abo٭ the distribution of all participation, X_{11} through X_{33}, by finding only t٭ subgroup or category in which the individual observations fall. To do th٭ we must break down the total variance

$$\frac{\sum\sum(X_{ij}-\overline{X})^2}{n-1}$$

into its component parts. For each observation of X_{ij}, the following equali٭ holds:

(8-26) $(X_{ij}-\overline{X}) = (X_{ij}-\overline{X}_j) + (\overline{X}_j-\overline{X})$

Verbally, this means that the distance between any observation and t٭ grand mean is equal to the sum of two components: (1) the distance betwee٭ the observation and the mean of its group, and (2) the distance between t٭ mean of the group and the grand mean. By summing and squaring each ٭ these terms for the whole sample, we get

(8-27) $\underset{\substack{\text{total sum of squares}\\\text{(SST)}}}{\sum_i\sum_j(X_{ij}-\overline{X})^2} = \underset{\substack{\text{within-group sum}\\\text{of squares}\\\text{(SSW)}}}{\sum_i\sum_j(X_{ij}-\overline{X}_j)^2} + \underset{\substack{\text{between-group sum}\\\text{of squares}\\\text{(SSB)}}}{\sum_i\sum_j(X_j-\overline{X})^2}$

We can readily find SSW = .003356 from (8-24). From (8-27) we fin٭ SSB = .006847, and we can then calculate SST:

(8-28) $\text{SST} = \sum\sum X_{ij}^2 - \frac{(\sum\sum X_{ij})^2}{n}$

$$= 29.344105 - \frac{(31.113)^2}{33} = .010203$$

The total sample $mk = n = 33$. We can see that (8-26) holds:

.010203 = .003356 + .006847
(SST)   (SSW)   (SSB)

Now each of these terms can be legitimately used as the numerator in a٭ estimate of the population variance. The denominators, however, var٭ greatly. The total sum of squares can be used if we treat the three subsample٭ as one large sample. In this case, the denominator is $n-1$, the degrees ٭ freedom. The SSW term can be used in the weighted average formula an٭ the degrees of freedom is $n-k$, where k is the number of samples (sub٭ groups). And the final term, SSB, can be used when the denominator ٭ $k-1$.

We have divided the total variance into two separate parts: SST/$(n-1$ has been subdivided into SSW/$(n-k)$ and SSB/$(k-1)$. As stated in the pre٭

vious illustration, if $\mu_1 = \mu_2 = \mu_3$, then the value $SSW/(n-k)$ will be close to the value of $SSB/(k-1)$. Suppose we look at the data from a different angle. Suppose we wanted to find a set of subgroups for X which helped account for the distribution of X, that is, subgroups that helped predict the distribution of X. The better the set of subgroups chosen, the higher is between-group variance in relation to the within-group variance. For example, if the values of X within each subgroup were equal, all the variance of X would be accounted for by the scheme of classification. So, the relative magnitude of the between-group variance is an indicator of how much of the total variance is being accounted for with the set of subgroups chosen.

The point here is that if the null hypothesis $H_o: \mu_1 = \mu_2 = \mu_3$ is rejected, we are also concluding that the set of subgroups accounts for a significant amount of the variance of the dependent variable. The ratio of the between-group sum of squares to the total sum of squares is a measure of how successful the particular scheme of classification is. This is called the *amount of variance* accounted for by the independent variable. In the preceding illustration, $SSB/SST = .006847/.010203 = .67$. But, of course, we established that this was not significant. If this ratio were higher, then the numerator of the F ratio (8-23) would have been higher and perhaps F would have been significant.

Now we can show a relationship among the F ratio, the correlation coefficient, and analysis of variance. In analysis of variance we have identified the ratio of the between-group variance to the total variance as the "variance accounted for" by a particular set of subgroupings. We decided whether this "variance accounted for" is significant by constructing an F ratio of between-group variance to within-group variance. The square of the correlation coefficient r^2 for simple correlation and R^2 for multiple correlation is frequently identified as the percent variance accounted in an association of two or more variables, and it is analogous to the between-group sum of squares to the total sum of squares. Therefore, $1-r^2$ (or $1-R^2$) may be treated as the ratio of within-group sum of squares to total sum of squares. The ratio of r^2 (or R^2) to $1-r^2$ (or $1-R^2$) has interesting properties:

$$\frac{r^2}{1-r^2} = \frac{SSB/SST}{SSW/SST}$$

The SST term cancels out and, when we divide each term by its respective degrees of freedom, we have constructed an F ratio of

(8-29) $$\frac{r^2/(k-1)}{(1-r^2)/(n-k)}$$

which is distributed $F_{(k-1),(n-k)}$, where k is the number of variables making up $r(R)$ and n is the sample size. Using the F ratio to test hypotheses about $r(R)$ should provide no difficulties.

Example 8–5

In Example 8-4 the correlation coefficient between percent Democratic county committee vacancies and percent Democratic vote in 1969 was calculated as $r = -.6484$. Therefore, $r^2 = (-.6484)^2 = .4204$. The degrees of freedom of the numerator is $k - 1$, where k is the number of variables. The degrees of freedom of the denominator is $n - k = 20 - 2 = 18$. The appropriate F ratio is

$$F = \frac{.4204/(2-1)}{.5796/(20-2)} = \frac{.4204}{.0305} = 13.8$$

In Table A-5 (Appendix) the critical value of $F_{1,19}$ is

$$P(F_{1,19} \geq 8.18) = .01$$

The conclusion is that the relationship in the data between committee vacancies and party strength is significant at the .01 level; that is, there is less than 1 chance in 100 that the pattern is due to chance.

TWO-WAY ANALYSIS OF VARIANCE, SINGLE OBSERVATIOI

In our consideration of two-way analysis of variance models, we shall b concerned only with uses of the models as measures of the association (distributions. The single observation-per-cell model assumes that th dependent variable is normally distributed within each subcategory of eac of the independent variables. Further, the model assumes that the tw independent variables are independent of each other.

Table 8-5 presents data from a six-candidate contest for local electior

Table 8-5

Six-Candidate Contest

Ballot position	Republican	Independent	Democrat	$\sum X_i$	$\bar{X}_i$
1	51	44	54	149	49.7
2	48	46	52	146	48.7
3	46	41	50	137	45.7
4	49	43	51	143	47.7
5	47	42	49	138	46.0
6	48	43	49	140	46.7
$\sum X_j$	289	259	305		$\bar{\bar{X}} = 47.4$
$\bar{X}_j$	48.16	43.16	50.83		

Some state election laws take ballot position of candidates into account in their election procedures because of the common belief (justifiably) that candidates listed higher on the ballot get more voter attention than candidates listed lower on the ballot. Michigan requires that ballot positions be systematically rotated from polling place to polling place in order to offset the advantage of position. Table 8-5 shows election results in hundreds of votes for each party's candidates by ballot position. For example, the Republican candidates received 5100 votes from polling places that listed them first, 4800 from those that listed them second, etc.

It seems reasonable to assume that party and ballot position are independent. Our problem is to test whether party and ballot position account for a significant proportion of the variance in partisan voting in this election. This can be done by partitioning the total variance in voting into three components: (1) the variance due to the row attribute (ballot position); (2) the variance due to the column attribute (party); and (3) the sample variance of the residual variance. Once we have estimates of these three things, we can set up the appropriate F ratios and perform a significance test on the contribution of each attribute to the total variance of the dependent variable. In one-way analysis of variance we take the F ratio of the between-group variance to the within-group variance. The within-group variance is the sample variance and the between-group variance is the variance accounted for by the classification scheme. Now two F ratios are necessary:

$$F_1 = \frac{\text{variance between rows}}{\text{sample variance}} \qquad F_2 = \frac{\text{variance between columns}}{\text{sample variance}}$$

As in one-way analysis of variance, if the classification schemes are independent of the dependent variable, the variance between rows and the variance between columns will not be significantly different from the sample variance.

This two-way analysis of variance problem is solved in a manner analogous to the one-way problem illustrated previously. In that illustration we had k columns with m observations per column. Formula (8-23) produces an estimate of the between-group variance. For this problem we have $k = 3$ columns and $m = 6$ rows. The variance between columns is $m \sum (\overline{X}_j - \overline{X})^2/(k-1)$, the same as (8-23). There are k columns and m observations per column. The variance between rows is analogous: $k \sum (\overline{X}_i - \overline{X})^2/(m-1)$. Here there are m rows and k observations per row. Thus, we have formulas for estimating column and row variances.

Now we turn to the problem of estimating sample variance. The sample variance of X will be the residual variance after the effects of the column variance and the row variance have been removed from the total variance of the dependent variable. For some observations of X_{ij}, it is the difference between X_{ij} and the grand mean, minus the influences of the column and row means:

$$\underset{\substack{\text{total}\\\text{deviation}}}{(X_{ij}-\bar{X})} - \underset{\substack{\text{row}\\\text{influence}}}{(\bar{X}_i-\bar{X})} - \underset{\substack{\text{column}\\\text{influence}}}{(\bar{X}_j-\bar{X})} = \text{residual, or sample variance}$$

If the column and row variables have no effect on X, then $\bar{X}_i = \bar{X}_j = \bar{X}$ and all the variance in X is sampling variance. The preceding expression can be simplified by removing parentheses: $(X_{ij}-\bar{X}_i-\bar{X}_j+\bar{X})$. This is the residual deviation of X_{ij}. To find the sample variance, or residual variance, we sum the squared deviations and divide by the degrees of freedom:

$$(8\text{-}30) \qquad \frac{\displaystyle\sum_i\sum_j(X_{ij}-\bar{X}_i-\bar{X}_j+\bar{X})^2}{(k-1)(m-1)}$$

Computational simplifications for column and row sum of squares are

$$k\sum(\bar{X}_j-\bar{X})^2 = k\left[\sum \bar{X}_j^2 - m\bar{X}^2\right]$$
$$m\sum(\bar{X}_i-\bar{X})^2 = m\left[\sum \bar{X}_i^2 - k\bar{X}^2\right]$$

Another method of finding the residual sum of squares is to subtract column and row sums from the total sum of squares. The total sum of squares is expressed and simplified as

$$(8\text{-}31) \qquad \sum_i\sum_j(X_{ij}-\bar{X})^2 = \sum_i\sum_j X_{ij}^2 - mk\bar{X}^2$$

Therefore, the residual sum of squares is

Residual sum of squares $=$

$$\sum_i\sum_j X_{ij}^2 - mk\bar{X}^2 - m\left[\sum \bar{X}_i^2 - k\bar{X}^2\right] - k\left[\sum \bar{X}_j^2 - m\bar{X}^2\right]$$

Given the data in Table 8-5, we can find $\sum \bar{X}_i^2$, $\sum \bar{X}_j^2$ and $\sum\sum X_{ij}^2$.

$$\sum \bar{X}_i^2 = 13{,}502.65 \qquad \sum \bar{X}_j^2 = 6751.86 \qquad \sum_i\sum_j X_{ij}^2 = 40{,}653$$

The following calculations can be performed.

Total:
$$\sum_i\sum_j X_{ij}^2 - mk\bar{X}^2 = 40{,}653 - 18(2244.86)$$
$$= 40{,}653 - 40{,}407.48$$
$$= 245.52$$

Column:
$$k(\sum \bar{X}_j - m\bar{X}^2) = 3[13{,}502.65 - 6(2244.86)]$$
$$= 3[13{,}502.65 - 13{,}469.16]$$
$$= 100.47$$

Row:
$$m(\textstyle\sum X_i^2 - k\bar{X}^2) = 6[6751.86 - 3(2244.86)]$$
$$= 6[6751.86 - 6734.58]$$
$$= 103.68$$

The sample, or residual, sum of squares is $245.52 - 100.47 - 103.68 = 41.37$. As analysis of variance problems become more complex, a tabular summary of critical information is a useful device. See Table 8-6.

Table 8-6

Analysis of Variance, Ballot Position, and Party Label on Voting

Source of variance	Sum of squares	Degrees of freedom	Variance estimate
Between rows	103.68	5	20.736
Between columns	100.47	2	50.235
Residual	41.37	10	4.137
Total	245.52	17	

Now that we have these data, we can construct the two F ratios of interest and test the original hypotheses. The null hypotheses of these tests are that there is no relationship between ballot position and voting and that there is no relationship between party label and voting. $F_1 = 20.736/4.137 = 5.012$. From Table A-5, we find the critical levels for $d_1 = m - 1 = 5$ and $d_2 = (m-1)(k-1) = 10$. The critical levels of F are $F \geqslant 3.333$ at the .05 level of significance and $F \geqslant 5.64$ at the .01 level of significance. The computed value of F lies between these values; thus, we conclude that if we reject the null hypothesis, there is less than 1 chance in 20 but greater than 1 chance in 100 that we would be making a mistake.

Let us turn now to F_2 ($50.235/4.137 = 12.14$). The respective degrees of freedom in this case are 2 and 10. The critical values of $F_{2,10}$ are 4.10 and 7.56. Here we find that party labels account for a significant amount of the variance in voting at the .01 level or better.

A TWO-WAY ANALYSIS OF VARIANCE, MULTIPLE OBSERVATIONS

Unlike the model presented in the preceding section, this model assumes that the two attributes subdividing the main variable are not necessarily independent of each other, although all other assumptions are the same. The model we present now does not require that assumption and it enables the measurement of the interaction of the attributes. In order to measure this interaction, multiple observations per cell are necessary. When we obtain these data, it is possible to calculate the column variance, the row variance, the sample variance, and the *interaction* variance. These four statistics are used to construct three F ratios, which provide us with the tools to test the significance of the amount of variance of the dependent variable accounted for by the attributes and their interaction.

$$F_1 = \frac{\text{variance between rows}}{\text{sample variance}}$$

$$F_2 = \frac{\text{variance between columns}}{\text{sample variance}}$$

$$F_3 = \frac{\text{interaction variance}}{\text{sample variance}}$$

The main restriction of this model is that the variances within cells must be homogeneous; that is, they cannot be significantly different from each other and therefore from the total sample variance. See Table 8-7. We have n

Table   8-7

Column and Row Matrix

		Column attribute		
Row attribute	A	$X_{111}, X_{112}, ..., X_{11n}$	$X_{121}, X_{122}, ..., X_{12n}$	$X_{131}, X_{132}, ..., X_{13n}$
	B	$X_{211}, X_{212}, ..., X_{21n}$	$X_{221}, X_{222}, ..., X_{22n}$	$X_{231}, X_{232}, ..., X_{23n}$
	C	$X_{311}, X_{312}, ..., X_{31n}$	$X_{321}, X_{322}, ..., X_{32n}$	$X_{331}, X_{332}, ..., X_{33n}$

observations of the variable X per cell of the matrix and, as in the previous illustration, there are k columns and m rows. Estimation of the column and row variances is analogous to the method just described. Column variance is equal to $\left(nm\sum(\overline{X}_j - \overline{X})^2/(k-1)\right)$, and the row variance is equal to $\left(nk\sum(\overline{X}_i - \overline{X})^2/(m-1)\right)$. The interaction variance is equal to n times the residual variance, as calculated from (8-30).

(8-32)   Interaction variance $= \dfrac{n\sum_i\sum_j(\overline{X}_{ij} - \overline{X}_i - \overline{X}_j + \overline{X})^2}{(m-1)(k-1)}$

But, of course, here we are dealing with the mean of a set of observations per cell, $\overline{X}_{ij}$, rather than the single observation in the cell, X_{ij}, as in (8-31). If there is no interaction between the attributes, the expected value of $\overline{X}_{ij}$ will be equal to $(-\bar{X}_i - \bar{X}_j + \bar{X})$ and the interaction variance will be equal to zero. That is, the two attributes must be systematically related or the $(-\bar{X}_i - \bar{X}_j)$ terms will cancel out the $(+\bar{X}_{ij} + \bar{X})$ terms.

The residual variance is found by subtracting the three components from the total variance of X, but a shorter method exists. Let X_{ije} be the eth observation in cell X_{ij}. Then

$$(8\text{-}33) \qquad \text{residual variance} = \frac{\sum_i \sum_j \sum_e (X_{ije} - \bar{X}_{ij})^2}{mk(n-1)}$$

It may become evident that it is computationally more convenient to calculate the total sum of squares and then subtract three-component sums of squares to avoid calculating a fourth. The total sum of squares is simply the sum of the squared derivations of all observations of X from the grand mean:

$$(8\text{-}34) \qquad \text{Total sum of squares} = \sum_i \sum_j \sum_e (X_{ije} - \bar{X})^2$$

The results of this model can be summarized in a table similar to Table 8-6. Having the data in Table 8-8, the appropriate F ratios could be constructed and the hypotheses tested.

Table 8-8

Two-Way Analysis of Variance, Multiple Observations

Source of variance	Sum of squares	Degrees of freedom	Estimate of variance
Columns	SS Columns	$k-1$	$\hat{\sigma}_2$ column
Rows	SS Rows	$m-1$	$\hat{\sigma}_2$ rows
Interaction	SS Interaction	$(m-1)(k-1)$	$\hat{\sigma}_2$ interaction
Residual	SS Residual	$mk(n-1)$	$\hat{\sigma}_2$ residual
Total	SS Total	$(kmn)-1$	$\hat{\sigma}_2$ total

It is unfortunate that analysis of variance is not widely used in political research because the technique seems to deserve more attention than it is usually given. Some interesting suggestions for application come to mind. In international relations a number of economic and social indicators, measurable by interval scales, are of interest. These could be cross-classified by nominal scales of nations, bloc or coalition membership, type of government, type of party systems, type of economic systems, etc. Survey research data can be explored by analysis of variance also. Multiple values per cell could consist of observations of a particular variable for a number of subsamples; any number of interesting attributes are included in most surveys. For a simple example one could cross-classify partisan attitudes in regions of the United States by, say, occupation and religion. The problem of voter turnout by office level, as previously analyzed by one-way analysis of variance, could be reanalyzed with a larger sample of carefully selected election districts, and additional control variables could be tested. These are just a few of the possible uses of the analysis of variance models we have presented. Numerous other applications are possible and numerous other analyses of variance models are available. We have sought to present the analysis of variance models that are most likely to be useful to the political researcher and suggest some of the more obvious applications.

SUMMARY

In this chapter we have presented the F ratio and two sets of statistical models to which it can be applied: correlation and analysis of variance. The F ratio is the ratio of two χ^2 variables divided by their respective degrees of freedom. Since the null hypothesis of tests employing the F ratio is that two variables are from the same population, the population variance in the denominators of each χ^2 value cancels out, and the F ratio is the ratio of two variance estimates. This factor enables tests of the equality of variances using the F ratio. For these tests, the ratio is always constructed so that the larger estimate is the numerator; thus $F > 1.0$.

The sample correlation coefficient r is a measure of the association of two distributions. In order to calculate r, certain important assumptions must be made about variables X and Y:

1. Both X and Y are normally distributed.

2. If X and Y are related, the relationship is linear.

3. Both variables are measured by at least an interval scale.

4. X and Y are independent; this means that the null hypothesis of a test is $H_o: r_{XY} = 0$.

The statistic r ranges between -1 (perfect negative correlation) to $+1$ (perfect positive correlation). If r is not equal to zero, we reject the null hypothesis and conclude that X and Y are not independent. A significance test for r is available through the use of the F ratio.

Analysis of variance is used for two purposes: (1) to test for the difference of means in a number of samples, and (2) to measure the degree of association between one normally distributed variable measured by an interval scale and one or more variables measured by less than an interval scale. The strategy of this technique is to divide the variance of the dependent variable into components due to random factors and components due to the presence of an attribute (independent variable). If the component due to the attribute does not account for a significant amount of the variance of the dependent variable, it will not be significantly different from the component due to random factors. This is determined by the use of an F ratio. As the attribute accounts for more of the variance of the dependent variable, it gets larger than the sample variance.

Three analyses of variance models were discussed here and each required slightly different assumptions. One-way analysis of variance assumes that the dependent variable is normally distributed and that each of its subgroups is normally distributed. It is not necessary to assume that each subgroup has the same variance. Two-way analysis of variance, single observations per cell, makes the same assumptions about the dependent variable, but it also assumes that the two attributes are independent of each other. Two-way analysis of variance, multiple observations per cell, makes the same assumptions about the dependent variable and also assumes homogeneous variances (that is, the variances of the cells are equal). It also allows the attributes to be dependent on one another and measures the degree of their interaction.

NOTES   Chapter 8

1. A two-tailed test would be useful in one of the analysis of variance models presented later in this chapter. The model measures the interaction between two independent variables. This is done with an F ratio, which is not restricted to values of $F \geqslant 1.0$.

2. Simon makes a dubious assumption that true correlation is causation, but the assumption is not necessary for use of the technique. For an extension of this technique, see Blalock (1964).

3. A random effects model is one where the attribute subdividing the variable is randomly selected from a population of attributes. For example, in setting up a quality control experiment on a population of machines which produce the same product, one might select a sample of machines and study the characteristics of their output. The variable being studied would be the characteristics of the machines' output and the attribute would be the sample of machines. For a thorough discussion of random effects models, see Yamane (1970, pp. 732–752).

REFERENCES   Chapter 8

Blalock, Hubert. *Social Statistics*. New York: McGraw-Hill, 1960.

Blalock, Hubert, *Causal Inferences in Non-experimental Research*. Chapel Hill: University of North Carolina Press, 1964.

Fisher, Ronald A. *Statistical Methods for Research Workers*. New York: Hafner, 1948.

Rai, Kul B. "The Relationship between Foreign Policy Indicators and Voting Patterns in the U.N. General Assembly." Ph.D. Thesis, University of Rochester, 1969.

Simon, Herbert A. "Spurious Correlations; a Causal Interpretation," *Journal of the American Statistical Association*, Vol. 49 (September, 1954).

Yamane, Taro, *Statistics, An Introductory Analysis*, 2d ed. New York: Harper & Row, 1967. (See especially chap. 21.)

Chapter 9

LINEAR REGRESSION

SIMPLE LINEAR REGRESSION

The term *regression* is attributed to Sir Francis Galton. In his studies on heredity, Galton observed the phenomenon that the sons of tall fathers are not so tall as their fathers and the sons of short fathers are not so short as their fathers; he labeled it "regression to mediocrity." For the examples we discuss in this chapter, the word "regression" may not appear quite appropriate to you, but we do not propose to start an argument about the appropriateness of this term. For our purpose, regression means a statistical model used for hypothesis testing.

In Chapter 1 we discussed the relationship between cognitive models and the use of statistical models to test them. From cognitive models, which are designed to explain a phenomenon, we draw hypotheses that we test by using statistical models. This process is illustrated in Chapter 1 with a hypothesis that voters would be more likely to vote Republican (R), the more business interests (I) they had. Symbolically, this relationship was expressed by the linear equation

$$R = a + bI$$

To test this hypothesis, we wish to estimate the parameter b, the slope of the line relating the variables R and I. The linear regression model is the appropriate statistical technique for estimating b. There are a number of possible variations on the linear regression model and all are derived from two basic types: simple linear regression and multiple linear regression. In simple linear regression, only two variables are considered; in multiple linear regression, more than two variables are considered. We discuss simple linear regression in the first part of the chapter and multiple linear regression in the second part.[1]

For political research we may want to test hypotheses concerning a variety of simple relationships. For example, we could explore the relationship between the nationwide votes polled by a party in legislative elections and the number or percentage of seats won by it; between voter registration in a large city and the voter turnout in that state; or between employment in cities and frequency of riots. Regression is suitable to test hypotheses of the following nature: As the votes polled by a party in the elections increase, the number or percentage of seats won by it increases; as the voter registration in a large city increases, voter turnout in that state increases; and as employment in cities increases, the frequency of riots decreases. The simple determination of a positive or a negative effect is possible, as in correlation analysis. However, in addition to the sign of a relationship, the regression analysis gives us the slope of the line relating the variables. That is, we can estimate the marginal impact of one variable on another. While investigating such relationships we must be certain that the relationships are indeed basically bivariate; that is, the relationships under investigation are such that the consideration of more than two variables is not necessary for a meaningful analysis.

In setting up hypotheses to test with simple linear regression analysis, we first identify the dependent and independent variables. The independent variable must have been observed in a time frame preceding the observation of the dependent variable. We attempt to account for fluctuations in the dependent variable with the distribution of the antecedent independent variable. Thus, in the examples given above, the number or percentage of seats won by a political party in the elections, voter turnout in a state, and frequency of riots are the dependent variables; and votes polled by a party, voter registration in a large city, and employment in cities are the independent variables.

The model which simple linear regression is used to estimate is expressed as

$$(9\text{-}1) \qquad Y = \alpha + \beta X$$

where Y is the dependent variable, X is the independent variable, and α and β are population parameters.

$\alpha + \beta X$ is not a line passing through the individual Y values; instead, it is a line passing through the means of the subpopulations of Y. We assume that for each fixed value of X there is a subpopulation of Y; thus, we get a number of values of the means of these subpopulations.

To use simple linear regression, we must assume that expression (9-1) reasonably represents the relationship between X and Y in the population; that is, we must assume that X and Y are indeed linearly related. Our problem is to estimate values of α and β from a sample of the population. We use a and b to represent estimates of α and β, and we use a sample of X and Y to represent the whole population of X and Y. The equation we use for the regression model to estimate is

$$(9\text{-}2) \qquad Y_c = a + bX$$

This second equation is in fact an estimate of the first equation. We use the second equation to make inferences about the population, based on the data in the sample. It should be evident that if we calculate a and b from the data provided in our sample, the assumptions we make about the distributions of X and Y are critical to the values we produce for a and b. For example, if Y and X were perfectly correlated, we would have to know only two sets of coordinates in order to discover $Y = a + bX$. Suppose we knew that when $X = 2$, $Y = 5$, and when $X = 3$, $Y = 7$. The graph of the linear equation inferred from these coordinates is presented in Figure 9-1. In this case, Y_c (estimated values of Y) = Y (actual values of Y).

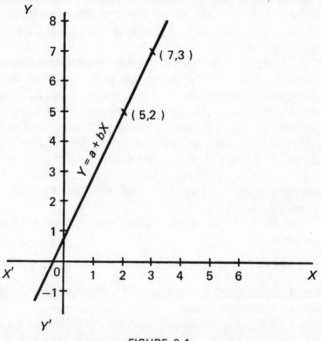

FIGURE 9-1

The value of $a = 1$, the Y intercept of $a + bX$. The value of b is the ratio of a change in Y to a change in $X = (5-7)/(2-3) = -2/-1 = 2$. So, if we assumed that Y and X were perfectly correlated, the equation $Y = a + bX$ would be $Y = 1 + 2X$. But, of course, most of the interesting variables in the world are not perfectly correlated (in fact, that's what makes them interesting to the statistician).

Statistical models deal with random variables, that is, variables that can be described by some probability function. The element of randomness suggests that if we try to describe any bivariate or multivariate relationship containing at least one random variable, there will always be some variations not accounted for in the random variable. In regression analysis we must always assume that Y is a normally distributed random variable. Therefore, no matter how well the distribution of X accounts for fluctuations in Y, there will always be some fluctuations not accounted for in Y. These residual fluctuations will result purely from chance. This error must be taken into account in expressing our basic regression model.

In the case of the *population*, an individual Y may be expressed as the expected value of Y, given a fixed X, plus a certain error or disturbance term, for which we write ε (epsilon). In the case of a *sample*, an individual Y may be expressed as Y_c, plus a certain error or disturbance term, for which we write e. Thus, for the population, an individual $Y = E(Y|X) + \varepsilon$; and for a sample, an individual $Y = Y_c + e$. We discuss below the population error term in some detail along with the assumptions of simple linear regression, and we discuss the sample error term later in the chapter.

Before we demonstrate the use of simple linear regression, it is important that we state explicitly all assumptions pertaining to it.

Assumptions of Simple Linear Regression

1. *The relationship between X (independent variable) and Y (dependent variable) is linear.*

You may question the frequency of linearly related variables in the field of politics. Your question is justified because many political variables are not linearly related. But, on the other hand, several political variables are approximately linear in the relatively narrow range of values that we typically observe, and if you know your data well enough, you can use simple linear regression—provided, of course, your data meet the other assumptions of the model.

2. *For each value of X the values of Y are normally distributed.*

If for each value of Y the values of X are normally distributed, the two form a bivariate normal distribution.

The second assumption should be clear to you if you realize that the total population has a large number of observations and for each value of X there are several values of Y and for each value of Y there are several values of X.

3. *The variance of each subpopulation of Y (it is usually written $\sigma^2 y \cdot x$) is the same and is independent of X.*

This assumption is called *homoscedasticity*.

4. *We make the following assumptions about ε, the error term.*

a. *All values of ε are independent of each other.*

b. *The ε has a normal distribution.*

c. $E(\varepsilon) = 0$.

d. $\text{Var}(\varepsilon) = $ *variance of each subpopulation of Y; that is, $\sigma^2 y \cdot x$.*

The error term can be expressed as $\varepsilon = Y - E(Y|X)$, since $Y = E(Y|X) + \varepsilon$. Substantively, the error term may have two meanings. It may represent random error, which is perfectly acceptable; but it may also represent a certain gap in the information that we have. The error term may be due to some unknown variables, hopefully not very important in our analysis. If the error term contains an important independent variable, it will contaminate other estimates produced by the model.

The assumptions regarding ε are not at all subtle. If the values of ε are not independent of each other, it indicates that we have ignored an important explanatory (independent) variable or variables. That ε has a normal distribution is suggested by the Central Limit theorem. $E(\varepsilon) = 0$ because the values of ε are randomly clustered around $\alpha + \beta X$; some of these values are positive and others are negative. The variance of ε can be explained by the following algebraic equations:

$$\text{Var}(\varepsilon) = E(\varepsilon - E(\varepsilon))^2 = E(\varepsilon - 0)^2 = E(\varepsilon)^2$$

Now the variance of each subpopulation of Y is clearly the following:

$$\text{Var}(Y) = E(Y - E(Y|X))^2$$
$$= E(\varepsilon)^2$$

since $\varepsilon = Y - E(Y|X)$. Hence, $\text{Var}(\varepsilon) = \text{Var}(Y)$.

Least Squares Method

We can now turn to the method of calculating sample regression equation $Y_c = a + bX$. Remember that the *population regression coefficients* are written α and β, and the *sample regression coefficients* are written a and b; a and b are estimates of α and β derived from a sample of the population. So the next question is: How do we arrive at values for a and b?

We estimate α and β with the least squares method. By this method, we find the line $a + bX$ such that the sum of the squared deviations of the observed values of Y from this line is at a minimum. Just as we use ε to express the difference between Y and $E(Y|X)$, we use e to express the difference between Y and Y_c. Thus, we minimize $\sum e^2$.

The least squares method entails deriving two equations called *normal equations*, which we explain with verbal reasoning and some elementary algebra. We stated that the line $a + bX$ must minimize $\sum e^2$. The only point on the line at which e will always equal zero is where $Y = \bar{Y}$ and $X = \bar{X}$; so we conclude that $a + bX$ must pass through the coordinates $(\bar{Y}, \bar{X})$. Thus,

$$\bar{Y} = a + b\bar{X}$$
$$n\bar{Y} = \sum Y, \qquad n\bar{X} = \sum X \quad \text{(where } n \text{ is the sample size)}$$
$$n(\bar{Y}) = n(a + b\bar{X})$$

so that we get the first normal equation:

(9-3) $\sum Y = na + b\sum X$

Each individual case is represented as

$$Y = a + bX$$

Multiplying each side of the equation by X does not destroy the relationship:

$$YX = aX + bX^2$$

Then, summing, we get the second normal equation:

(9-4) $\sum YX = a\sum X + b\sum X^2$

With these two equations, we can solve for a and b. From

$$\sum Y = na + b\sum X$$

we get

(9-5) $a = \dfrac{\sum Y}{n} - b\dfrac{\sum X}{n}$

The value of b is derived as follows:

$$\sum XY = a\sum X + b\sum X^2$$
$$= \left(\frac{\sum Y}{n} - b\frac{\sum X}{n}\right)\sum X + b\sum X^2$$
$$= \frac{\sum X\sum Y - b(\sum X)^2 + nb\sum X^2}{n}$$
$$= \frac{\sum X\sum Y + b(n\sum X^2 - (\sum X)^2)}{n}$$
$$= \frac{\sum X\sum Y}{n} + b\frac{n\sum X^2 - (\sum X)^2}{n}$$

Therefore

(9-6) $b = \left(\dfrac{n\sum XY - \sum X\sum Y}{n}\right)\left(\dfrac{n}{n\sum X^2 - (\sum X)^2}\right)$

$$= \frac{n\sum XY - \sum X\sum Y}{n\sum X^2 - (\sum X)^2}$$

Formulas (9-5) and (9-6) are quite easy to work with, if the number of observations is not large. However, if the number of observations is large, it may be better to make use of a computer than to work by hand or with a desk calculator. You do not have to be an expert in computer programming in order to use a computer for the purpose of simple (or even multiple) linear regression. You must, of course, know the basic fundamentals of the computer language that you are making use of. Then you can use one of the computer programs that are already written (canned programs).

Some Examples

Example 9-1

The data of this example are hypothetical and are presented in Table 9-1.

Table 9-1

Data for Example 9-1

X	Y
1	2
2	4
3	5
4	6

For this example a and b can be derived by formulas (9-5) and (9-6) as follows:

$$b = \frac{n\sum XY - \sum X \sum Y}{n\sum X^2 - (\sum X)^2}$$

$$= \frac{4(49) - 170}{4(30) - 100} = \frac{196 - 170}{120 - 100} = \frac{26}{20} = 1.3$$

$$a = \frac{\sum Y}{n} - b\frac{\sum X}{n}$$

$$= \frac{17}{4} - 1.3 \times \frac{10}{4} = \frac{17 - 13}{4} = 1.0$$

The calculation is

$$X = 1, \qquad Y_c = a + bX = 1 + (1.3)1 = 2.3$$

$$X = 2, \qquad Y_c = a + bX = 1 + (1.3)2 = 3.6$$

$$X = 3, \qquad Y_c = a + bX = 1 + (1.3)3 = 4.9$$

$$X = 4, \qquad Y_c = a + bX = 1 + (1.3)4 = 6.2$$

The corresponding values of Y and Y_c for the values of X are written as follows:

X	Y	Y_c
1	2	2.3
2	4	3.6
3	5	4.9
4	6	6.2

The values of X, Y, and Y_c are illustrated in Figure 9-2 also. The points clustered around Y_c (that is, around $a+bX$) are the actual Y values.

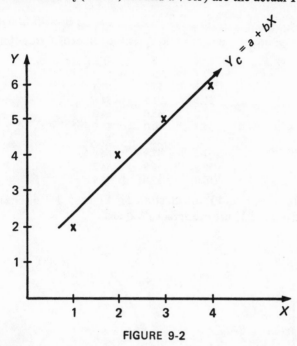

FIGURE 9-2

Example 9–2

The data of the second example are taken from *Statistical Abstracts of the United States* and are presented in Table 9-2.

Table   9-2

Data for Example 9–2

Year of Elections	X % of votes polled by the Democrats for the elections to the House	Y % of seats won by the Democrats in the House
1952	49.7	48.7
1954	52.5	53.3
1956	51.1	53.8
1958	56.2	65.0
1960	54.7	60.0
1962	52.5	59.3
1964	57.2	67.8
1966	50.9	56.9
1968	50.0	55.8

In this example we computed the values of a and b as well as of Y_c for you. The values of a and b are

$$a = -46.4 \qquad b = 2.0$$

The corresponding values of Y and Y_c for the values of X are as follows:

X	Y	Y_c
49.7	48.7	51.8
52.5	53.3	57.3
51.1	53.8	54.6
56.2	65.0	64.6
54.7	60.0	61.7
52.5	59.3	57.3
57.2	67.8	66.6
50.9	56.9	54.2
50.0	55.8	52.4

The values of X, Y, and Y_c are illustrated in Figure 9-3 also. The points clustered around Y_c are the actual Y values.

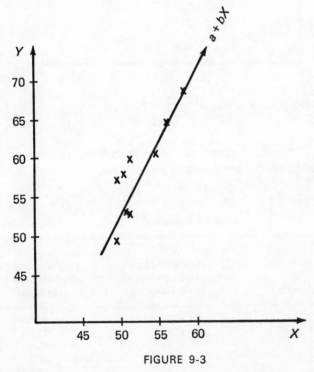

FIGURE 9-3

Example 9–3

The data for this example are taken from *Connecticut State Register and Manual* and are presented in Table 9-3. The figures are expressed in thousands for simplicity.

Table   9-3

Data for Example 9–3

Year of elections	Voter registration in Connecticut, in thousands	Votes for Democratic presidential candidate in Connecticut, in thousands
1948	1034	423
1952	1185	482
1956	1242	405
1960	1321	657
1964	1373	826
1968	1435	621

For this third example the values of a and b as well as of Y_c have been computed for you. The values of a and b are

$$a = -476.9 \quad b = 0.8$$

The corresponding values of Y and Y_c for the values of X are as follows:

X	Y	Y_c
1034	423	378.0
1185	482	502.9
1242	405	549.9
1321	657	615.3
1373	826	658.3
1435	621	709.6

The values of X, Y, and Y_c are illustrated in Figure 9-4 also. The points clustered around Y_c are the actual Y values.

In simple linear regression, b is the most useful statistic. As mentioned earlier, it is the slope of the regression line $a + bX$. With a unit change in X, b indicates the estimated average change in Y. Thus, in Example 9-1, a unit increase in X makes an estimated average increase of 1.3 in Y; in Example 9-2, an increase of 1 percent in the votes polled by the Democrats makes an estimated average increase of 2 percent in the seats won by the Democrats; and in Example 9-3, an increase of 1000 registered voters in Connecticut makes an estimated average increase of 800 votes polled by a Democratic presidential candidate in Connecticut. To remind you once again, these examples are samples drawn from populations. For every fixed value of X we expect a number of the values of Y that are normally distributed. If you realize this, it will make sense to talk in terms of estimated averages.

We want to emphasize again that the regression model enables us to test specific hypotheses. In each of the three examples discussed above, we hypothesize that the value of b would be positive; that is, in each example,

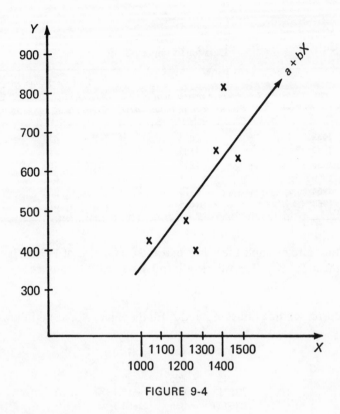

FIGURE 9-4

higher values of X would produce higher values of Y. Clearly, the regression analysis shows that we accept our hypotheses—or rather we accept the cognitive models—that relate X and Y in each case positively. In fact, the precision brought in by the exact value of b in each case gives a certain predictive value to our cognitive models. Often, this element of prediction in regression is overly emphasized. Our point, however, is that the over-emphasis on prediction in regression tends to make one overlook the main use of the statistical models, that is, hypothesis testing.

A word of caution is essential here. Although it may not be immediately apparent to you, the inclusion of Example 9-3 is intended to show you the limitations of the simple linear regression. We discuss this in the subsequent sections.

Standard Error of Estimate

Thus far we have learned when to use simple linear regression and how to use it. We now want to develop a measure of the quality of our estimate, given by the sample regression line. In particular, we want a measure of how close the estimated values of the dependent variable, represented by the sample regression line, are to the observed values of the dependent variable. If the estimated values of Y are not close enough to the observed values of Y, our sample regression line represents a poor estimate, and despite the introduction of precise-sounding numbers we do not improve much our knowledge of the variables under investigation.

The measure that indicates the distance of the observed values of Y from the estimated values of Y is called *standard error of estimate*. It is also called *sample standard deviation of regression* or *standard deviation of regression*. It is an estimate of the population standard deviation (that is, $\sigma y \cdot x$) and is written $\hat{\sigma} y \cdot x$. (Note that $\sigma^2 y \cdot x$ has been mentioned earlier in this chapter as the variance of each subpopulation.) The derived *standard error of estimate* is

$$(9\text{-}7) \qquad \hat{\sigma} y \cdot x = \left(\frac{\sum (Y - Y_c)^2}{n-2} \right)^{\frac{1}{2}}$$

If we square $\hat{\sigma} y \cdot x$, it becomes unexplained sample variance. The denominator of the expression (9-7) is our old friend the degrees of freedom, and in the present case, as in others, makes our estimate unbiased. Note that $\sum (Y - Y_c)^2 = \sum e^2$.

The formula $((\sum (Y - Y_c)^2)/(n-2))^{\frac{1}{2}}$ is somewhat difficult to work with because of its numerator, since we have to calculate every value of Y_c. The numerator can be written $(\sum Y^2 - (a \sum Y + b \sum XY))^{\frac{1}{2}}$, and this makes the calculations less tedious.

The *standard error of estimate* ($\hat{\sigma} y \cdot x$) in Examples 9-1, 9-2, and 9-3 is 0.4, 2.8, and 123.7, respectively. For Example 9-1, we show below the derivation of the *standard error of estimate*. For Examples 9-2 and 9-3, the values of the *standard error of estimate* have been computed for you.

The *standard error of estimate* for Example 9-1 is derived as follows:

$$\hat{\sigma} y \cdot x = \left(\frac{\sum Y^2 - (a \sum Y + b \sum XY)}{n-2} \right)^{\frac{1}{2}}$$

$$= \left(\frac{81 - (1 \times 17 + 1.3 \times 49)}{4-2} \right)^{\frac{1}{2}}$$

$$= \left(\frac{81 - 80.7}{2} \right)^{\frac{1}{2}} = \left(\frac{.3}{2} \right)^{\frac{1}{2}} = .4$$

Since we assume normal distribution of Y in our population, we expect approximately 2/3 of the observed values of Y to fall within $\pm \hat{\sigma} y \cdot x$ of our estimated regression line, and 95 percent of the observed values of Y to fall within $\pm 1.96 \hat{\sigma} y \cdot x$ of our estimated regression line. In Example 9-1, all observed values of Y are within $\pm \hat{\sigma} y \cdot x$ as well as within $\pm 1.96 \hat{\sigma} y \cdot x$ of the regression line; in Example 9-2, 77 percent of the observed values of Y are within $\pm \hat{\sigma} y \cdot x$ of the regression line, and all observed values of Y are within $\pm 1.96\hat{\sigma}y \cdot x$ of the regression line; and in Example 9-3, 2/3 of the observed values of Y are within $\pm \hat{\sigma}y \cdot x$ of the regression line and all observed values of Y are within $\pm 1.96\hat{\sigma}y \cdot x$ of the regression line. You might question why these discrepancies occur. The reason is the small size of our samples (Hoel, 1966, pp. 219–220). When we deal with small samples, it is worthwhile to check how much discrepancy is due to size of the sample.

Of greater concern to us is the size of the *standard error of estimate*. If the *standard error of estimate* becomes unduly large (note that as $\hat{\sigma}y \cdot x$ approaches zero, our estimate improves), it means that we have done one or both of the following: (1) we have excluded from our analysis certain important explanatory (independent) variable or variables; (2) we have made a sampling or measurement error. The first of these is more serious, for it indicates that simple linear regression is not appropriate for the analysis of our data and what is needed is multivariate analysis. If we make a sampling or measurement error, we can do the bivariate (simple) linear regression analysis again after correcting our error. In the examples we presented, the *standard error of estimate* in Example 9-3 is quite large, and it is apparently due to the exclusion of certain important explanatory variables such as expenditure on campaigning and the issues in the elections. As suggested above, we included this example to show the limitations of simple linear regression. Just because we have quantitative data at hand, it does not mean that we should have great expectations from statistical models. We would like to emphasize that the use of simple linear regression in the first two examples is quite appropriate.

Coefficient of Determination

Whereas $\hat{\sigma}y^2 \cdot x$ gives the unexplained sample variance, r^2 (called the *coefficient of determination*) gives the explained proportion of the total sample variance. We denote the total sample variance by σy^2. With the use of regression, we attempt to explain a part, in fact as much as possible, of this total sample variance.

Since r^2 is the explained proportion of the total sample variance, we write it as follows:

$$(9\text{-}8) \qquad r^2 = \frac{\text{explained variance}}{\text{total variance}}$$

$$= \frac{\text{total variance} - \text{unexplained variance}}{\text{total variance}}$$

$$= 1 - \frac{\text{unexplained variance}}{\text{total variance}}$$

$$= 1 - \frac{\hat{\sigma}y^2 \cdot x}{\sigma y^2}$$

We might look at the problem this way: In Chapter 3 we said that the mean of a variable (Y) was the "best guess" we could make about the value of a randomly chosen observation of the variable. When we apply the regression model, we have assumed that the values of Y are, at least in part, a linear function of some independent variable X. If this assumption is true, then the values of X plugged into the linear function $a+bX$ should enable us to make better guesses of Y than $\bar{Y}$ provides. The *coefficient of determination* is a measure of how much better $a+bX$ is as a guess of Y than $\bar{Y}$ is as a guess of Y.

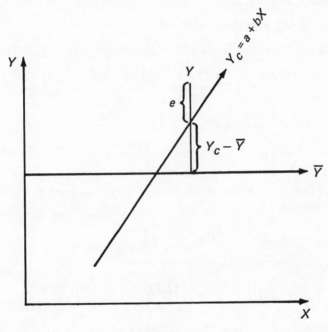

FIGURE 9-5

In Chapter 3 we also pointed out that

$$\text{Var}(Y) = \frac{\Sigma(Y-\bar{Y})^2}{n-1}$$

Figure 9-5 shows how $\text{Var}(Y)$ can be broken down into two components. The unexplained variance, $Y-Y_c$, is the variance of Y around the regression line, presumably due to random fluctuations in Y. The remainder, $Y_c-\bar{Y}$, is a measure of how much we improve our guess of Y, knowing X over our guess of Y, if we know only $\bar{Y}$.

We write

(9-9) $\underset{\text{total}}{(Y-\bar{Y})} = \underset{\text{unexplained}}{(Y-Y_c)} + \underset{\text{explained}}{(Y_c-\bar{Y})}$

By squaring and summing each side we get

$$\underset{\substack{\text{total sum of}\\\text{squares}}}{\sum(Y-\overline{Y})^2} = \underset{\substack{\text{unexplained}\\\text{sum of}\\\text{squares}}}{\sum(Y-Y_c)^2} + \underset{\substack{\text{explained}\\\text{sum of}\\\text{squares}}}{\sum(Y_c-\overline{Y})^2} + 2\sum(Y-Y_c)(Y_c-\overline{Y})$$

It can be easily shown that $2\sum(Y-Y_c)(Y_c-\overline{Y}) = 0$:

$$2\sum(Y-Y_c)(Y_c-\overline{Y}) = 2\left(\sum YY_c - \sum Y\overline{Y} - \sum Y_c^2 + \sum Y_c\overline{Y}\right)$$

$$= 2\left(\sum Y_c\overline{Y} - \sum Y\overline{Y}\right)$$

since $\sum YY_c = \sum Y_c^2$.

$$2\sum(Y-Y_c)(Y_c-\overline{Y}) = 0$$

since $\sum Y_c$ (that is, $\sum(a+bX)) = \sum Y$, which is $na+b\sum X$. Thus,

$$(9\text{-}10)\qquad \underset{\substack{\text{total sum of}\\\text{squares}}}{\sum(Y-\overline{Y})^2} = \underset{\substack{\text{unexplained}\\\text{sum of}\\\text{squares}}}{\sum(Y-Y_c)^2} + \underset{\substack{\text{explained}\\\text{sum of}\\\text{squares}}}{\sum(Y_c-\overline{Y})^2}$$

We now show that

$$(9\text{-}11)\qquad r^2 = \frac{\sum(Y_c-\overline{Y})^2}{\sum(Y-\overline{Y})^2}$$

We first define r, the correlation coefficient discussed in Chapter 8, and r^2 as follows:

$$(9\text{-}12)\qquad r = \frac{\sum xy}{\left((\sum x^2)(\sum y^2)\right)^{1/2}}$$

and

$$(9\text{-}13)\qquad r^2 = \frac{(\sum xy)^2}{(\sum x^2)(\sum y^2)}$$

where $x = X-\overline{X}$ and $y = Y-\overline{Y}$. Now

$$\frac{\sum(Y_c-\overline{Y})^2}{\sum(Y-\overline{Y})^2} = \frac{\sum(a+bX-\overline{Y})^2}{\sum y^2}$$

$$= \frac{\sum(\overline{Y}-b\overline{X}+bX-\overline{Y})^2}{\sum y^2}$$

$$= \frac{\sum(bX-b\overline{X})^2}{\sum y^2}$$

$$= \frac{b^2\sum x^2}{\sum y^2}$$

$$= \frac{(\sum xy)^2}{(\sum x^2)^2}\cdot\frac{\sum x^2}{\sum y^2}$$

since $b = \sum xy / \sum x^2$. This can be easily derived from formula (9-6) for b. Then

$$\frac{\sum(Y_c - \overline{Y})^2}{\sum(Y - \overline{Y})^2} = \frac{(\sum xy)^2}{(\sum x^2)(\sum y^2)} = r^2$$

For the purpose of calculation, the following formula is the most convenient:

$$(9\text{-}14) \qquad r^2 = \frac{[n\sum XY - (\sum X)(\sum Y)]^2}{(n\sum X^2 - (\sum X)^2)(n\sum Y^2 - (\sum Y)^2)}$$

In Examples 9-1, 9-2, and 9-3, r^2 is 0.97, 0.81, and 0.54, respectively. For Example 9-1, we show below the derivation of r^2. For Examples 9-2 and 9-3 the values of r^2 have been computed for you. In Example 9-1, r^2 indicates that, with the help of X, we can explain practically all variation in Y. In Example 9-2, r^2 indicates that, with the help of percentage of votes polled by the Democrats for the elections to the House, we can explain most of the variation in the percentage of seats won by the Democrats in the House in different years. In Example 9-3, r^2 indicates that, with the help of voter registration in Connecticut, we can explain only about half of the variation in the votes for Democratic presidential candidates in Connecticut in different years. The values of r^2 in the three examples further confirm that the use of simple linear regression is not so much justified in Example 9-3 as in the first two examples. The relatively low value of r^2 in the third example apparently is due, as we have already suggested, to the exclusion of certain important variables.

In Example 9-1, r^2 is derived as follows:

$$r^2 = \frac{[n\sum XY - (\sum X)(\sum Y)]^2}{(n\sum X^2 - (\sum X)^2)(n\sum Y^2 - (\sum Y)^2)}$$

$$= \frac{(4 \times 49 - 170)^2}{(4 \times 30 - 100)(4 \times 81 - 289)}$$

$$= \frac{(196 - 170)^2}{(20)(35)} = \frac{(26)^2}{700} = 0.97$$

Note that the maximum value of r^2 is 1.0, or 100 percent of the variance. We get the maximum value of r^2 when all Y points lie on Y_c. Since

$$r^2 = \frac{\sum(Y_c - \overline{Y})^2}{\sum(Y - \overline{Y})^2}$$

when $Y_c = Y$,

$$r^2 = 1$$

The minimum value of r^2 is zero. We get the minimum value of r^2 when $b = 0$. This happens because

$$Y_c = a + bX = \overline{Y} - b\overline{X} + bX = \overline{Y}$$

Thus, the numerator in the preceding formula for r^2 becomes zero, which makes $r^2 = 0$. Verbally, this means that $a + bX$ is not a better guess of Y than $\overline{Y}$.

Significance Test and Confidence Interval

We now want to make sure that β is not equal to zero and therefore that X and Y are not independent. For, if β is equal to zero and X and Y are independent, we do not achieve anything by regression analysis. Specifically, we wish to test the null hypothesis that $\beta = 0$. The confidence interval is the interval that contains a certain percentage of the values of β.

For performing significance test and finding confidence interval, we assume that we take a large number of samples from a population and thus have several values of b. This distribution of b is normal, with parameters as follows:

(9-15) $E(b) = \beta$

(9-16) $\sigma(b) = \dfrac{\hat{\sigma}y \cdot x}{\sum (X - \overline{X})^2}$

Of course, for small n, we must rely on the t-distribution rather than the normal distribution to test hypotheses. However, for samples with $n \geqslant 30$, the normal distribution can be used. Both t- and normal tests are constructed in the same manner, that is,

(9-17) $\dfrac{b - E(b)}{\sigma b} = \dfrac{b - \beta}{\sigma b}$

Since the null hypothesis is $\beta = 0$, the result of (9-17) reduces to $b/\sigma b$.

Obviously, for our three examples, the t-test is applicable. The t-statistic (that is, $b/\sigma b$) is as follows in the three cases:

Example 9-1: $t = 6.5$

Example 9-2: $t = 5.0$

Example 9-3: $t = 2.7$

The values of t for Examples 9-2 and 9-3 have been computed for you. The value of t for Example 9-1 is derived as follows:

$$t = \frac{b}{\sigma b} = \frac{1.3}{0.2} = 6.5$$

If we check Table A-3 (Appendix), we find that these values are significant at the .05 significance level (note that the degrees of freedom in the first, second, and the third example are $n-2$ (that is, 2, 7, and 4, respectively). This means that b in each example is significantly different from zero and that all three samples are from populations in which β is not equal to zero and X and Y are not independent. In other words, we reject the null hypothesis that β is equal to zero, and therefore accept the alternative hypothesis that β is not equal to zero.

For constructing confidence interval use the t-table (Table A-3) and the method outlined in Chapter 6. The 95 percent confidence intervals for our three cases are as follows:

Example 9-1: $b \pm 4.3\sigma b = 1.3 \pm 4.3(0.2) = 1.3 \pm .86$

Example 9-2: $b \pm 2.4\sigma b = 2.0 \pm 2.4(0.4) = 2.0 \pm .96$

Example 9-3: $b \pm 2.8\sigma b = 0.8 \pm 2.8(0.3) = 0.8 \pm .84$

These confidence intervals contain 95 percent of the values of β in each of the three cases when several samples are drawn from each of the three populations.

MULTIPLE LINEAR REGRESSION

Due to the complexity of the political phenomena, a great many political research questions require the consideration of more than one independent variable to explain the dependent variable. Multiple linear regression is appropriate for analyzing such questions. We have indicated earlier that the single variable, voter registration, is not adequate for explaining votes for the Democratic presidential candidate in Connecticut. There are any number of such cases in political science research. Political alienation can be explained by a number of independent variables such as age, education, and race; foreign aid can be explained by a number of independent variables such as geographical situation, ideology, and trade; and voting in the United Nations General Assembly can be explained by a number of independent variables such as membership in alliances, foreign aid, and trade.

Since we deal with a number of variables in multiple linear regression, we have to decide which of the independent variables should be included in the analysis and which should be excluded. The solution of this problem lies in the development of a certain theory regarding the relationships we study. This theory, of course, is based on a cognitive model. Once a theory is developed, testable relationships among variables can be deduced. We can then operationalize these relationships in clearly stated hypotheses and then test these hypotheses by using multiple linear regression.

It is not possible to place a maximum on the number of independent variables that should be used, although some statisticians (see Ezekiel and Fox, 1959) suggest that stable results are not possible with more than five independent variables. Keeping the number of independent variables within a reasonable limit (we do not want to specify an exact limit) does help in the interpretation of the results and in making the analysis more meaningful. What should be kept in mind is that every added variable sacrifices a degree of freedom. Each degree of freedom sacrificed increases the size of the *standard error of estimate* (because degrees of freedom is the denominator) and thus reduces the likelihood of significant results.

The calculations in multiple linear regression are often tedious, especially if the number of independent variables is more than two or three and if the number of observations in the sample is large. When you use multiple linear regression, you are likely to make use of a computer. We feel that it is more important that you understand the assumptions and limitations of the multiple linear regression model than learn how to do complex calculations. We do not ignore the calculations altogether, but we emphasize the assumptions and limitations of the model in the following discussion so that when you want to use this model, you can make an intelligent decision about its use.

Assumptions of Multiple Linear Regression

Five assumptions are made.

1. *The relationship between Y (dependent variable) and X's (independent variables) is linear.*

The first assumption is clear enough. Remember that the regression line in the simple linear regression passes through the mean values of $(Y|X)$, and Y_c in the sample estimates this line. We extend this notion to the multiple linear regression. Since we have more than two variables, the relationship between independent variables and the dependent variable is graphically depicted as a plane instead of a line. This plane has $k+1$ dimensions, assuming that there are k independent variables; that is, there is one dimension for each variable. Figure 9-6 shows such a plane for one dependent and two independent variables.

We write the population and the sample regression equations with k independent variables as follows:

(9-18) $Y = \alpha + \beta_1 X_1 + \beta_2 X_2 + \cdots + \beta_k X_k$ (population)

(9-19) $Y_c = a + b_1 X_1 + b_2 X_2 + \cdots + b_k X_k$ (sample)

Y_c estimates the expected value of Y and not individual Y values. The parameters of these equations, α and β's in equation (9-18) and a and b's in equation (9-19), are constants; a and b's are the estimates of α and β's,

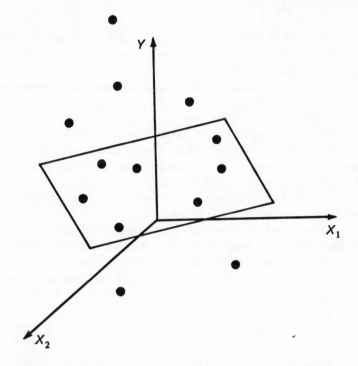

FIGURE 9-6

respectively. α or a represents the height of the regression plane as it intercepts the Y-axis and β_i or b_i represents the slope of the regression plane as it passes through the $(Y|X_i)$-axis. The b's, with which we are more concerned for the interpretation of the regression equations, are called *partial regression coefficients*. Each of the b's indicates the estimated average change in the dependent variable, with a unit change in an independent variable, when other independent variables are held constant. That is, each b_i represents the partial contribution of X_i to the variance of Y.

2. *The distribution of the population is multivariate normal; that is, there is normal distribution of each variable about all other variables.*

You perhaps find it easier to think in terms of distributions of Y values for fixed X's. We assume that such distributions of Y values for fixed X's are normal. In fact, it is possible to use multiple linear regression by assuming that each X_i is fixed but that $(Y|X_i)$ is normally distributed. However, we assume multivariate normal distribution, since it helps satisfy other assumptions also.

3. *The error or the disturbance terms are uncorrelated.*

Note that, whereas in simple linear regression we refer to only one error term (although it has several values, depending upon the number of observations), in multiple linear regression we refer to more than one error term. We do this because of the inclusion of more than one independent variable in multiple linear regression. We write a population error term ε_i and a sample error term e_i.

We assume normal distribution of each ε_i and make the following two important assumptions about it: (1) $E(\varepsilon_i) = 0$ and (2) $\text{Var}(\varepsilon_i) = \sigma^2$.

4. *The variances are the same.*

Here, again, we extend our simple linear regression model. We have a number of subpopulations of Y for fixed X's, each with the same variance, and we also have a number of error terms, each with the same variance as that of the subpopulations of Y.

5. *None of the independent variables has exact linear relationship with any of the other independent variables.*

If any of the independent variables has perfect linear relationship with another independent variable or with several of them, it becomes impossible to estimate the separate influences of the independent variables on the dependent variable. This problem is called *multicollinearity* and is so important that we devote a separate section of this chapter to it.

Least Squares Method

For our sample regression we estimate the population parameters α and β's by the least squares method; that is, with the same method by which we estimated α and β in simple linear regression. Thus, we wish to find a and b's that set

(9-20)

$$\sum e^2 = \sum (Y - a - b_1 X_1 - b_2 X_2 - \cdots - b_k X_k)^2 = \text{minimum}$$

We get the following *normal equations*:

(9-21)

$$\sum Y = na + b_1 \sum X_1 + b_2 \sum X_2 + \cdots + b_k \sum X_k$$

(n is the sample size)

(9-22)

$$\sum X_1 Y = a \sum X_1 + b_1 \sum X_1^2 + b_2 \sum X_1 X_2 + \cdots + b_k \sum X_1 X_k$$

(9-23)

$$\sum X_2 Y = a \sum X_2 + b_1 \sum X_1 X_2 + b_2 \sum X_2^2 + \cdots + b_k \sum X_2 X_k$$

. . . .

(9-24)

$$\sum X_k Y = a \sum X_k + b_1 \sum X_1 X_k + b_2 \sum X_2 X_k + \cdots + b_k \sum X_k^2$$

For particular cases in which we use multiple linear regression, we can solve the *normal equations* and get the values of a and b's. However, general solutions to the equations have been devised to obtain these values. We suggest the following formulas for a and b's:

(9-25) $a_{1.23} = \bar{X}_1 - b_{12.3}\bar{X}_2 - b_{13.2}\bar{X}_3$

(9-26) $b_{12.3} = \dfrac{b_{12} - (b_{13})(b_{32})}{1 - (b_{23})(b_{32})}$

(9-27) $b_{13.2} = \dfrac{b_{13} - (b_{12})(b_{23})}{1 - (b_{32})(b_{23})}$

Formulas (9-25), (9-26), and (9-27) are for two independent variables. In order to avoid confusion when interpreting the subscripts in these formulas, we depart briefly from our usual notation and now denote the dependent variable as X_1 and the two independent variables as X_2 and X_3. The notation is analogous to that used to represent partial r in Chapter 8. The symbol $a_{1.23}$ indicates that variable 1 is dependent and variables 2 and 3 are independent. The symbol $b_{12.3}$ means that variable 1 is dependent and variable 3 is held constant; that is, $b_{12.3}$ is the *partial regression coefficient* of variable 2. The value $b_{13.2}$ indicates that variable 1 is dependent, variable 2 is held constant, and the *partial regression coefficient* is for variable 3; b_{12} is a simple regression coefficient of the independent variable 2 when variable 1 is dependent.

We want to emphasize that b_{12} and $b_{12.3}$ are not the same even though 1 and 2 in both expressions represent the same variables. By introducing the third variable and holding it constant, we adjust for the influence of this variable while we measure the influence of variable 2 on variable 1. In b_{12} we make no such adjustment. Consequently, b_{12} might include some of the influence of variable 3 on variable 1.

For three independent variables the formulas are

(9-28) $a_{1.234} = \bar{X}_1 - b_{12.34}\bar{X}_2 - b_{13.24}\bar{X}_3 - b_{14.23}\bar{X}_4$

(9-29) $b_{12.34} = \dfrac{b_{12.3} - (b_{14.3})(b_{42.3})}{1 - (b_{24.3})(b_{42.3})}$

(9-30) $b_{13.24} = \dfrac{b_{13.2} - (b_{14.2})(b_{43.2})}{1 - (b_{34.2})(b_{43.2})}$

(9-31) $b_{14.23} = \dfrac{b_{14.2} - (b_{13.2})(b_{34.2})}{1 - (b_{43.2})(b_{34.2})}$

Note that $a_{1.234}$ indicates that variable 1 is dependent and variables 2, 3, and 4 are independent; $b_{12.34}$ is the *partial regression coefficient* of variable 2 when variable 1 is dependent and variables 3 and 4 are held constant. The remaining symbols are to be read similarly. By following the reasoning presented in Chapter 8 for partial r, you should be able to write the expression for any partial b.

You may now realize how cumbersome it is to calculate a and b's when more than two independent variables are involved. In fact, if n is large, the calculation of a and b's, even with two independent variables, is quite tedious. We have given the foregoing formulas as tools if you choose to use them, and—most important—so that you can see what is involved in producing these coefficients. Instead of lengthy computations we present examples that have been worked out on a computer.

Some Examples

Our examples are from two studies, one concerned with explaining voting patterns in the United Nations General Assembly on the basis of foreign policy indicators (see Rai, 1969) and the other concerned with explaining election turnout and partisan vote in a local election in Monroe County, New York, on the basis of certain political and social characteristics of the election districts, year of the election, and campaign activities in the districts (data from Blydenburgh, 1968). A number of regression equations are analyzed in both studies. However, we discuss one equation from each study to illustrate the use of multiple linear regression for the study of politics.

In each of the studies a theoretical discussion is first presented with regard to the relationship between the dependent and the independent variables under consideration. On the basis of this discussion, the relevant independent variables are selected and certain hypotheses are presented that are tested by an appropriate regression model.

Example 9–4

In the regression model we present here from the study on U.N. voting, the United States and 60 developing nations from Africa, Asia, Middle East, and Latin America are included. The dependent variable in this model is an index of agreement,[2] varying from 0 percent to 100 percent, between the United States and each of the 60 developing nations on 53 roll-call votes on the colonial issues of the Twentieth General Assembly session (1965). The independent variables include U.S. economic aid, Soviet economic aid, U.S. military aid, Soviet military aid, trade with the United States, trade with the Soviet Union, alliance with the United States,[3] Communist party membership as a percentage of the working-age (15–64) population, per capita gross domestic product, former colonial status, and anti-United States demonstrations.[4]

The economic aid has been measured in terms of per capita aid received by a developing nation from the United States or the Soviet Union, as the case may be. The U.S. military aid has been presented in thousands of dollars received by a developing nation from the United States. Three variables—Soviet military aid, alliance with the United States, and former colonial status—are represented as dummy variables. A dummy variable is one that is coded 1 if the characteristic in which we are interested is present; it is zero otherwise. Later in this chapter we discuss the uses and special problems of dummy variables in regression analysis. In trade, both exports and imports are included, and the two variables on trade measure the percentage of a developing nation's total annual trade with the United States or the Soviet Union, as the case may be. The Communist party membership for small and large nations has been standardized by the introduction of the working-age population. Per capita gross domestic product has been used because data on per capita gross national product, which is a more familiar measure, are not available for every year and the study covered several years.[5] The exact number of the anti-United States demonstrations in each of the 60 countries (in 1965) has been considered.

The values of the b's in this equation are given in Table 9-4. The respective standard errors of the b's are given in parentheses following the estimate.

Table   9-4

The Values of b's

Dependent variable	Independent variables	b's	Standard errors
Index of agreement with the U.S. on the colonial questions of the 20th General Assembly session	U.S. economic aid	−0.11	(0.18)
	Soviet economic aid	−1.98	(0.92)
	U.S. military aid	0.02	(0.02)
	Soviet military aid	−4.23	(3.13)
	Trade with the U.S.	19.35	(8.44)
	Trade with the Soviet Union	−4.24	(18.15)
	Alliance with the U.S.	13.86	(3.16)
	Communist Party membership	−7.73	(6.33)
	Per capita gross domestic product	1.22	(0.48)
	Former colonial status	−5.29	(2.44)
	Anti-U.S. demonstrations	−3.22	(1.85)

As mentioned earlier, the b's indicate the estimated average change in the dependent variable, with a unit change in the independent variables. Thus, an increase of $1.00 per capita United States

economic aid decreases the average index of agreement with the
United States by .11 percent. An increase of $1.00 per capita Soviet
economic aid decreases, as expected, the average index of agreement
with the United States by about 2 percent. The remaining b's are
interpreted similarly. The interpretation of the b's for the dummy
variables, however, is somewhat different. For example, the interpretation of the b for the alliance variable is that alliance with the
United States increases the average index of agreement with the
United States by about 14 percent.

Example 9–5

In the equation from the study on the election turnout and partisan
vote, we included the dependent variable on the partisan vote and
three demographic independent variables. The dependent variable in
this case is the percent Democratic vote of the two-party vote in a
district. Thirty-five districts, from which a ward supervisor was elected
in Monroe County, New York, in a recent year, are considered. We
designate the independent variables as Po, $\bar{H}$, and $\bar{R}$, where Po equals
the proportion of housing units in a district which are owner-occupied;
$\bar{H}$ equals the average value of owner-occupied dwellings in an election
district; and $\bar{R}$ equals the average rent paid by renter-occupants.

The values of the b's are given in Table 9-5. The standard errors
of the b's are enclosed by parentheses.

Table   9-5

The Values of b's

Dependent variable	Independent variables	b's	Standard errors
Percent Democratic vote	Po	−0.03	(0.18)
of the two-party vote	$\bar{H}$	−1.78	(0.30)
	$\bar{R}$	−0.49	(0.23)

The values of the b's indicate that increases in Po, $\bar{H}$, and $\bar{R}$ lead
to decline in the Democratic support among the voters. Of particular
interest is the b of $\bar{H}$. A unit increase in $\bar{H}$ decreases the average
percent Democratic vote (of the two-party vote) by close to 2 percent.

Betas and b's

Although b's are generally used for the interpretation of regression
equations, one problem with them is that they cannot be compared with

each other because of the different measurement units of the independent variables. Thus, we cannot decide on the basis of the magnitude of different b's whether one independent variable is relatively more important than another independent variable in explaining the dependent variable. In order to remedy this problem, we standardize b's. The standardized b's are called β coefficients[6] or *beta weights*, and are comparable. Beta weights are derived as follows:

$$(9\text{-}32) \qquad \beta_1 \text{ (beta weight of independent variable 1)} = b_1 \frac{\sigma_1}{\sigma y}$$

where σ_1 is the standard deviation of independent variable 1 and σy is the standard deviation of the dependent variable. Similarly,

$$(9\text{-}33) \qquad \beta_2 = b_2 \frac{\sigma_2}{\sigma y}$$

$$(9\text{-}34) \qquad \beta_3 = b_3 \frac{\sigma_3}{\sigma y}$$

$$\vdots$$

$$(9\text{-}35) \qquad \beta_k = b_k \frac{\sigma_k}{\sigma y}$$

Despite the apparent attractiveness of the beta weights, the b's are commonly used in the study of politics. The reasons for ignoring the beta weights are that they are cumbersome for the interpretation of the regression results and that they have somewhat questionable value, even for comparing the relative importance of the independent variables. For, while the interpretation of a b is straightforward, in interpreting a beta weight we say that with one standard deviation change in a certain independent variable, the change in the dependent variable will be the beta weight of that independent variable multiplied by the standard deviation of the dependent variable. The value of the beta weights in explaining the relative importance of the independent variables is somewhat questionable because of the artificiality imposed by the beta weights on the data. In the field of politics, the independent variables often interact in having their impact on the dependent variable. Therefore, when we say that the explanatory value of an independent variable is twice or thrice as much as that of another independent variable, we miss this essential point of the interaction of these. two variables.

The b's are thus much more useful for our purpose than are beta weights. However, to illustrate beta weights further, we give their values from our example on the U.N. voting in Table 9-6.

Table   9-6

Values of Beta Weights

Dependent variable	Independent variables	Beta weights
Index of agreement with the U.S. on the colonial questions of the 20th General Assembly session	U.S. economic aid	−0.05
	Soviet economic aid	−0.14
	U.S. military aid	0.06
	Soviet military aid	−0.12
	Trade with the U.S.	0.23
	Trade with the Soviet Union	−0.02
	Alliance with the U.S.	0.48
	Communist party membership	−0.09
	Per capita gross domestic product	0.19
	Former colonial status	−0.19
	Anti-U.S. demonstrations	−0.11

From Table 9-6 it is apparent that the most important explanatory variable is alliance with the United States, and next in relative importance is trade with the United States. The values of the beta weights of these two variables indicate that the former is about twice as important as the latter in explaining U.N. voting. However, this conclusion should be accepted, keeping in mind the considerations discussed above. In interpreting the relative importance of the other independent variables, the same considerations should be kept in mind.

Standard Error of Estimate

After calculating b's and beta weights, we want some measure of the quality of our model. Specifically, we want to answer three questions: (1) How far are the observations from the estimated points of the regression plane? (2) What percentage of the variance is explained by the regression? (3) Are the b's, when considered individually as well as together, significantly different from zero? We consider the first question in this section and the second and the third questions in the subsequent sections.

In order to know how far the observations are from the estimated points of the regression plane, we need to estimate the standard deviation of the population for Y. The estimated standard deviation of the population for Y is called *standard error of estimate*, or *standard deviation of regression*. We state without proof that the *standard error of estimate* is

$$(9\text{-}36) \qquad \hat{\sigma} = \left(\frac{\sum (Y - Y_c)^2}{n - k - 1} \right)^{1/2}$$

where $\hat{\sigma}$ is used because we estimate σ, the population standard deviation.

Note that the numerator $\sum(Y-Y_c)^2 = \sum e^2$. The denominator, $n-k-1$, indicates the degrees of freedom.

For the purpose of calculation, the following formula is available:

$$(9\text{-}37) \qquad \hat{\sigma} = \left(\frac{\sum y^2 - (b_1 \sum x_1 y + b_2 \sum x_2 y + \cdots + b_k \sum x_k y)}{n-k-1}\right)^{1/2}$$

where

$$y = (Y-\bar{Y})$$

$$x_1 = (X_1 - \bar{X}_1)$$

$$x_2 = (X_2 - \bar{X}_2) \cdots x_k = (X_k - \bar{X}_k)$$

It is easier to understand the *standard error of estimate* in simple linear regression, since we can plot the observed and the estimated points in a rectangular coordinate system. This is impossible in multiple linear regression because of the several dimensions involved in the regression plane. Earlier in this chapter, Figure 9-6 was presented to give you an intuitive idea of a plane with one dependent and two independent variables. We do not, however, suggest that the *standard error of estimate* be ignored. Instead, we suggest that it should be considered, but only after the data and the estimated values are carefully studied. If you know your data and the estimated values well enough, then the *standard error of estimate* will certainly give you an intuitive idea of how far the observations are from the estimated points of the regression plane. The data for the two examples that we have mentioned above are so extensive that we decided not to include them in this book. We mention here the *standard error of estimate* of Example 9-4 (U.N. voting) only, which is 5.68, and we suggest, because of our knowledge of the data and the estimated values, that this error is rather small. This means that our estimated values are close to our observations.

Coefficient of Multiple Determination

The *coefficient of multiple determination*, denoted by R^2, indicates how much of the variation in the dependent variable is explained by the independent variables under consideration. In the study of politics, we often want to explain why variation occurs in a political variable under measured variable conditions. Part of this explanation is provided by R^2, for this measure indicates whether the independent variables, which we select to explain the variation in the dependent variable, are important enough to do this job.

As we explained while discussing simple linear regression,

$$\underset{\substack{\text{total sum of}\\\text{squares}}}{\sum(Y-\bar{Y})^2} = \underset{\substack{\text{unexplained}\\\text{sum of}\\\text{squares}}}{\sum(Y-Y_c)^2} + \underset{\substack{\text{explained}\\\text{sum of}\\\text{squares}}}{\sum(Y_c-\bar{Y})^2}$$

The ratio of the explained sum of squares to the total sum of squares is R^2.

That is,

$$(9\text{-}38) \qquad R^2 = \frac{\sum (Y_c - \overline{Y})^2}{\sum (Y - \overline{Y})^2}$$

Because of Y_c in (9-38), the equation is not a very convenient formula for calculating R^2. As in other cases, convenient formulas are available. We suggest the following formula:

$$(9\text{-}39) \qquad R^2 = \frac{b_1 \sum x_1 y + b_2 \sum x_2 y + \cdots + b_k \sum x_k y}{\sum y^2}$$

where

$$y = (Y - \overline{Y})$$

$$x_1 = (X_1 - \overline{X})$$

$$x_2 = (X_2 - \overline{X}_2) \cdots x_k = (X_k - \overline{X}_k)$$

R^2 in our examples on the U.N. voting and the partisan vote is 0.84 and 0.62, respectively. Thus, the independent variables under consideration explain 84 percent of the variance in Example 9-4 and 62 percent of the variance in Example 9-5.

Significance Test of b's

We now want to find out whether the b's, considered individually, are significant, that is, whether they are significantly different from zero. We can also say that we want to know whether the β's of the population regression equation, considered individually, are equal to zero. If $\beta_1 = 0$ (that is, if b_1 is not significantly different from zero), then X_1 and Y are independent and there is no relationship between them. We can say the same about the β's and the b's of the other independent variables. We emphasize, however, that our purpose here is to test each β and b individually.

As in simple linear regression, we generally use the t-test, but in samples with $n \geq 30$, the normal test can be used. We assume that each b has a normal distribution and that $E(b_i) = \beta_i$. We construct the t-statistic as follows:

$$(9\text{-}40) \qquad t = \frac{b_i - E(b_i)}{\sigma b_i} = \frac{b_i - \beta_i}{\sigma b_i}$$

Once again the null hypothesis is $\beta_i = 0$; therefore,

$$t = \frac{b_i}{\sigma b_i}$$

where σb_i is the standard error of b_i.

We now illustrate the t-test further and, as above, we set $t = b_i/\sigma b_i$. For using the t-test, we need degrees of freedom that are $n-k-1$, n being the sample size and k being the number of independent variables. With this information we can find out from Table A-3 whether the b's are individually significant. The significance level generally used is .05. However, it is possible to avoid consulting the t-table most of the time. For a one-tail test and at .05 significance level, the value of t varies between 2.02 for 5 degrees of freedom and 1.65 for 500 degrees of freedom. We can therefore use the following rule:

If $b_i/\sigma b_i > 2$, b_i is significant, and if $b_i/\sigma b_i \leqslant 2$, b_i is not significant.

Using this rule we find in Example 9-4 that the b's of the following variables are significant: Soviet economic aid, trade with the United States, alliance with the United States, per capita gross domestic product, and former colonial status. The remaining independent variables thus do not contribute to the explanation of the U.N. voting. In Example 9-5, the independent variables whose b's are significant are $\bar{H}$ and $\bar{R}$. Thus, Po does not contribute to the explanation of the partisan vote.

Significance Test of the Regression

Now we want to test the null hypothesis that $\beta_1 = \beta_2 = \cdots = \beta_k = 0$; that is, we wish to test the whole regression model. If every β (population regression coefficient) is equal to zero, there is no relationship between the dependent variable and any of the independent variables. In other words, if every β is equal to zero, the dependent variable and each of the independent variables are independent.

We use the F test for the test of the regression. We construct the F ratio as follows:

$$(9\text{-}41) \qquad F = \frac{(\sum(Y_c - \bar{Y})^2)/k}{(\sum(Y - Y_c)^2)/(n-k-1)}$$

This is the same variance ratio test for testing R^2 as that presented in Chapter 8. Note that k and $n-k-1$ are degrees of freedom and that n is the number of observations in the sample and k is the number of independent variables.

If we divide the numerator and the denominator of (9-41) by $\sum(Y - \bar{Y})^2$, we get

$$(9\text{-}42) \qquad F = \frac{((\sum(Y_c - \bar{Y})^2)/(\sum(Y - \bar{Y})^2))/k}{((\sum(Y - Y_c)^2)/(\sum(Y - \bar{Y})^2))/(n-k-1)}$$

and this is equal to

$$(9\text{-}43) \qquad F = \frac{R^2/k}{(1-R^2)/(n-k-1)}$$

We use Table A-5 to find whether the value of F that we get is significant. The significance level usually considered is .05.

The F ratios in Examples 9-4 and 9-5 are 22.73 and 12.95, respectively. In Example 9-4, $k = 11$ and $n - k - 1 = 48$, the sample size being 60. In Example 9-5, $k = 3$ and $n - k - 1 = 31$, the sample size being 35. The F ratio in both examples is significant at the .05 significance level. In fact, in both examples, it is also significant at .01 significance level. This means that in both examples we reject the null hypothesis that all the β's are equal to zero.

As a general rule, the closer the F ratio is to zero, the less likely it is to be significant. In order to get an intuitive idea of the F test, note that $F = 0$ if $Y_c = \overline{Y}$. This means that the explained variation is zero and the introduction of the independent variables does not add to the explanation of the dependent variable. If the observed points are far away from the estimated points, $\sum (Y_c - \overline{Y})^2$ becomes small and $\sum (Y - Y_c)^2$ becomes large, thus making F small and consequently less likely to be significant. On the other hand, if the observed points are clustered closely around the estimated points, $\sum (Y_c - \overline{Y})^2$ becomes large and $\sum (Y - Y_c)^2$ becomes small, thus making F large and consequently more likely to be significant. The importance of the distance between the Y_c values and $\overline{Y}$ goes back to something we said at the beginning of this chapter. If we had to guess the values of the variable Y, one good guess would be $\overline{Y}$. But by finding a set of independent variables (X's) we might be able to improve that guess with Y_c.

Multicollinearity

We sometimes face a problem in the use of multiple linear regression when all or some of the independent variables are highly correlated with one another. Because of such high correlation it becomes difficult, and in some cases impossible, to determine the separate influence of each independent variable on the dependent variable. This problem is called *multicollinearity*.

Multicollinearity occurs in two cases: (1) One or more of the independent variables have an exact linear relationship with at least one other of the independent variables; and (2) none of the independent variables has exact linear relationship with another independent variable, but correlations between some of the independent variables are quite high. In the first case, which may be called *perfect* multicollinearity, the method of multiple linear regression does not work.

The second case, when the correlations between some of the independent variables are high, needs further elaboration. A simple correlation is considered high for the purpose of multicollinearity if it is .8 or more. Such multicollinearity leads to two consequences: (1) the size of the standard errors of the b's increases (Johnston, 1963); and (2) the size of R^2 decreases (Ferber, 1949). Both consequences undermine the results of the regression analysis. One way to solve the problem is to drop one of the variables from the analysis. This decision must be based on purely theoretical, and therefore mathematically arbitrary, considerations. In the original analysis of U.N. voting, we first included geographical location among the independent variables. But we found geographical location to be highly correlated with the alliance variable, so we dropped geography because we consider alliance more important for explaining the voting outcome in the United Nations.

Another method used to solve the problem of multicollinearity is to apply regression twice, first dropping one independent variable and then dropping the other independent variable. This step might be appropriate when we think that both independent variables, although highly correlated, are more or less equally important for the explanation of the dependent variable and that both should be included as control variables so that their effect on other independent variables can be evaluated.

Dummy Variables

In studying politics we sometimes encounter variables that are dichotomous by necessity or by convenience. Winning and losing, voting and not voting, living or dying are necessarily dichotomous variables. In other cases we may not be able to get the quantitative values of certain variables that we need for a discrete interval scale measurement; or even if the quantitative values are available, we may think that we can do an equally good job of our analysis by using two broad categories. In such cases we make use of what is known as *dummy* (or dichotomous) variables.

We mentioned earlier that some of the independent variables in Example 9-4 are represented as dummy variables. A dummy variable has only two values: It is coded 1 if the attribute of interest is present and it is coded 0 for the absence of the attribute. For example, alliance with the United States is a dummy variable in Example 9-4. If a country is in alliance with the United States, the alliance variable is coded 1, and if a country is not in alliance with the United States, it is coded 0.

When we use one or more of the independent variables as dummy variables, our interpretation of the regression results is not very precise. However, the interpretation of the regression coefficient of a dummy variable is straightforward. The regression coefficient is the slope of the line relating Y and X_i; that is, the ratio of a change in Y to a change in X_i. If X_i is a dummy variable, then the change in X_i is always equal to 1. Therefore, the regression coefficient is directly interpretable as the impact on the dependent variable of the presence of the attribute of interest. For example, the coefficient for the alliance variable is 13.86, so we conclude that the presence of alliance with the United States produces an average increase of 13.86 in the agreement index.

If we use dummy variables, we have to be aware of a serious limitation on their use. If we use more than one independent variable as dummy variables and the observations of each dummy variable are different from the observations of every other dummy variable, even though all observations of the sample are included in the dummy variables considered, we are likely to get enormous amounts of standard errors. This would be the case if the following four geographical dummy variables were included in Example 9-4: Africa, Asia, Latin America, and Middle East. To overcome this problem, two methods are suggested: (1) set the intercept term equal to zero, or (2) drop one of the dummy variables (Suits, 1957).

SUMMARY

In Chapter 8 we explained the determination of a positive or a negative relationship between variables through the use of correlation analysis. Regression analysis goes beyond this. It helps us estimate the character of the relationship between variables.

Although nonlinear regression is available, in this chapter we discuss only linear regression. Linear regression has been used more widely than nonlinear regression in political research. Also, linear regression is easier than nonlinear regression to comprehend and interpret.

Two variations of linear regression have been considered: simple linear regression and multiple linear regression. In simple linear regression only two variables, one dependent and the other independent, are considered. In multiple linear regression, more than two variables, one dependent and the others independent, are considered.

Simple Linear Regression

For using simple linear regression, we make the following assumptions:

1. The relationship between Y (dependent variable) and X (independent variable) is linear.
2. For each value of X the values of Y are normally distributed.
3. The variance of each subpopulation of $Y(\sigma^2 y \cdot x)$ is the same and is independent of X.
4. The values of ε, the population error term, are independent of each other and ε is normally distributed with zero mean and $\sigma^2 y \cdot x$ variance.

As in other parametric statistical models, we have investigated a sample in linear regression and have made inferences about the whole population. In simple linear regression the sample regression model is written as

$$Y_c = a + bX$$

This equation is an estimate of

$$Y = \alpha + \beta X$$

where α and β are population coefficients. We estimate α and β with the least squares method, which minimizes $\sum (Y - Y_c)^2$. Here, a is the estimate of α and b is the estimate of β.

In interpreting regression results, b is the most useful statistic. It is the slope of the regression line and indicates average change in Y with a unit change in X.

After we develop the sample regression model, we want to ascertain the quality of our estimate, given by the line $a + bX$. The measure used to ascertain the quality of our estimate is called the *standard error of estimate* and is written $\hat{\sigma}y \cdot x$. The *standard error of estimate* indicates the distance of the observed values of Y from the estimated values of Y. Notationally,

$$\hat{\sigma}y \cdot x = \left(\frac{\sum (Y - Y_c)^2}{n-2}\right)^{\frac{1}{2}}$$

If we square $\hat{\sigma}y \cdot x$, we get $\hat{\sigma}^2 y \cdot x$, the unexplained sample variance. On the other hand, *coefficient of determination*, written r^2, gives the explained proportion of the total sample variance. In a sense, r^2 is a measure of how much better $a + bX$ is as a guess of Y than $\bar{Y}$ is a guess of Y. r^2 varies between 0 and 1. We get the minimum value of r^2 when $Y_c = \bar{Y}$ and we get its maximum value when $Y_c = Y$.

It is essential to ascertain that β is not equal to zero and X and Y are not independent. For this, the t-test is used. If $n \geqslant 30$, the normal test can be used. With the help of a t-table (Table A-3, Appendix) we can also construct the confidence interval for β.

Multiple Linear Regression

The assumptions of multiple linear regression are the following:

1. The relationship between Y (dependent variable) and X's (independent variables) is linear.
2. The distributions of Y for fixed X's are normal. Often, multivariate normal distribution is assumed.
3. The error terms are unrelated. We have more than one error term and each ε_i is assumed to be normally distributed with zero mean and σ^2 variance.
4. The variances are the same.

We write the population and the sample equations as follows:

$$Y = \alpha + \beta_1 X_1 + \beta_2 X_2 + \cdots + \beta_k X_k \quad \text{(population)}$$
$$Y_c = a + b_1 X_1 + b_2 X_2 + \cdots + b_k X_k \quad \text{(sample)}$$

where a and b's are estimates of α and β's, respectively. We get the estimates of α and β's with the least squares method, which minimizes $\sum(Y-Y_c)^2$.

In interpreting regression results, b's are most useful; b's are called *partial regression coefficients*. Each of the b's indicates the average change in Y with a unit change in an independent variable, when other independent variables are held constant.

Also, b's can be standardized and the standardized b's can be used to compare the relative importance of the independent variables. However, we have argued that standardized b's are not so useful as they appear to be.

As in the case of simple linear regression, we ascertain the quality of our estimate with the *standard error of estimate*, written as $\hat{\sigma}$. The error $\hat{\sigma}$ is equal to

$$\left(\frac{\sum(Y-Y_c)^2}{n-k-1}\right)^{\frac{1}{2}}$$

The explained variance is denoted by R^2 and is called the *coefficient of multiple determination*.

We use the t-test (normal test can be used for $n \geqslant 30$) to test for each β_i (that is, to find whether it is equal to zero). In explaining t-test, standard errors of b's were explained. We use F test for the entire regression.

In using multiple linear regression, we must be careful about avoiding multicollinearity; otherwise, the separate influences of the independent variables on the dependent variable cannot be ascertained.

The last section of this chapter has been devoted to dummy variables, and it has been emphasized that they must be used carefully.

NOTES   Chapter 9

1. Although nonlinear regression model is available, we discuss only linear regression in this book, since linear regression is easier to comprehend and interpret than nonlinear regression.

2. This index of agreement was devised by Arend Lijphart (1963) on the basis of the Rice-Beyle technique.

3. None of the countries in this study is a member of the Soviet alliance system. Hence, there is no independent variable on alliance with the Soviet Union.

4. No anti-Soviet demonstrations are reported in 1965 (in the 60 countries under study) in the *New York Times*. So we don't have an independent variable on the anti-Soviet demonstrations.

5. Domestic product differs from national product by the exclusion of income received from abroad.

6. These β coefficients are different from β's, the *population regression coefficients*.

REFERENCES   Chapter 9

Blydenburgh, John C. "Two Attempts to Measure the Effects of Precinct-Level Campaigning Activities." Ph.D. Thesis, University of Rochester, 1968.

Ezekiel, M., and K. A. Fox. *Methods of Correlation and Regression Analysis*. New York: Wiley, 1959.

Ferber, Robert. *Market Research*. New York: McGraw-Hill, 1949, p. 363.

Hoel, Paul G. *Elementary Statistics*. New York: Wiley, 1966, pp. 219–220.

Johnston, J. *Econometric Methods*. New York: McGraw-Hill, 1963.

Lijphart, Arend. "The Analysis of Bloc Voting in the General Assembly: A Critique and a Proposal," *American Political Science Review*, Vol. 57 (December 1963), pp. 902–917.

Rai, Kul B. "The Relationship between Foreign Policy Indicators and Voting Patterns in the U.N. General Assembly." Ph. D. Thesis, University of Rochester, 1969.

Suits, D. B. "Use of Dummy Variables in Regression Equations," *Journal of American Statistical Association*, Vol. 52 (December 1957), pp. 548–551.

APPENDIXES

Table   A-1

Normal Distribution

This table presents the area under the normal curve between a perpendicular erected at various points on the baseline and the right tail. The baseline is represented in units of Z.

Z	.00	.01	.02	.03	.04	.05	.06	.07	.08	.09
0.0	.5000	.4960	.4920	.4880	.4840	.4801	.4761	.4721	.4681	.4681
0.1	.4602	.4562	.4522	.4483	.4443	.4404	.4364	.4325	.4286	.4247
0.2	.4207	.4168	.4129	.4090	.4052	.4013	.3974	.3936	.3897	.3859
0.3	.3821	.3783	.3745	.3707	.3669	.3632	.3594	.3557	.3520	.3483
0.4	.3446	.3409	.3372	.3336	.3300	.3264	.3264	.3192	.3156	.3121
0.5	.3085	.3050	.3015	.2981	.2946	.2912	.2877	.2843	.2810	.2776
0.6	.2743	.2709	.2676	.2643	.2611	.2578	.2546	.2514	.2483	.2451
0.7	.2420	.2389	.2358	.2327	.2296	.2266	.2236	.2206	.2177	.2148
0.8	.2119	.2090	.2061	.2033	.2005	.1977	.1949	.1922	.1894	.1867
0.9	.1841	.1814	.1788	.1762	.1736	.1711	.1685	.1660	.1635	.1611
1.0	.1587	.1562	.1530	.1515	.1492	.1469	.1446	.1423	.1401	.1379
1.1	.1357	.1335	.1314	.1292	.1271	.1251	.1230	.1210	.1190	.1170
1.2	.1151	.1131	.1112	.1093	.1075	.1056	.1038	.1020	.1003	.0985
1.3	.0968	.0951	.0934	.0918	.0901	.0885	.0869	.0853	.0838	.0823
1.4	.0808	.0793	.0788	.0764	.0749	.0735	.0721	.0708	.0694	.0681
1.5	.0668	.0655	.0643	.0630	.0618	.0606	.0594	.0582	.0571	.0559
1.6	.0548	.0537	.0526	.0516	.0505	.0495	.0485	.0475	.0465	.0455
1.7	.0446	.0436	.0427	.0418	.0409	.0401	.0392	.0384	.0375	.0367
1.8	.0359	.0351	.0344	.0336	.0329	.0322	.0314	.0307	.0301	.0294
1.9	.0287	.0281	.0274	.0268	.0262	.0256	.0250	.0244	.0239	.0233
2.0	.0228	.0222	.0217	.0212	.0207	.0202	.0917	.0192	.0188	.0183
2.1	.0179	.0174	.0170	.0166	.0162	.0158	.0154	.0150	.0146	.0143
2.2	.0139	.0136	.0132	.0129	.0125	.0122	.0119	.0116	.0113	.0110
2.3	.0107	.0104	.0102	.0099	.0096	.0094	.0091	.0089	.0087	.0084
2.4	.0082	.0080	.0078	.0075	.0073	.0071	.0069	.0068	.0066	.0064
2.5	.0062	.0060	.0059	.0057	.0055	.0054	.0052	.0051	.0049	.0048
2.6	.0047	.0045	.0044	.0043	.0041	.0040	.0039	.0038	.0037	.0036
2.7	.0035	.0034	.0033	.0032	.0031	.0030	.0029	.0028	.0027	.0026
2.8	.0026	.0025	.0024	.0023	.0023	.0022	.0021	.0021	.0020	.0019
2.9	.0019	.0018	.0018	.0017	.0016	.0016	.0015	.0015	.0014	.0014
3.0	.00135	.0013	.0013	.0012	.0012	.0011	.0011	.0011	.0010	.0010
3.5	.0002326									
4.5	.0000317									
5.0	.000000287									

Table   A-2

Random Numbers

Line/Col.	(1)	(2)	(3)	(4)	(5)	(6)	(7)	(8)	(9)	(10)	(11)	(12)	(13)	(14)
1	10480	15011	01536	02011	81647	91646	69179	14194	62590	36207	20969	99570	91291	90700
2	22368	46573	25595	85393	30995	89198	27982	53402	93965	34095	52666	19174	39615	99505
3	24130	48360	22527	97265	76393	64809	15179	24830	49340	32081	30680	19655	63348	58629
4	42167	93093	06243	61680	07856	16376	39440	53537	71341	57004	00849	74917	97758	16379
5	37570	39975	81837	16656	06121	91782	60468	81305	49684	60672	14110	06927	01263	54613
6	77921	06907	11008	42751	27756	53498	18602	70659	90655	15053	21916	81825	44394	42880
7	99562	72905	56420	69994	98872	31016	71194	18738	44013	48840	63213	21069	10634	12952
8	96301	91977	05463	07972	18876	20922	94595	56869	69014	60045	18425	84903	42508	32307
9	89579	14342	63661	10281	17453	18103	57740	84378	25331	12566	58678	44947	05585	56941
10	85475	36857	43342	53988	53060	59533	38867	62300	08158	17983	16439	11458	18593	64952
11	28918	69578	88231	33276	70997	79936	56865	05859	90106	31595	01547	85590	91610	78188
12	63553	40961	48235	03427	49626	69445	18663	72695	52180	20847	12234	90511	33703	90322
13	09429	93969	52636	92737	88974	33488	36320	17617	30015	08272	84115	27156	30613	74952
14	10365	61129	87529	85689	48237	52267	67689	93394	01511	26358	85104	20285	29975	89868
15	07119	97336	71048	08178	77233	13916	47564	81056	97735	85977	29372	74461	28551	90707
16	51085	12765	51821	51259	77452	16308	60756	92144	49442	53900	70960	63990	75601	40719
17	02368	21382	52404	60268	89368	19885	55322	44819	01188	65255	64835	44919	05944	55157
18	01011	54092	33362	94904	31273	04146	18594	29852	71585	85030	51132	01915	92747	64951
19	52162	53916	46369	58586	23216	14513	83149	98736	23495	64350	94738	17752	35156	35749
20	07056	97628	33787	09998	42698	06691	76988	13602	51851	46104	88916	19509	25625	58104
21	48663	91245	85828	14346	09172	30168	90229	04734	59193	22178	30421	61666	99904	32812
22	54164	58492	22421	74103	47070	25306	76468	26384	58151	06646	21524	15227	96909	44592
23	32639	32363	05597	24200	13363	38005	94342	28728	35806	06912	17012	64161	18296	22851
24	29334	27001	87637	87308	58731	00256	45834	15398	46557	41135	10367	07684	36188	18510
25	02488	33062	28834	07351	19731	92420	60952	61280	50001	67658	32586	86679	50720	94953
26	81525	72295	04839	96423	24878	82651	66566	14778	76797	14780	13300	87074	79666	95725
27	29676	20591	68086	26432	46901	20849	89768	81536	86645	12659	92259	57102	80428	25280
28	00742	57392	39064	66432	84673	40027	32832	61362	98947	96067	64760	64584	96096	98253
29	05366	04213	25669	26422	44407	44048	37937	63904	45766	66134	75470	66520	34693	90449
30	91921	26418	64117	94305	26766	25940	39972	22209	71500	64568	91402	42416	07844	69618
31	00582	04711	87917	77341	42206	35126	74087	99547	81817	42607	43808	76655	62028	76630
32	00725	69884	62797	56170	86324	88072	76222	36086	84637	93161	76038	65855	77919	88006
33	69011	65797	95876	55293	18988	27354	26575	08625	40801	59920	29841	80150	12777	48501
34	25976	57948	29888	88604	67917	48708	18912	82271	65424	69774	33611	54262	85963	03547
35	09763	83473	73577	12908	30883	18317	28290	35797	05998	41688	34952	37888	38917	88050
36	91567	42595	27958	30134	04024	86385	29880	99730	55536	84855	29080	09250	79656	73211
37	17955	56349	90999	49127	20044	59931	06115	20542	18059	02008	73708	83517	36103	42791
38	46503	18584	18845	49618	02304	51038	20655	58727	28168	15475	56942	53389	20562	87338
39	92157	89634	94824	78171	84610	82834	09922	25417	44137	48413	25555	21246	35509	20468
40	14577	62765	35605	81263	39667	47358	56873	56307	61607	49518	89656	20103	77490	18062
41	98427	07523	33362	64270	01638	92477	66969	98420	04880	45585	46565	04102	46880	45709
42	34914	63976	88720	82765	34476	17032	87589	40836	32427	70002	70663	88863	77775	69348
43	70060	28277	39475	46473	23219	53416	94970	25832	69975	94884	19661	72828	00102	66794
44	53976	54914	06990	67245	68350	82948	11398	42878	80287	88267	47363	46634	06541	97809
45	76072	29515	40980	07391	58745	25774	22987	80059	39911	96189	41151	14222	60697	59583
46	90725	52210	83974	29992	65831	38857	50490	83765	55657	14361	31720	57375	56228	41546
47	64364	67412	33339	31926	14883	24413	59744	92351	97473	89286	35931	04110	23726	51900
48	08962	00358	31662	25388	61642	34072	81249	35648	56891	69352	48373	45578	78547	81788
49	95012	68379	93526	70765	10593	04542	76463	54328	02349	17247	28865	14777	62730	92277
50	15664	10493	20492	38391	91132	21999	59516	81652	27195	48223	46751	22923	32261	85653

Source: Reprinted from Samuel M. Selby, *Standard Mathematical Tables,* 17th ed. (Cleveland: The Chemical Rubber Co., 1969), "A Table of 14,000 Random Units," pp. 626–27. © Copyright by The Chemical Rubber Co., with the kind permission of the publisher.

Table A-2

Random Numbers (*continued*)

Line/Col.	(1)	(2)	(3)	(4)	(5)	(6)	(7)	(8)	(9)	(10)	(11)	(12)	(13)	(14)
51	16408	81899	04153	53381	79401	21438	83035	92350	36693	31238	59649	91754	72772	02338
52	18629	81953	05520	91962	04739	13092	97662	24822	94730	06496	35090	04822	86772	98289
53	73115	35101	47498	87637	99016	71060	88824	71013	18735	20286	23153	72924	35165	43040
54	57491	16703	23167	49323	45021	33132	12544	41035	80780	45393	44812	12515	98931	91202
55	30405	83946	23792	14422	15059	45799	22716	19792	09983	74353	68668	30429	70735	25499
56	16631	35006	85900	98275	32388	52390	16815	69298	82732	38480	73817	32523	41961	44437
57	96773	20206	42559	78985	05300	22164	24369	54224	35083	19687	11052	91491	60383	19746
58	38935	64202	14349	82674	66523	44133	00697	35552	35970	19124	63318	29686	03387	59846
59	31624	76384	17403	53363	44167	64486	64758	75366	76554	31601	12614	33072	60332	92325
60	78919	19474	23632	27889	47914	02584	37680	20801	72152	39339	34806	08930	85001	87820
61	03931	33309	57047	74211	63445	17361	62825	39908	05607	91284	68833	25570	38818	46920
62	74426	33278	43972	10119	89917	15665	52872	73823	73144	88662	88970	74492	51805	99378
63	09066	00903	20795	95452	92648	45454	09552	88815	16553	51125	79375	97596	16296	66092
64	42238	12426	87025	14267	20979	04508	64535	31355	86064	29472	47689	05974	52468	16834
65	16153	08002	26504	41744	81959	65642	74240	56302	00033	67107	77510	70625	28725	34191
66	21457	40742	29820	96783	29400	21840	15035	34537	33310	06116	95240	15957	16572	06004
67	21581	57802	02050	89728	17937	37621	47075	42080	97403	48626	68995	43805	33386	21597
68	55612	78095	83197	33732	05810	24813	86902	60397	16489	03264	88525	42786	05269	92532
69	44657	66999	99324	51281	84463	60563	79312	93454	68876	25471	93911	25650	12682	73572
70	91340	84979	46949	81973	37949	61023	43997	15263	80644	43942	89203	71795	99533	50501
71	91227	21199	31935	27022	84067	05462	35216	14486	29891	68607	41867	14951	91696	85065
72	50001	38140	66321	19924	72163	09538	12151	06878	91903	18749	34405	56087	82790	70925
73	65390	05224	72958	28609	81406	39147	25549	48542	42627	45233	57202	94617	23772	07896
74	27504	96131	83944	41575	10573	08619	64482	73923	36152	05184	94142	25299	84387	34925
75	37169	94851	39117	89632	00959	16487	65536	49071	39782	17095	02330	74301	00275	48280
76	11508	70225	51111	38351	19444	66499	71945	05422	13442	78675	84081	66938	93654	59894
77	37449	30362	06694	54690	04052	53115	62757	95348	78662	11163	81651	50245	34971	52924
78	46515	70331	85922	38329	57015	15765	97161	17869	45349	61796	66345	81073	49106	79860
79	30986	81223	42416	58353	21532	30502	32305	86482	05174	07901	54339	58861	74818	46942
80	63798	64995	46583	09765	44160	78128	83991	42865	92520	83531	80377	35909	81250	54238
81	82486	84846	99254	67632	43218	50076	21361	64816	51202	88124	41870	52689	51275	83556
82	21885	32906	92431	09060	64297	51674	64126	62570	26123	05155	59194	52799	28225	85762
83	60336	98782	07408	53458	13564	59089	26445	29789	85205	41001	12535	12133	14645	23541
84	43937	46891	24010	25560	86355	33941	25786	54990	71899	15475	95434	98227	21824	19585
85	97656	63175	89303	16275	07100	92063	21942	18611	47348	20203	18534	03862	78095	50136
86	03299	01221	05418	38982	55758	92237	26759	86367	21216	98442	08303	56613	91511	75928
87	79626	06486	03574	17668	07785	76020	79924	25651	83325	88428	85076	72811	22717	50585
88	85636	68335	47539	03129	65651	11977	02510	26113	99447	68645	34327	15152	55230	93448
89	18039	14367	61337	06177	12143	46609	32989	74014	64708	00533	35398	58408	13261	47908
90	08362	15656	60627	36478	65648	16764	53412	09013	07832	41574	17639	82163	60859	75567
91	79556	29068	04142	16268	15387	12856	66227	38358	22478	73373	88732	09443	82558	05250
92	92608	82674	27072	32534	17075	27698	98204	63863	11951	34648	88022	56148	34925	57031
93	23982	25835	40055	67006	12293	02753	14827	22235	35071	99704	37543	11601	35503	85171
94	09915	96306	05908	97901	28395	14186	00821	80703	70426	75647	76310	88717	37890	40129
95	50937	33300	26695	62247	69927	76123	50842	43834	86654	70959	79725	93872	28117	19233
96	42488	78077	69882	61657	34136	79180	97526	43092	04098	73571	80799	76536	71255	64239
97	46764	86273	63003	93017	31204	36692	40202	35275	57306	55543	53203	18098	47625	88684
98	03237	45430	55417	63282	90816	17349	88298	90183	36600	78406	06216	95787	42579	90730
99	86591	81482	52667	61583	14972	90053	89534	76036	49199	43716	97548	04379	46370	28672
100	38534	01715	94964	87288	65680	43772	39560	12918	86537	62738	19636	51132	25739	56947

Table A-3

Percentage Points of the *t* Distribution

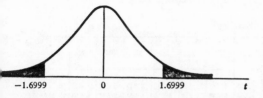

Example
for 29 degrees of freedom
P(t > 1.6999) = .05
P(t < −1.6999) = .05

−1.6999   0   1.6999   *t*

ϕ \ α	.25	.20	.15	.10	.05	.025	.01	.005	.0005
1	1.000	1.376	1.963	3.078	6.314	12.706	31.821	63.657	636.619
2	.816	1.061	1.386	1.886	2.920	4.303	6.965	9.925	31.598
3	.765	.978	1.250	1.638	2.353	3.182	4.541	5.841	12.941
4	.741	.941	1.190	1.533	2.132	2.776	3.747	4.604	8.610
5	.727	.920	1.156	1.476	2.015	2.571	3.365	4.032	6.859
6	.718	.906	1.134	1.440	1.943	2.447	3.143	3.707	5.959
7	.711	.896	1.119	1.415	1.895	2.365	2.998	3.499	5.405
8	.706	.889	1.108	1.397	1.860	2.306	2.896	3.355	5.041
9	.703	.883	1.100	1.383	1.833	2.262	2.821	3.250	4.781
10	.700	.879	1.093	1.372	1.812	2.228	2.764	3.169	4.587
11	.697	.876	1.088	1.363	1.796	2.201	2.718	3.106	4.437
12	.695	.873	1.083	1.356	1.782	2.179	2.681	3.055	4.318
13	.694	.870	1.079	1.350	1.771	2.160	2.650	3.012	4.221
14	.692	.868	1.076	1.345	1.761	2.145	2.624	2.977	4.140
15	.691	.866	1.074	1.341	1.753	2.131	2.602	2.947	4.073
16	.690	.865	1.071	1.337	1.746	2.120	2.583	2.921	4.015
17	.689	.863	1.069	1.333	1.740	2.110	2.567	2.898	3.965
18	.688	.862	1.067	1.330	1.734	2.101	2.552	2.878	3.922
19	.688	.861	1.066	1.328	1.729	2.093	2.539	2.861	3.883
20	.687	.860	1.064	1.325	1.725	2.086	2.528	2.845	3.850
21	.686	.859	1.063	1.323	1.721	2.080	2.518	2.831	3.819
22	.686	.858	1.061	1.321	1.717	2.074	2.508	2.819	3.792
23	.685	.858	1.060	1.319	1.714	2.069	2.500	2.807	3.767
24	.685	.857	1.059	1.318	1.711	2.064	2.492	2.397	3.745
25	.684	.856	1.058	1.316	1.708	2.060	2.485	2.787	3.725
26	.684	.856	1.058	1.315	1.706	2.056	2.479	2.779	3.707
27	.684	.855	1.057	1.314	1.703	2.052	2.473	2.771	3.690
28	.683	.855	1.056	1.313	1.701	2.048	2.467	2.763	3.674
29	.683	.854	1.055	1.311	1.699	2.045	2.462	2.756	3.659
30	.683	.854	1.055	1.310	1.697	2.042	2.457	2.750	3.646
40	.681	.851	1.050	1.303	1.684	2.021	2.423	2.704	3.551
60	.679	.848	1.046	1.296	1.671	2.000	2.390	2.660	3.460
120	.677	.845	1.041	1.289	1.658	1.980	2.358	2.617	3.373
∞	.674	.842	1.036	1.282	1.645	1.960	2.326	2.576	3.291

SOURCE: This table is abridged from Table III of Fisher & Yates: *Statistical Tables for Biological, Agricultural and Medical Research* published by Oliver & Boyd Ltd., Edinburgh, and by permission of the authors and publishers.

Table   A-4

Chi-Square

Probability

df	.99	.98	.95	.90	.80	.70	.50	.30	.20	.10	.05	.02	.01	.001
1	.0²157	.0²628	.00393	.0158	.0642	.148	.455	1.074	1.642	2.706	3.841	5.412	6.635	10.827
2	.0201	.0404	.103	.211	.446	.713	1.386	2.408	3.219	4.605	5.991	7.824	9.210	13.815
3	.115	.185	.352	.584	1.005	1.424	2.366	3.665	4.642	6.251	7.815	9.837	11.341	16.268
4	.297	.429	.711	1.064	1.649	2.195	3.357	4.878	5.989	7.779	9.488	11.668	13.277	18.465
5	.554	.752	1.145	1.610	2.343	3.000	4.351	6.064	7.289	9.236	11.070	13.388	15.086	20.517
6	.872	1.134	1.635	2.204	3.070	3.828	5.348	7.231	8.558	10.645	12.592	15.033	16.812	22.457
7	1.239	1.564	2.167	2.833	3.822	4.671	6.346	8.383	9.803	12.017	14.067	16.622	18.475	24.322
8	1.646	2.032	2.733	3.490	4.594	5.527	7.344	9.524	11.030	13.362	15.507	18.168	20.090	26.125
9	2.088	2.532	3.325	4.168	5.380	6.393	8.343	10.656	12.242	14.684	16.919	19.679	21.666	27.877
10	2.558	3.059	3.940	4.865	6.179	7.267	9.342	11.781	13.442	15.987	18.307	21.161	23.209	29.588
11	3.053	3.609	4.575	5.578	6.989	8.148	10.341	12.899	14.631	17.275	19.675	22.618	24.725	31.264
12	3.571	4.178	5.226	6.304	7.807	9.034	11.340	14.011	15.812	18.549	21.026	24.054	26.217	32.909
13	4.107	4.765	5.892	7.042	8.634	9.926	12.340	15.119	16.985	19.812	22.362	25.472	27.688	34.528
14	4.660	5.368	6.571	7.790	9.467	10.821	13.339	16.222	18.151	21.064	23.685	26.873	29.141	36.123
15	5.229	5.985	7.261	8.547	10.307	11.721	14.339	17.322	19.311	22.307	24.996	28.259	30.578	37.697
16	5.812	6.614	7.962	9.312	11.152	12.624	15.338	18.418	20.465	23.542	26.296	29.633	32.000	39.252
17	6.408	7.255	8.672	10.085	12.002	13.531	16.338	19.511	21.615	24.769	27.587	30.995	33.409	40.790
18	7.015	7.906	9.390	10.865	12.857	14.440	17.338	20.601	22.760	25.989	28.869	32.346	34.805	42.312
19	7.633	8.567	10.117	11.651	13.716	15.352	18.338	21.689	23.900	27.204	30.144	33.687	36.191	43.820
20	8.260	9.237	10.851	12.443	14.578	16.266	19.337	22.775	25.038	28.412	31.410	35.020	37.566	45.315
21	8.897	9.915	11.591	13.240	15.445	17.182	20.337	23.858	26.171	29.615	32.671	36.343	38.932	46.797
22	9.542	10.600	12.338	14.041	16.314	18.101	21.337	24.939	27.301	30.813	33.924	37.659	40.289	48.268
23	10.196	11.293	13.091	14.848	17.187	19.021	22.337	26.018	28.429	32.007	35.172	38.968	41.638	49.728
24	10.856	11.992	13.848	15.659	18.062	19.943	23.337	27.096	29.553	33.196	36.415	40.270	42.980	51.179
25	11.524	12.697	14.611	16.473	18.940	20.867	24.337	28.172	30.675	34.382	37.652	41.566	44.314	52.620
26	12.198	13.409	15.379	17.292	19.820	21.792	25.336	29.246	31.795	35.563	38.885	42.856	45.642	54.052
27	12.879	14.125	16.151	18.114	20.703	22.719	26.336	30.319	32.912	36.741	40.113	44.140	46.963	55.476
28	13.565	14.847	16.928	18.939	21.588	23.647	27.336	31.391	34.027	37.916	41.337	45.419	48.278	56.893
29	14.256	15.574	17.708	19.768	22.475	24.577	28.336	32.461	35.139	39.087	42.557	46.693	49.588	58.302
30	14.953	16.306	18.493	20.599	23.364	25.508	29.336	33.530	36.250	40.256	43.773	47.962	50.892	59.703

For larger values of df, the expression $\sqrt{2\chi^2} - \sqrt{2df - 1}$ may be used as a normal deviate with unit variance, remembering that the probability for χ^2 corresponds with that of a single tail of the normal curve.

Source: Taken from Table IV of R. A. Fisher and F. Yates, *Statistical Tables for Biological, Agricultural and Medical Research* (1948 ed.), published by Oliver & Boyd Ltd., Edinburgh, and by permission of the authors and publishers.

Table A-5

Percentage Points of the F Distribution

5% (Roman Type) and 1% (Bold Face Type) Points for the Distribution of F

n_1 degrees of freedom (for greater mean square)

Each cell shows the 5% point (roman) over the 1% point (bold), written as 5% / 1%.

n_2	1	2	3	4	5	6	7	8	9	10	11	12	14	16	20	24	30	40	50	75	100	200	500	∞
1	161 / 4,052	200 / 4,999	216 / 5,403	225 / 5,625	230 / 5,764	234 / 5,859	237 / 5,928	239 / 5,981	241 / 6,022	242 / 6,056	243 / 6,082	244 / 6,106	245 / 6,142	246 / 6,169	248 / 6,208	249 / 6,234	250 / 6,258	251 / 6,286	252 / 6,302	253 / 6,323	253 / 6,334	254 / 6,352	254 / 6,361	254 / 6,366
2	18.51 / 98.49	19.00 / 99.00	19.16 / 99.17	19.25 / 99.25	19.30 / 99.30	19.33 / 99.33	19.36 / 99.34	19.37 / 99.36	19.38 / 99.38	19.39 / 99.40	19.40 / 99.41	19.41 / 99.42	19.42 / 99.43	19.43 / 99.44	19.44 / 99.45	19.45 / 99.46	19.46 / 99.47	19.47 / 99.48	19.47 / 99.48	19.48 / 99.49	19.49 / 99.49	19.49 / 99.49	19.50 / 99.50	19.50 / 99.50
3	10.13 / 34.12	9.55 / 30.82	9.28 / 29.46	9.12 / 28.71	9.01 / 28.24	8.94 / 27.91	8.88 / 27.67	8.84 / 27.49	8.81 / 27.34	8.78 / 27.23	8.76 / 27.13	8.74 / 27.05	8.71 / 26.92	8.69 / 26.83	8.66 / 26.69	8.64 / 26.60	8.62 / 26.50	8.60 / 26.41	8.58 / 26.35	8.57 / 26.27	8.56 / 26.23	8.54 / 26.18	8.54 / 26.14	8.53 / 26.12
4	7.71 / 21.20	6.94 / 18.00	6.59 / 16.69	6.39 / 15.98	6.26 / 15.52	6.16 / 15.21	6.09 / 14.98	6.04 / 14.80	6.00 / 14.66	5.96 / 14.54	5.93 / 14.45	5.91 / 14.37	5.87 / 14.24	5.84 / 14.15	5.80 / 14.02	5.77 / 13.93	5.74 / 13.83	5.71 / 13.74	5.70 / 13.69	5.68 / 13.61	5.66 / 13.57	5.65 / 13.52	5.64 / 13.48	5.63 / 13.46
5	6.61 / 16.26	5.79 / 13.27	5.41 / 12.06	5.19 / 11.39	5.05 / 10.97	4.95 / 10.67	4.88 / 10.45	4.82 / 10.27	4.78 / 10.15	4.74 / 10.05	4.70 / 9.96	4.68 / 9.89	4.64 / 9.77	4.60 / 9.68	4.56 / 9.55	4.53 / 9.47	4.50 / 9.38	4.46 / 9.29	4.44 / 9.24	4.42 / 9.17	4.40 / 9.13	4.38 / 9.07	4.37 / 9.04	4.36 / 9.02
6	5.99 / 13.74	5.14 / 10.92	4.76 / 9.78	4.53 / 9.15	4.39 / 8.75	4.28 / 8.47	4.21 / 8.26	4.15 / 8.10	4.10 / 7.98	4.06 / 7.87	4.03 / 7.79	4.00 / 7.72	3.96 / 7.60	3.92 / 7.52	3.87 / 7.39	3.84 / 7.31	3.81 / 7.23	3.77 / 7.14	3.75 / 7.09	3.72 / 7.02	3.71 / 6.99	3.69 / 6.94	3.68 / 6.90	3.67 / 6.88
7	5.59 / 12.25	4.74 / 9.55	4.35 / 8.45	4.12 / 7.85	3.97 / 7.46	3.87 / 7.19	3.79 / 7.00	3.73 / 6.84	3.68 / 6.71	3.63 / 6.62	3.60 / 6.54	3.57 / 6.47	3.52 / 6.35	3.49 / 6.27	3.44 / 6.15	3.41 / 6.07	3.38 / 5.98	3.34 / 5.90	3.32 / 5.85	3.29 / 5.78	3.28 / 5.75	3.25 / 5.70	3.24 / 5.67	3.23 / 5.65
8	5.32 / 11.26	4.46 / 8.65	4.07 / 7.59	3.84 / 7.01	3.69 / 6.63	3.58 / 6.37	3.50 / 6.19	3.44 / 6.03	3.39 / 5.91	3.34 / 5.82	3.31 / 5.74	3.28 / 5.67	3.23 / 5.56	3.20 / 5.48	3.15 / 5.36	3.12 / 5.28	3.08 / 5.20	3.05 / 5.11	3.03 / 5.06	3.00 / 5.00	2.98 / 4.96	2.96 / 4.91	2.94 / 4.88	2.93 / 4.86
9	5.12 / 10.56	4.26 / 8.02	3.86 / 6.99	3.63 / 6.42	3.48 / 6.06	3.37 / 5.80	3.29 / 5.62	3.23 / 5.47	3.18 / 5.35	3.13 / 5.26	3.10 / 5.18	3.07 / 5.11	3.02 / 5.00	2.98 / 4.92	2.93 / 4.80	2.90 / 4.73	2.86 / 4.64	2.82 / 4.56	2.80 / 4.51	2.77 / 4.45	2.76 / 4.41	2.73 / 4.36	2.72 / 4.33	2.71 / 4.31
10	4.96 / 10.04	4.10 / 7.56	3.71 / 6.55	3.48 / 5.99	3.33 / 5.64	3.22 / 5.39	3.14 / 5.21	3.07 / 5.06	3.02 / 4.95	2.97 / 4.85	2.94 / 4.78	2.91 / 4.71	2.86 / 4.60	2.82 / 4.52	2.77 / 4.41	2.74 / 4.33	2.70 / 4.25	2.67 / 4.17	2.64 / 4.12	2.61 / 4.05	2.59 / 4.01	2.56 / 3.96	2.55 / 3.93	2.54 / 3.91
11	4.84 / 9.65	3.98 / 7.20	3.59 / 6.22	3.36 / 5.67	3.20 / 5.32	3.09 / 5.07	3.01 / 4.88	2.95 / 4.74	2.90 / 4.63	2.86 / 4.54	2.82 / 4.46	2.79 / 4.40	2.74 / 4.29	2.70 / 4.21	2.65 / 4.10	2.61 / 4.02	2.57 / 3.94	2.53 / 3.86	2.50 / 3.80	2.47 / 3.74	2.45 / 3.70	2.42 / 3.66	2.41 / 3.62	2.40 / 3.60
12	4.75 / 9.33	3.88 / 6.93	3.49 / 5.95	3.26 / 5.41	3.11 / 5.06	3.00 / 4.82	2.92 / 4.65	2.85 / 4.50	2.80 / 4.39	2.76 / 4.30	2.72 / 4.22	2.69 / 4.16	2.64 / 4.05	2.60 / 3.98	2.54 / 3.86	2.50 / 3.78	2.46 / 3.70	2.42 / 3.61	2.40 / 3.56	2.36 / 3.49	2.35 / 3.46	2.32 / 3.41	2.31 / 3.38	2.30 / 3.36
13	4.67 / 9.07	3.80 / 6.70	3.41 / 5.74	3.18 / 5.20	3.02 / 4.86	2.92 / 4.62	2.84 / 4.44	2.77 / 4.30	2.72 / 4.19	2.67 / 4.10	2.63 / 4.02	2.60 / 3.96	2.55 / 3.85	2.51 / 3.78	2.46 / 3.67	2.42 / 3.59	2.38 / 3.51	2.34 / 3.42	2.32 / 3.37	2.28 / 3.30	2.26 / 3.27	2.24 / 3.21	2.22 / 3.18	2.21 / 3.16

Table A-5

Percentage Points of the F Distribution (continued)

5% (Roman Type) and 1% (Bold Face Type) Points for the Distribution of F

n_1 degrees of freedom (for greater mean square)

Each cell shows the 5% point (Roman) / 1% point (Bold).

n_2	1	2	3	4	5	6	7	8	9	10	11	12	14	16	20	24	30	40	50	75	100	200	500	∞	n_2
14	4.60/8.86	3.74/6.51	3.34/5.56	3.11/5.03	2.96/4.69	2.85/4.46	2.77/4.28	2.70/4.14	2.65/4.03	2.60/3.94	2.56/3.86	2.53/3.80	2.48/3.70	2.44/3.62	2.39/3.51	2.35/3.43	2.31/3.34	2.27/3.26	2.24/3.21	2.21/3.14	2.19/3.11	2.16/3.06	2.14/3.02	2.13/3.00	14
15	4.54/8.68	3.68/6.36	3.29/5.42	3.06/4.89	2.90/4.56	2.79/4.32	2.70/4.14	2.64/4.00	2.59/3.89	2.55/3.80	2.51/3.73	2.48/3.67	2.43/3.56	2.39/3.48	2.33/3.36	2.29/3.29	2.25/3.20	2.21/3.12	2.18/3.07	2.15/3.00	2.12/2.97	2.10/2.92	2.08/2.89	2.07/2.87	15
16	4.49/8.53	3.63/6.23	3.24/5.29	3.01/4.77	2.85/4.44	2.74/4.20	2.66/4.03	2.59/3.89	2.54/3.78	2.49/3.69	2.45/3.61	2.42/3.55	2.37/3.45	2.33/3.37	2.28/3.25	2.24/3.18	2.20/3.10	2.16/3.01	2.13/2.96	2.09/2.89	2.07/2.86	2.04/2.80	2.02/2.77	2.01/2.75	16
17	4.45/8.40	3.59/6.11	3.20/5.18	2.96/4.67	2.81/4.34	2.70/4.10	2.62/3.93	2.55/3.79	2.50/3.68	2.45/3.59	2.41/3.52	2.38/3.45	2.33/3.35	2.29/3.27	2.23/3.16	2.19/3.08	2.15/3.00	2.11/2.92	2.08/2.86	2.04/2.79	2.02/2.76	1.99/2.70	1.97/2.67	1.96/2.65	17
18	4.41/8.28	3.55/6.01	3.16/5.09	2.93/4.58	2.77/4.25	2.66/4.01	2.58/3.85	2.51/3.71	2.46/3.60	2.41/3.51	2.37/3.44	2.34/3.37	2.29/3.27	2.25/3.19	2.19/3.07	2.15/3.00	2.11/2.91	2.07/2.83	2.04/2.78	2.00/2.71	1.98/2.68	1.95/2.62	1.93/2.59	1.92/2.57	18
19	4.38/8.18	3.52/5.93	3.13/5.01	2.90/4.50	2.74/4.17	2.63/3.94	2.55/3.77	2.48/3.63	2.43/3.52	2.38/3.43	2.34/3.36	2.31/3.30	2.26/3.19	2.21/3.12	2.15/3.00	2.11/2.92	2.07/2.84	2.02/2.76	2.00/2.70	1.96/2.63	1.94/2.60	1.91/2.54	1.90/2.51	1.88/2.49	19
20	4.35/8.10	3.49/5.85	3.10/4.94	2.87/4.43	2.71/4.10	2.60/3.87	2.52/3.71	2.45/3.56	2.40/3.45	2.35/3.37	2.31/3.30	2.28/3.23	2.23/3.13	2.18/3.05	2.12/2.94	2.08/2.86	2.04/2.77	1.99/2.69	1.96/2.63	1.92/2.56	1.90/2.53	1.87/2.47	1.85/2.44	1.84/2.42	20
21	4.32/8.02	3.47/5.78	3.07/4.87	2.84/4.37	2.68/4.04	2.57/3.81	2.49/3.65	2.42/3.51	2.37/3.40	2.32/3.31	2.28/3.24	2.25/3.17	2.20/3.07	2.15/2.99	2.09/2.88	2.05/2.80	2.00/2.72	1.96/2.63	1.93/2.58	1.89/2.51	1.87/2.47	1.84/2.42	1.82/2.38	1.81/2.36	21
22	4.30/7.94	3.44/5.72	3.05/4.82	2.82/4.31	2.66/3.99	2.55/3.76	2.47/3.59	2.40/3.45	2.35/3.35	2.30/3.26	2.26/3.18	2.23/3.12	2.18/3.02	2.13/2.94	2.07/2.83	2.03/2.75	1.98/2.67	1.93/2.58	1.91/2.53	1.87/2.46	1.84/2.42	1.81/2.37	1.80/2.33	1.78/2.31	22
23	4.28/7.88	3.42/5.66	3.03/4.76	2.80/4.26	2.64/3.94	2.53/3.71	2.45/3.54	2.38/3.41	2.32/3.30	2.28/3.21	2.24/3.14	2.20/3.07	2.14/2.97	2.10/2.89	2.04/2.78	2.00/2.70	1.96/2.62	1.91/2.53	1.88/2.48	1.84/2.41	1.82/2.37	1.79/2.32	1.77/2.28	1.76/2.26	23
24	4.26/7.82	3.40/5.61	3.01/4.72	2.78/4.22	2.62/3.90	2.51/3.67	2.43/3.50	2.36/3.36	2.30/3.25	2.26/3.17	2.22/3.09	2.18/3.03	2.13/2.93	2.09/2.85	2.02/2.74	1.98/2.66	1.94/2.58	1.89/2.49	1.86/2.44	1.82/2.36	1.80/2.33	1.76/2.27	1.74/2.23	1.73/2.21	24
25	4.24/7.77	3.38/5.57	2.99/4.68	2.76/4.18	2.60/3.86	2.49/3.63	2.41/3.46	2.34/3.32	2.28/3.21	2.24/3.13	2.20/3.05	2.16/2.99	2.11/2.89	2.06/2.81	2.00/2.70	1.96/2.62	1.92/2.54	1.87/2.45	1.84/2.40	1.80/2.32	1.77/2.29	1.74/2.23	1.72/2.19	1.71/2.17	25
26	4.22/7.72	3.37/5.53	2.98/4.64	2.74/4.14	2.59/3.82	2.47/3.59	2.39/3.42	2.32/3.29	2.27/3.17	2.22/3.09	2.18/3.02	2.15/2.96	2.10/2.86	2.05/2.77	1.99/2.66	1.95/2.58	1.90/2.50	1.85/2.41	1.82/2.36	1.78/2.28	1.76/2.25	1.72/2.19	1.70/2.15	1.69/2.13	26

Table A-5

Percentage Points of the F Distribution (continued)

5% (Roman Type) and 1% (Bold Face Type) Points for the Distribution of F

ϕ_1 degrees of freedom (for greater mean square)

Each cell shows the 5% point (Roman) over the 1% point (Bold Face).

ϕ_2	1	2	3	4	5	6	7	8	9	10	11	12	14	16	20	24	30	40	50	75	100	200	500	∞	ϕ_2
27	4.21 **7.68**	3.35 **5.49**	2.96 **4.60**	2.73 **4.11**	2.57 **3.79**	2.46 **3.56**	2.37 **3.39**	2.30 **3.26**	2.25 **3.14**	2.20 **3.06**	2.16 **2.98**	2.13 **2.93**	2.08 **2.83**	2.03 **2.74**	1.97 **2.63**	1.93 **2.55**	1.88 **2.47**	1.84 **2.38**	1.80 **2.33**	1.76 **2.25**	1.74 **2.21**	1.71 **2.16**	1.68 **2.12**	1.67 **2.10**	27
28	4.20 **7.64**	3.34 **5.45**	2.95 **4.57**	2.71 **4.07**	2.56 **3.76**	2.44 **3.53**	2.36 **3.36**	2.29 **3.23**	2.24 **3.11**	2.19 **3.03**	2.15 **2.95**	2.12 **2.90**	2.06 **2.80**	2.02 **2.71**	1.96 **2.60**	1.91 **2.52**	1.87 **2.44**	1.81 **2.35**	1.78 **2.30**	1.75 **2.22**	1.72 **2.18**	1.69 **2.13**	1.67 **2.09**	1.65 **2.06**	28
29	4.18 **7.60**	3.33 **5.42**	2.93 **4.54**	2.70 **4.04**	2.54 **3.73**	2.43 **3.50**	2.35 **3.33**	2.28 **3.20**	2.22 **3.08**	2.18 **3.00**	2.14 **2.92**	2.10 **2.87**	2.05 **2.77**	2.00 **2.68**	1.94 **2.57**	1.90 **2.49**	1.85 **2.41**	1.80 **2.32**	1.77 **2.27**	1.73 **2.19**	1.71 **2.15**	1.68 **2.10**	1.65 **2.06**	1.64 **2.03**	29
30	4.17 **7.56**	3.32 **5.39**	2.92 **4.51**	2.69 **4.02**	2.53 **3.70**	2.42 **3.47**	2.34 **3.30**	2.27 **3.17**	2.21 **3.06**	2.16 **2.98**	2.12 **2.90**	2.09 **2.84**	2.04 **2.74**	1.99 **2.66**	1.93 **2.55**	1.89 **2.47**	1.84 **2.38**	1.79 **2.29**	1.76 **2.24**	1.72 **2.16**	1.69 **2.13**	1.66 **2.07**	1.64 **2.03**	1.62 **2.01**	30
32	4.15 **7.50**	3.30 **5.34**	2.90 **4.46**	2.67 **3.97**	2.51 **3.66**	2.40 **3.42**	2.32 **3.25**	2.25 **3.12**	2.19 **3.01**	2.14 **2.94**	2.10 **2.86**	2.07 **2.80**	2.02 **2.70**	1.97 **2.62**	1.91 **2.51**	1.86 **2.42**	1.82 **2.34**	1.76 **2.25**	1.74 **2.20**	1.69 **2.12**	1.67 **2.08**	1.64 **2.02**	1.61 **1.98**	1.59 **1.96**	32
34	4.13 **7.44**	3.28 **5.29**	2.88 **4.42**	2.65 **3.93**	2.49 **3.61**	2.38 **3.38**	2.30 **3.21**	2.23 **3.08**	2.17 **2.97**	2.12 **2.89**	2.08 **2.82**	2.05 **2.76**	2.00 **2.66**	1.95 **2.58**	1.89 **2.47**	1.84 **2.38**	1.80 **2.30**	1.74 **2.21**	1.71 **2.15**	1.67 **2.08**	1.64 **2.04**	1.61 **1.98**	1.59 **1.94**	1.57 **1.91**	34
36	4.11 **7.39**	3.26 **5.25**	2.86 **4.38**	2.63 **3.89**	2.48 **3.58**	2.36 **3.35**	2.28 **3.18**	2.21 **3.04**	2.15 **2.94**	2.10 **2.86**	2.06 **2.78**	2.03 **2.72**	1.98 **2.62**	1.93 **2.54**	1.87 **2.43**	1.82 **2.35**	1.78 **2.26**	1.72 **2.17**	1.69 **2.12**	1.65 **2.04**	1.62 **2.00**	1.59 **1.94**	1.56 **1.90**	1.55 **1.87**	36
38	4.10 **7.35**	3.25 **5.21**	2.85 **4.34**	2.62 **3.86**	2.46 **3.54**	2.35 **3.32**	2.26 **3.15**	2.19 **3.02**	2.14 **2.91**	2.09 **2.82**	2.05 **2.75**	2.02 **2.69**	1.96 **2.59**	1.92 **2.51**	1.85 **2.40**	1.80 **2.32**	1.76 **2.22**	1.71 **2.14**	1.67 **2.08**	1.63 **2.00**	1.60 **1.97**	1.57 **1.90**	1.54 **1.86**	1.53 **1.84**	38
40	4.08 **7.31**	3.23 **5.18**	2.84 **4.31**	2.61 **3.83**	2.45 **3.51**	2.34 **3.29**	2.25 **3.12**	2.18 **2.99**	2.12 **2.88**	2.07 **2.80**	2.04 **2.73**	2.00 **2.66**	1.95 **2.56**	1.90 **2.49**	1.84 **2.37**	1.79 **2.29**	1.74 **2.20**	1.69 **2.11**	1.66 **2.05**	1.61 **1.97**	1.59 **1.94**	1.55 **1.88**	1.53 **1.84**	1.51 **1.81**	40
42	4.07 **7.27**	3.22 **5.15**	2.83 **4.29**	2.59 **3.80**	2.44 **3.49**	2.32 **3.26**	2.24 **3.10**	2.17 **2.96**	2.11 **2.86**	2.06 **2.77**	2.02 **2.70**	1.99 **2.64**	1.94 **2.54**	1.89 **2.46**	1.82 **2.35**	1.78 **2.26**	1.73 **2.17**	1.68 **2.08**	1.64 **2.02**	1.60 **1.94**	1.57 **1.91**	1.54 **1.85**	1.51 **1.80**	1.49 **1.78**	42
44	4.06 **7.24**	3.21 **5.12**	2.82 **4.26**	2.58 **3.78**	2.43 **3.46**	2.31 **3.24**	2.23 **3.07**	2.16 **2.94**	2.10 **2.84**	2.05 **2.75**	2.01 **2.68**	1.98 **2.62**	1.92 **2.52**	1.88 **2.44**	1.81 **2.32**	1.76 **2.24**	1.72 **2.15**	1.66 **2.06**	1.63 **2.00**	1.58 **1.92**	1.56 **1.88**	1.52 **1.82**	1.50 **1.78**	1.48 **1.75**	44
46	4.05 **7.21**	3.20 **5.10**	2.81 **4.24**	2.57 **3.76**	2.42 **3.44**	2.30 **3.22**	2.22 **3.05**	2.14 **2.92**	2.09 **2.82**	2.04 **2.73**	2.00 **2.66**	1.97 **2.60**	1.91 **2.50**	1.87 **2.42**	1.80 **2.30**	1.75 **2.22**	1.71 **2.13**	1.65 **2.04**	1.62 **1.98**	1.57 **1.90**	1.54 **1.86**	1.51 **1.80**	1.48 **1.76**	1.46 **1.72**	46
48	4.04 **7.19**	3.19 **5.08**	2.80 **4.22**	2.56 **3.74**	2.41 **3.42**	2.30 **3.20**	2.21 **3.04**	2.14 **2.90**	2.08 **2.80**	2.03 **2.71**	1.99 **2.64**	1.96 **2.58**	1.90 **2.48**	1.86 **2.40**	1.79 **2.28**	1.74 **2.20**	1.70 **2.11**	1.64 **2.02**	1.61 **1.96**	1.56 **1.88**	1.53 **1.84**	1.50 **1.78**	1.47 **1.73**	1.45 **1.70**	48

Table A-5

Percentage Points of the F Distribution (continued)

5% (Roman Type) and 1% (Bold Face Type) Points for the Distribution of F

n_1 degrees of freedom (for greater mean square). Each cell shows 5% (Roman) over 1% (Bold) values.

n_2	1	2	3	4	5	6	7	8	9	10	11	12	14	16	20	24	30	40	50	75	100	200	500	∞
50	4.03 / 7.17	3.18 / 5.06	2.79 / 4.20	2.56 / 3.72	2.40 / 3.41	2.29 / 3.18	2.20 / 3.02	2.13 / 2.88	2.07 / 2.78	2.02 / 2.70	1.98 / 2.62	1.95 / 2.56	1.90 / 2.46	1.85 / 2.39	1.78 / 2.26	1.74 / 2.18	1.69 / 2.10	1.63 / 2.00	1.60 / 1.94	1.55 / 1.86	1.52 / 1.82	1.48 / 1.76	1.46 / 1.71	1.44 / 1.68
55	4.02 / 7.12	3.17 / 5.01	2.78 / 4.16	2.54 / 3.68	2.38 / 3.37	2.27 / 3.15	2.18 / 2.98	2.11 / 2.85	2.05 / 2.75	2.00 / 2.66	1.97 / 2.59	1.93 / 2.53	1.88 / 2.43	1.83 / 2.35	1.76 / 2.23	1.72 / 2.15	1.67 / 2.06	1.61 / 1.96	1.58 / 1.90	1.52 / 1.82	1.50 / 1.78	1.46 / 1.71	1.43 / 1.66	1.41 / 1.64
60	4.00 / 7.08	3.15 / 4.98	2.76 / 4.13	2.52 / 3.65	2.37 / 3.34	2.25 / 3.12	2.17 / 2.95	2.10 / 2.82	2.04 / 2.72	1.99 / 2.63	1.95 / 2.56	1.92 / 2.50	1.86 / 2.40	1.81 / 2.32	1.75 / 2.20	1.70 / 2.12	1.65 / 2.03	1.59 / 1.93	1.56 / 1.87	1.50 / 1.79	1.48 / 1.74	1.44 / 1.68	1.41 / 1.63	1.39 / 1.60
65	3.99 / 7.04	3.14 / 4.95	2.75 / 4.10	2.51 / 3.62	2.36 / 3.31	2.24 / 3.09	2.15 / 2.93	2.08 / 2.79	2.02 / 2.70	1.98 / 2.61	1.94 / 2.54	1.90 / 2.47	1.85 / 2.37	1.80 / 2.30	1.73 / 2.18	1.68 / 2.09	1.63 / 2.00	1.57 / 1.90	1.54 / 1.84	1.49 / 1.76	1.46 / 1.71	1.42 / 1.64	1.39 / 1.60	1.37 / 1.56
70	3.98 / 7.01	3.13 / 4.92	2.74 / 4.08	2.50 / 3.60	2.35 / 3.29	2.23 / 3.07	2.14 / 2.91	2.07 / 2.77	2.01 / 2.67	1.97 / 2.59	1.93 / 2.51	1.89 / 2.45	1.84 / 2.35	1.79 / 2.28	1.72 / 2.15	1.67 / 2.07	1.62 / 1.98	1.56 / 1.88	1.53 / 1.82	1.47 / 1.74	1.45 / 1.69	1.40 / 1.62	1.37 / 1.56	1.35 / 1.53
80	3.96 / 6.96	3.11 / 4.88	2.72 / 4.04	2.48 / 3.56	2.33 / 3.25	2.21 / 3.04	2.12 / 2.87	2.05 / 2.74	1.99 / 2.64	1.95 / 2.55	1.91 / 2.48	1.88 / 2.41	1.82 / 2.32	1.77 / 2.24	1.70 / 2.11	1.65 / 2.03	1.60 / 1.94	1.54 / 1.84	1.51 / 1.78	1.45 / 1.70	1.42 / 1.65	1.38 / 1.57	1.35 / 1.52	1.32 / 1.49
100	3.94 / 6.90	3.09 / 4.82	2.70 / 3.98	2.46 / 3.51	2.30 / 3.20	2.19 / 2.99	2.10 / 2.82	2.03 / 2.69	1.97 / 2.59	1.92 / 2.51	1.88 / 2.43	1.85 / 2.36	1.79 / 2.26	1.75 / 2.19	1.68 / 2.06	1.63 / 1.98	1.57 / 1.89	1.51 / 1.79	1.48 / 1.73	1.42 / 1.64	1.39 / 1.59	1.34 / 1.51	1.30 / 1.46	1.28 / 1.43
125	3.92 / 6.84	3.07 / 4.78	2.68 / 3.94	2.44 / 3.47	2.29 / 3.17	2.17 / 2.95	2.08 / 2.79	2.01 / 2.65	1.95 / 2.56	1.90 / 2.47	1.86 / 2.40	1.83 / 2.33	1.77 / 2.23	1.72 / 2.15	1.65 / 2.03	1.60 / 1.94	1.55 / 1.85	1.49 / 1.75	1.45 / 1.68	1.39 / 1.59	1.36 / 1.54	1.31 / 1.46	1.27 / 1.40	1.25 / 1.37
150	3.91 / 6.81	3.06 / 4.75	2.67 / 3.91	2.43 / 3.44	2.27 / 3.14	2.16 / 2.92	2.07 / 2.76	2.00 / 2.62	1.94 / 2.53	1.89 / 2.44	1.85 / 2.37	1.82 / 2.30	1.76 / 2.20	1.71 / 2.12	1.64 / 2.00	1.59 / 1.91	1.54 / 1.83	1.47 / 1.72	1.44 / 1.66	1.37 / 1.56	1.34 / 1.51	1.29 / 1.43	1.25 / 1.37	1.22 / 1.33
200	3.89 / 6.76	3.04 / 4.71	2.65 / 3.88	2.41 / 3.41	2.26 / 3.11	2.14 / 2.90	2.05 / 2.73	1.98 / 2.60	1.92 / 2.50	1.87 / 2.41	1.83 / 2.34	1.80 / 2.28	1.74 / 2.17	1.69 / 2.09	1.62 / 1.97	1.57 / 1.88	1.52 / 1.79	1.45 / 1.69	1.42 / 1.62	1.35 / 1.53	1.32 / 1.48	1.26 / 1.39	1.22 / 1.33	1.19 / 1.28
400	3.86 / 6.70	3.02 / 4.66	2.62 / 3.83	2.39 / 3.36	2.23 / 3.06	2.12 / 2.85	2.03 / 2.69	1.96 / 2.55	1.90 / 2.46	1.85 / 2.37	1.81 / 2.29	1.78 / 2.23	1.72 / 2.12	1.67 / 2.04	1.60 / 1.92	1.54 / 1.84	1.49 / 1.74	1.42 / 1.64	1.38 / 1.57	1.32 / 1.47	1.28 / 1.42	1.22 / 1.32	1.16 / 1.24	1.13 / 1.19
1000	3.85 / 6.66	3.00 / 4.62	2.61 / 3.80	2.38 / 3.34	2.22 / 3.04	2.10 / 2.82	2.02 / 2.66	1.95 / 2.53	1.89 / 2.43	1.84 / 2.34	1.80 / 2.26	1.76 / 2.20	1.70 / 2.09	1.65 / 2.01	1.58 / 1.89	1.53 / 1.81	1.47 / 1.71	1.41 / 1.61	1.36 / 1.54	1.30 / 1.44	1.26 / 1.38	1.19 / 1.28	1.13 / 1.19	1.08 / 1.11
∞	3.84 / 6.64	2.99 / 4.60	2.60 / 3.78	2.37 / 3.32	2.21 / 3.02	2.09 / 2.80	2.01 / 2.64	1.94 / 2.51	1.88 / 2.41	1.83 / 2.32	1.79 / 2.24	1.75 / 2.18	1.69 / 2.07	1.64 / 1.99	1.57 / 1.87	1.52 / 1.79	1.46 / 1.69	1.40 / 1.59	1.35 / 1.52	1.28 / 1.41	1.24 / 1.36	1.17 / 1.25	1.11 / 1.15	1.00 / 1.00

The function, $F = e$ with exponent $2z$, is computed in part from Fisher's table VI (7). Additional entries are by interpolation, mostly graphical.

SOURCE: This table is reproduced from *Statistical Methods*, by George W. Snedecor (Ames, Iowa: The Iowa State University Press, 5th ed., 1956), pp. 246–249. By permission of the author and publishers.

Table   A-6

Values of r (Simple Correlation Coefficient) for
Different Levels of Significance

n	.1	.05	.02	.01	.001
1	.98769	.99692	.999507	.999877	.9999988
2	.90000	.95000	.98000	.990000	.99900
3	.8054	.8783	.93433	.95873	.99116
4	.7293	.8114	.8822	.91720	.97406
5	.6694	.7545	.8329	.8745	.95074
6	.6215	.7067	.7887	.8343	.92493
7	.5822	.6664	.7498	.7977	.8982
8	.5494	.6319	.7155	.7646	.8721
9	.5214	.6021	.6851	.7348	.8471
10	.4973	.5760	.6581	.7079	.8233
11	.4762	.5529	.6339	.6835	.8010
12	.4575	.5324	.6120	.6614	.7800
13	.4409	.5139	.5923	.6411	.7603
14	.4259	.4973	.5742	.6226	.7420
15	.4124	.4821	.5577	.6055	.7246
16	.4000	.4683	.5425	.5897	.7084
17	.3887	.4555	.5285	.5741	.6932
18	.3783	.4438	.5155	.5614	.6787
19	.3687	.4329	.5034	.5487	.6652
20	.3598	.4227	.4921	.5368	.6524
25	.3233	.3809	.4451	.4869	.5974
30	.2960	.3494	.4093	.4487	.5541
35	.2746	.3246	.3810	.4182	.5189
40	.2573	.3044	.3578	.3932	.4896
45	.2428	.2875	.3384	.3721	.4648
50	.2306	.2732	.3218	.3541	.4433
60	.2108	.2500	.2948	.3248	.4078
70	.1954	.2319	.2737	.3017	.3799
80	.1829	.2172	.2565	.2830	.3568
90	.1726	.2050	.2422	.2673	.3375
100	.1638	.1946	.2301	.2540	.3211

SOURCE: This table is abridged from Table VII of Fisher & Yates: *Statistical Tables for Biological, Agricultural and Medical Research* published by Oliver & Boyd Ltd., Edinburgh, and by permission of the authors and publishers.

Table   A-7

Squares, Square Roots, and Reciprocals

N	N^2	$\sqrt{N}$	$\sqrt{10N}$	$1/N$	N	N^2	$\sqrt{N}$	$\sqrt{10N}$	$1/N$ .0
					50	2 500	7.071 068	22.36068	2000000
1	1	1.000 000	3.162 278	1.0000000	51	2 601	7.141 428	22.58318	1960784
2	4	1.414 214	4.472 136	.5000000	52	2 704	7.211 103	22.80351	1923077
3	9	1.732 051	5.477 226	.3333333	53	2 809	7.280 110	23.02173	1886792
4	16	2.000 000	6.324 555	.2500000	54	2 916	7.348 469	23.23790	1851852
5	25	2.236 068	7.071 068	.2000000	55	3 025	7.416 198	23.45208	1818182
6	36	2.449 490	7.745 967	.1666667	56	3 136	7.483 315	23.66432	1785714
7	49	2.645 751	8.366 600	.1428571	57	3 249	7.549 834	23.87467	1754386
8	64	2.828 427	8.944 272	.1250000	58	3 364	7.615 773	24.08319	1724138
9	81	3.000 000	9.486 833	.1111111	59	3 481	7.681 146	24.28992	1694915
10	100	3.162 278	10.00000	.1000000	60	3 600	7.745 967	24.49490	1666667
11	121	3.316 625	10.48809	.09090909	61	3 721	7.810 250	24.69818	1639344
12	144	3.464 102	10.95445	.08333333	62	3 844	7.874 008	24.89980	1612903
13	169	3.605 551	11.40175	.07692308	63	3 969	7.937 254	25.09980	1587302
14	196	3.741 657	11.83216	.07142857	64	4 096	8.000 000	25.29822	1562500
15	225	3.872 983	12.24745	.06666667	65	4 225	8.062 258	25.49510	1538462
16	256	4.000 000	12.64911	.06250000	66	4 356	8.124 038	25.69047	1515152
17	289	4.123 106	13.03840	.05882353	67	4 489	8.185 353	25.88436	1492537
18	324	4.242 641	13.41641	.05555556	68	4 624	8.246 211	26.07681	1470588
19	361	4.358 899	13.78405	.05263158	69	4 761	8.306 624	26.26785	1449275
20	400	4.472 136	14.14214	.05000000	70	4 900	8.366 600	26.45751	1428571
21	441	4.582 576	14.49138	.04761905	71	5 041	8.426 150	26.64583	1408451
22	484	4.690 416	14.83240	.04545455	72	5 184	8.485 281	26.83282	1388889
23	529	4.795 832	15.16575	.04347826	73	5 329	8.544 004	27.01851	1369863
24	576	4.898 979	15.49193	.04166667	74	5 476	8.602 325	27.20294	1351351
25	625	5.000 000	15.81139	.04000000	75	5 625	8.660 254	27.38613	1333333
26	676	5.099 020	16.12452	.03846154	76	5 776	8.717 798	27.56810	1315789
27	729	5.196 152	16.43168	.03703704	77	5 929	8.774 964	27.74887	1298701
28	784	5.291 503	16.73320	.03571429	78	6 084	8.831 761	27.92848	1282051
29	841	5.385 165	17.02939	.03448276	79	6 241	8.888 194	28.10694	1265823
30	900	5.477 226	17.32051	.03333333	80	6 400	8.944 272	28.28427	1250000
31	961	5.567 874	17.60682	.03225806	81	6 561	9.000 000	28.46050	1234568
32	1 024	5.656 854	17.88854	.03125000	82	6 724	9.055 385	28.63564	1219512
33	1 089	5.744 563	18.16590	.03030303	83	6 889	9.110 434	28.80972	1204819
34	1 156	5.830 952	18.43909	.02941176	84	7 056	9.165 151	28.98275	1190476
35	1 225	5.916 080	18.70829	.02857143	85	7 225	9.219 544	29.15476	1176471
36	1 296	6.000 000	18.97367	.02777778	86	7 396	9.273 618	29.32576	1162791
37	1 369	6.082 763	19.23538	.02702703	87	7 569	9.327 379	29.49576	1149425
38	1 444	6.164 414	19.49359	.02631579	88	7 744	9.380 832	29.66479	1136364
39	1 521	6.244 998	19.74842	.02564103	89	7 921	9.433 981	29.83287	1123596
40	1 600	6.324 555	20.00000	.02500000	90	8 100	9.486 833	30.00000	1111111
41	1 681	6.403 124	20.24846	.02439024	91	8 281	9.539 392	30.16621	1098901
42	1 764	6.480 741	20.49390	.02380952	92	8 464	9.591 663	30.33150	1086957
43	1 849	6.557 439	20.73644	.02325581	93	8 649	9.643 651	30.49590	1075269
44	1 936	6.633 250	20.97618	.02272727	94	8 836	9.695 360	30.65942	1063830
45	2 025	6.708 204	21.21320	.02222222	95	9 025	9.746 794	30.82207	1052632
46	2 116	6.782 330	21.44761	.02173913	96	9 216	9.797 959	30.98387	1041667
47	2 209	6.855 655	21.67948	.02127660	97	9 409	9.848 858	31.14482	1030928
48	2 304	6.928 203	21.90890	.02083333	98	9 604	9.899 495	31.30495	1020408
49	2 401	7.000 000	22.13594	.02040816	99	9 801	9.949 874	31.46427	1010101
50	2 500	7.071 068	22.36068	.02000000	100	10 000	10.00000	31.62278	1000000

Index